T0385203

Combining deep knowledge of Jewish tradition with decades of experience as a senior diplomat, Daniel Taub has written a book that is erudite, insightful and unexpectedly hopeful. With its understanding of the power of story to touch the places logic alone cannot reach, it offers an approach to conflict - whether between nations or within a family - that is both readable and practical. It's part Malcolm Gladwell, part Talmudic essay and completely compelling.

Jonathan Freedland, author of *The Escape Artist*

Our debates have become truly toxic, making it hard to understand the positions and outlooks of others, as each group and sector closes itself off and the walls of divisiveness and hostility grow only higher. In today's divisive climate, the approach Daniel Taub offers, that it is actually in difference that the potential for inspiration and creative thinking lies, is as vital as the air we breathe.

Isaac Herzog, President of the State of Israel

Beyond Dispute is beautifully written with humour, wonderful anecdotes, and powerful quotes. Using the timeless wisdom of the Old Testament and the Jewish commentaries on the Scriptures, as well as his own experience representing Israel as Ambassador and diplomat at the United Nations, this book is packed full of treasures from both the ancient sources and the modern world.

Reverend Nicky Gumbel, developer of the Alpha Course

All too often we see our faith traditions as forces that divide us. This book is a timely reminder that they have the power to bring us together. With deep understanding and concrete examples drawn from a life spent in negotiation and mediation, Daniel Taub shows us how, as individuals and as a society, we can bring the wisdom of our traditions into our hardest conversations.

Sheikh Dr. Eyad Amer, Imam, Kafr Qasim, Israel

Beyond Dispute is an essential guide to navigating and mastering the dying art of civil disagreement – and doing so in a time riven by deep cultural, religious, and political divides. Drawing on classic Jewish wisdom and modern social psychology, it will be an indispensable resource for Jewish and non-Jewish readers alike.

Dan Senor, co-author of *Start Up Nation*, host of Call Me Back podcast

A timely and inspiring book speaking directly to one of the greatest challenges of our time. A wonderful combination of big-picture wisdom and nitty-gritty practical advice. No-one is better positioned to speak to this issues with hard earned wisdom and menschly humanity.

Nancy Katz, Professor of Public Policy Emeritus, Harvard University

At a time when civil discourse is under extreme attack, veteran diplomat and lifelong Talmud scholar Daniel Taub has produced perhaps the most important guide ever written to arguing not to vanquish but to reach truth. With wit and wide-ranging expertise, the book helps remind us that those with whom we argue are our opponents, not our enemies – and sometimes can even, through argument when conducted properly, become our allies and friends.

Rabbi Joseph Telushkin, author of *Words that Hurt, Words that Heal*

Daniel Taub makes a compelling case that the wisdom of the Talmud has much to teach us for our toughest negotiations and most difficult conversations. He draws on his experience as a negotiator and diplomat and shows how arguments, done well, can help us learn not only about ideas, but about ourselves.

Natan Sharansky, Russian Prisoner of Zion and human rights activist

We have stopped speaking to each other, because we have also stopped listening. *Beyond Dispute* mines the richness of one of the world's most ancient traditions for wisdom about one of our most pressing current problems. Like Daniel Taub himself, this book makes us clearer thinkers, better listeners and more optimistic about the world it is still not too late to fashion.

Daniel Gordis, author of *We Stand Divided*

Beyond Dispute

Rediscovering the Jewish Art of
Constructive Disagreement

Daniel Taub

HODDER &
STOUGHTON

First published in Great Britain in 2025 by Hodder Faith
An imprint of John Murray Press

I

Copyright © Daniel Taub 2025

A CIP catalogue record for this title is available from the British Library

Hardback ISBN 978 1 399 81506 2
Trade Paperback ISBN 978 1 399 81507 9
ebook ISBN 978 1 399 81508 6

Typeset in Sabon MT by Hewer Text UK Ltd, Edinburgh
Printed and bound in Great Britain by Clays Ltd, Elcograf S.p.A.

John Murray Press policy is to use papers that are natural, renewable and recyclable
products and made from wood grown in sustainable forests. The logging and
manufacturing processes are expected to conform to the environmental regulations of
the country of origin.

Carmelite House
50 Victoria Embankment
London EC4Y 0DZ

www.hodderfaith.com

John Murray Press, part of Hodder & Stoughton Limited
An Hachette UK company

The authorised representative in the EEA is Hachette Ireland, 8 Castlecourt Centre,
Dublin 15, D15 XTP3, Ireland (email: info@hbgi.ie)

For Zehava,
and our children and grandchildren.
May all their arguments be for the sake of heaven.

Contents

Introduction

Can We Talk?

Moscow, Russia, 1985.
A frosty early morning. I am standing at a busy intersection surrounded by bleak communist-era buildings. It is well below zero. Passers-by in heavy coats hurry by, hunched and silent, their breath rising in columns in the freezing air. On the street corners, Soviet policemen in long grey coats and fur hats keep a lookout and blow sharp whistles at any hint of dawdling.

Some fifty yards down the street a young man appears. Slight of build, with a wispy beard, and wearing a heavy anorak. Under his arm is a package wrapped in newspaper. This is the man I've been waiting for. With a slight nod of his head, he signals me to follow him.

Keeping my distance, he leads me away from the main square and down side streets, these too lined with oppressive concrete apartment blocks. As we walk further away from the centre, I notice other people walking in the same direction as us, also with newspaper packages under their arms.

Finally, the young man turns furtively into a nondescript apartment block. I follow and see that the other package-carriers are entering the building too. We climb several flights of stairs and enter a small apartment, crammed with people of all ages, including young children, sitting in groups around tables. One by one the newcomers unwrap their packages and take out the books they had been hiding inside them. The Talmud. And so they begin to study.

Despite decades of suppression by the Soviet authorities, a handful of Jews in Moscow were secretly keeping the flame of Jewish study alive with *samizdat* study groups like the one I attended. They did this even though their study books were

3

prohibited, and they could be arrested merely for having one in their possession.

Even as a visiting westerner I had tasted the severity of the prohibition. I was in Moscow visiting 'refuseniks', Jews who had applied to leave the Soviet Union to live in Israel but who were not permitted to leave. Most had lost their jobs as a consequence, and were under close state scrutiny.[1] I had been sent by a group of Jews in London who had campaigned for the Moscow refuseniks and regularly sent them basic necessities and Jewish items. Landing in Moscow my suitcase was full of kosher food and religious items, all of which, I insisted to the customs officials, were for my own personal use. But one item raised their suspicions. Since bringing in Jewish books was prohibited by the Soviet authorities, some friends had given me a copy of a tractate of the Talmud on small microfiche slides (this was before floppy disks or USB sticks) in the hope that the Moscow group could project these slides and study from them. From the customs guards' panicked reaction, it was clear they had never seen something like this before, and I was taken to a side room for investigation. When I was asked what was on the microfiche, I answered truthfully: 'That's a tractate of the Babylonian Talmud'. They picked up the phone and passed on the message. From what I could tell it sounded as though they had an expert on Judaica on the other end of the line, explaining the significance of the text. After a lengthy interrogation, I was released, but the microfiches were confiscated.

What was it about the Talmud, an Aramaic text dating back close to two millennia, that was such a threat to the mighty Soviet Union? Did the powers that be perhaps realise something about its potency and subversive nature that I hadn't fully grasped? Fifteen years later, during an encounter with another authoritarian regime, it became clearer to me where this power might lie.

Shepherdstown, USA, 2000.

Israeli military service had by no means prepared me for the luxury of the Shepherdstown US military base where our peace talks with Syria were to take place. More like a resort than an army base, it had been chosen precisely because it was idyllic and discreet yet still close enough to Washington for the President and Secretary of State to pop in. The US officials hosting the talks hoped that the pastoral setting might help Middle East negotiators imagine a different future for our peoples.

After decades of hostilities, this was the first direct negotiation ever between Israelis and Syrians. One of the few things we shared was a certain bemusement at the naïve idealism of our American hosts. They had invited us to attend in 'casual dress', and showed up, Secretary of State included, in jeans, plaid shirts and cowboy boots. The Syrians continued to wear formal suits and ties (they were all men), while our Israeli delegation hovered in a grey area of semi-formal attire. And one morning, after it seemed that our delegations might have made a smidgen of progress, the US State Department officials brought in a large basket of fruit, to represent, they said coyly, 'the fruits of peace'.

Beyond this shared bemusement at the Americans, there was little common ground. The delegation heads declaimed talking points across the table in the formal negotiation sessions, but that was the sum of the engagement between the sides. The Syrians were under firm instructions that there be no other interaction: no small talk, no handshakes, nothing beyond the most formal prepared statements by the delegation heads. The Americans had hoped that we would tackle issues like water and security as we indulged in leisurely walks among the trees, or exercised together on the gym treadmills, but the Syrians point-blank refused to enter any of the common spaces if any Israelis were present (one morning I went to the gym and was annoyed to discover that it had been closed 'for the use of the Syrian delegation').

I was taken aback. Our negotiations with the Palestinians, and with the Egyptians and Jordanians with whom we had previously reached peace treaties, were no less charged, but over coffee breaks and after hours we had long and lively discussions, not just about the conflict between us, but about literature, philosophy, sports, and our families. We were negotiators, but we were people too.

Not the Syrians. Occasionally a member of their team would forget himself and give a slight nod of the head, or a hand would begin to move forward in greeting, but a glance from another delegation member would quickly quash any move towards human engagement.

At first, I assumed this was simply a stark expression of the anti-normalisation policy of the Syrian regime towards Israel. But as it went on, I suspected that it was something else too. Fear of where such a real conversation might lead. Talking, without a safety net as it were, might open minds or, even worse, hearts. If the talks were even for a moment to step off the agreed line and depart from the official talking points, we might, heaven forbid, begin to develop a human relationship. Who knows how seditious that might be, and where it might lead?

A Talmudic principle asserts that from a 'No' you can learn a 'Yes', that is, from a prohibition you can derive a positive value. Did the ferocity with which the Soviet regime sought to supress Talmud study, and the insistence of the Syrian authorities on preventing any genuine personal interaction, suggest that they recognised a subversive power here? If so, what might it be? I was reminded of these questions two decades later, hidden behind a one-way mirror in Tel Aviv.

Tel Aviv, Israel, June 2022.

I am seated behind a one-way mirror, gazing into a small room. On the far side, oblivious to my presence, are a dozen students representing a diverse spectrum of Israeli society: Jews and Arabs, religious, ultraorthodox, and secular. They have been brought together to discuss a new online course we are developing on contentious issues within Israeli society: the exemption of the ultraorthodox and Arab communities from military service, the role of religious law in marriage and divorce, limitations on freedom of expression. Can we hope to nurture thoughtful and respectful discussion of these hot-button issues? The signs are not positive. Even through the thick glass, their raised voices can be heard. Tension is high and the tone is fraught - there are few if any grounds of consensus among the group. At some point in the discussion, one of the participants bursts out: 'I hate having discussions with people who don't agree with me!' Sadly, this seems to be almost the only thing the group can agree on.

When did 'Can we talk?' become a threat rather than an invitation? My focus group's tense discussion is not happening in a vacuum. From my travels abroad it is clear that Israel is not alone in seeing a harsher tone enter debates over sensitive issues, making constructive discussion much harder. I am often invited to speak on university campuses about my experiences as a diplomat and peace negotiator in the Middle East, and so get to see first-hand how toxic the discussion of Israeli–Palestinian issues has become. In many places the debate has shifted from being about what you can say, to whether you can say anything at all. Particularly concerning is the lack of ability or even will on the part of university administrations to articulate and fulfil their primary responsibility of creating spaces which are safe *for* ideas and not *from* them. Salman Rushdie made the point forcefully in a 2015 speech:

> The university is the place where young people should be challenged every day, where everything they know should be put into question, so that they can think and learn and grow up. And the idea that they should be protected from ideas that they might not like is the opposite of what a university should be. It's ideas that should be protected, the discussion of ideas that should be given a safe place. The university should be a safe space for the life of the mind. That's what it's for.[2]

Over the years, the list of toxic issues in the academic arena has grown far beyond the Middle East, with taboo subjects now encompassing gender, race, immigration, law enforcement, and more. There are, to be sure, legitimate grounds for challenging orthodoxies, and for recognising historical asymmetries reflected in our institutions and even our language. All too often, though, the tone is less corrective and more intimidating and unforgiving, often seeming to insist simultaneously, you *must* understand me, and you *can never* understand me.

This trend is not limited to academia. The media often plays a significant role in fanning the flames of anger and hostility and downplaying or marginalising models of consensus and agreement. I was a witness to this myself when heading the Israeli side of the Israel–Palestinian Culture of Peace negotiations in the late 1990s. When approached by journalists with questions about progress behind the door of the negotiating room, I explained that I wasn't permitted to divulge the content of the negotiations. However, I added, if they were interested in reporting on peace-building efforts between Israelis and Palestinians, I would be happy to introduce them to courageous organisations bringing together people on both sides – activists, bereaved families, children – so that they could write articles about these green shoots. I was surprised and disappointed that I had no takers. None at all. When I mentioned this to one of the journalists he looked at me as if I was a child, before explaining: 'No one wants to read about good Israelis and good Palestinians.'

Even more than traditional media, the rise of social media has ramped up these levels of toxicity. It seems paradoxical that social media, which many hoped would result in greater dialogue and empathy between different groups, should in fact have aggravated the situation. But, spurred by commercially-driven algorithms, the platforms' individually curated feeds continually assure us not only that we are right in our views, but stir up in us an ever-greater anger at those who oppose us. A recent Pew survey in the US reported that two thirds of social media users now say they find it 'stressful and frustrating' to talk about politics with people they disagree with. Even more troubling was the finding that dialogue, when it does happen, seems to actually decrease empathy and understanding.[3]

As worrying as what *is* said is the prevailing sense that some things *cannot* be said. A recent study by the Cato Institute found that over 60 per cent of respondents agreed with the statement, 'The political climate these days prevents me from saying things I believe because others might find them offensive', and that as many as one third feared losing their job or job prospects if their true opinions became known.[4]

Flight or fight

Look in your local bookshop or online bookstore, and you will find we are not only polarised in relation to the issues we discuss, but we are polarised in relation to the very idea of argument itself. It quickly becomes clear that books on the subject of argument predominantly fall into one of two categories.

One group sees argument as a conflict to be avoided at all costs. With titles like *How to Stop Arguing*, and *How to Have Argument-Free Relationships*, they see argument as a threat to friendly and productive interactions. Indeed an early example of this approach is Dale Carnegie's 1936 best-seller *How to win friends and influence people,* which remains popular today. Alongside much considered and valuable advice, Carnegie writes: 'I have come to the conclusion that there is only one way under high heaven to get the best of an argument – and that is to avoid it.' Warning that any argument is bound to damage our relationships, he explains: 'You can't win an argument; you can't because if you lose it, you lose it; and if you win it, you lose it.'[5]

The second, and by far the larger, group, is of books which see argument as a battle to be won, and offer purportedly infallible tools and tricks to outsmart and defeat the opposition. A recent example is a book by British-American journalist and television host Mehdi Hasan. A fiercely sharp debater and interviewer, the book is revealingly titled *Win Every Argument* – a title which raises the intriguing question as to which side of an argument will win if *both* sides have read the book. While the book does contain practical advice on subjects like preparation and fact-checking, for Hasan argument is unquestionably a competition to be won. The goal is not to learn, but to shine. As Hasan advises his readers: 'Get it right, and you'll intimidate your opponent from the get-go while dazzling any audience in attendance.'[6]

Argument, so much of the current wisdom suggests, is a battle to be won or a conflict to be avoided – fight or flight. Is there another way?

I believe there is a third model of conducting our most difficult conversations, one that requires neither browbeating nor soft-pedalling. And I found it in my own tradition, in the distinctively Jewish approach to argument.

Here all along

Shortly after observing the Tel Aviv focus group, I was invited to help mediate an acrimonious dispute between two Jewish communal organisations (the precise bone of contention is of little relevance). Both sides were convinced of the rightness of their case, with their mutually shared conviction that they were serving a higher purpose only adding intensity to their fervour.

I was struck by the fact that both sides of the dispute chose to frame their positions in terms of traditional Jewish values. They were not, it became clear, so vehemently at odds *despite* their shared tradition, but rather *because* of it. Beyond the specific issue at hand, the dispute touched on deeply engrained issues of loyalty, identity, and insecurity. As with the focus group students, the subjects under discussion were real and substantive, but they were also trapdoors into hidden depths of perception and loyalty that unleashed intense levels of emotion.

Might those same deep streams of loyalty and identity that

resulted in acrimony also contain insights and practices for handling differences?

Many tribal and indigenous societies have their own traditional rituals and processes for dealing with conflict. Among the Kpelle people of Liberia, for example, disputes are often settled through a 'mo-meni-sai' or palava hut meeting, while in New Zealand, the Maori practice of 'Whakawhanaungatanga,' involves the entire *whanau* or extended family in a process that seeks to restore relationships and ensure future harmony. While these processes have practical value in themselves, much of their force derives from the fact that they derive from the same deep well of tradition as the loyalties and group identities playing out invisibly beneath the surface of the conflict of the moment, and so embody some of the moral and psychological force needed to help outweigh those differences. They hold out the possibility that by engaging constructively with views that differ from our own we are not necessarily betraying our tribal traditions; we may in fact be channelling them.

I was witness to a striking example of the force of traditional conflict resolution methods when co-mediating a dispute in a community mediation centre in Jerusalem. The dispute was between two Arab residents of the city, and my co- mediator was the highly respected Sheikh Dr Eyad Amer. The two disputants were making little progress, and one in particular, a passionate young man, was clearly about to explode into violence. At this point Sheikh Eyad asked me if I would mind if he departed from our agreed mediation protocol and adopt a different approach. With nothing to lose, I agreed. The Sheikh moved from speaking Hebrew to Arabic and spoke to the young man not as a mediator to a disputant, but in the caring but authoritative tone of a father to a son. The change in the young man's attitude was extraordinary. Before long he was no longer insisting on his position but humbly asking the Sheikh's advice on how he could extricate himself from the situation in which he found himself.

Considering the dispute I had witnessed between leaders

representing Jewish organisations, I began to wonder what might it mean for the argument to be conducted in a Jewish manner, that is to say, in accordance with insights on addressing differences taken from within the Jewish tradition?

The very idea might seem comical to anyone with the remotest familiarity with the raucous nature of Jewish life ('That's the synagogue I *don't* pray in!') or the colourful imagery of Yiddish curses ('May all your teeth fall out except one – and that one should give you toothache!'). *Broyges* – emotive arguing with a heavy dose of grievance and umbrage – sometimes seems to be a Jewish national sport.

It might seem surprising too to anyone who has followed the fraught public debates in Israel over recent years, where arguments over issues like the powers of the Supreme Court to review governmental decisions or, more painfully, the price that should be paid for the return of the hostages taken in the tragic massacre of October 7, 2023, have at times threatened to tear Israeli society apart. But the wisdom of the Jewish approach to argument should not be judged by the behaviour of Jewish communities or the Jewish state. Twentieth century American Jewish leader and rabbi Abraham Joshua Heschel may have been poignantly accurate when he described the Jews as 'A messenger who has forgotten his message'.

A key part of this message is the value of the right kind of argument, both as a way of containing the disparate elements of fractured societies, and as an engine of intellectual creativity. A history of arguing and scholarly wrangling has given birth to great Jewish works, including the Talmud, an extraordinary compendium of constructive debate. Over the millennia, this rigorous but adaptable corpus of wisdom has maintained Jewish life, survived dispersions, generated scholars, and nurtured Jewish innovation and creativity. Jewish tradition, and particularly the rabbinic or post-biblical tradition, seems to have developed an alchemy for turning difference into insight, and passionate debate into a source of renewable intellectual energy.

I had studied the Talmud since childhood but I had never before thought of it as a source of practical guidance for dealing with contentious contemporary debates. This was even more striking since so much of my work as a diplomat and negotiator (not to mention home life as the parent of six lively and opinionated kids) should have encouraged me to keep my eyes open for better ways of handling difference and discussion of fractious issues. But when I revisited its pages in this new frame of mind I was struck by how fresh and relevant its approach seemed to be. Could an ancient tradition really help us talk about the things that matter most?

A *third way*

The approach I rediscovered within Jewish tradition rejects both flight and fight. Rather than advising, like Carnegie, that you should avoid arguments because there is no way can you win, the Jewish approach suggests the opposite, that if you seek the truth, you cannot fail: either you win the argument, or, if you lose, you learn and grow.

Nor does the Jewish tradition see argument as a battle to be won. It is not so much a combat zone but more a joint enterprise, and its disputants are not sole custodians of the truth but collaborative explorers in search of it. Argument is not a fight but a process, an opportunity to engage in a joint expedition. It's a framing that seeks to create a safe space not by outlawing controversial opinions, but by welcoming them, helping us to build communities and societies that are resilient enough to face new and challenging ideas without fear.

From this perspective flow several tools and practices which characterise debate within the Jewish tradition. Many of these are ancient; others have developed over time and been honed through centuries of intellectual engagement. Looking at them again I was struck by how many these practices presage insights and techniques proposed today in cognitive theory and decision-making analysis.

Strikingly, many of these tools and practices are not designed to sharpen our intellects or tighten our logic. Rather they focus on the personal or moral sphere – humility, joy, admitting our influences, telling our personal stories and so on – reflecting a conviction that tempering rigour with compassion doesn't compromise our search for truth but is a critical element of the process.

Still, from the Aramaic pages of the Talmud to today's noisy debates on Facebook and Twitter/X seemed like an awful long journey. So, after researching and teaching some of the ideas I was rediscovering in different colleges in Israel, I suggested that we might road-test them in practice, by setting up a Difficult Conversations 'laboratory' to bring together students from different parts of the ideological spectrum. Israeli society provided fertile ground for finding vocal disputants, from left and right wing, religious and secular. There was no shortage of contentious issues, from the demand of the ultra-Orthodox sector to allow gender segregation, to rewriting the national anthem to be more inclusive of minorities, and from permitting racial profiling for reasons of security to imposing limits on the immigration of Ukrainian refugees. The goal of the laboratory was not, the participants learned, to resolve these issues, or even to change people's minds, but rather to see whether new ways of thinking and talking could lead to deeper understanding and help preserve and even deepen relationships between the disputants.

I have since facilitated 'laboratories' of this kind among many different and diverse groups. It has been an extraordinary learning experience and often an inspiring one. I am enormously grateful to the participants who, with courage and openness, have entered into uncharted waters. Participant feedback suggests that, while it is rare for students to flip sides on the most charged issues, it is also uncommon for them to leave such a process without having acquired an extra dose of understanding regarding the nuance of the situation, or an element of unexpected respect for the alternative viewpoint.

These tools and approaches, I should make clear at the outset, will not resolve every conflict, or defuse all tensions within our difficult conversations. As we will see, our differences are rooted in the core of our most deeply embedded identities and loyalties and no simple technique, or trick of the mind, will sidestep these ties, nor would we want them to. Still, these ways of thinking about difference, and of talking about it, have the potential to make our arguments more focused and effective. When we disagree, they can help us identify where the difference actually lies, and whether indeed this is a difference that needs a practical solution. While they are unlikely to dissolve frictions across the barricades in fiery campus protests, they may help us identify when and why these environments are unable to offer productive conversations, and help develop alternative environments which can. They can, importantly, help us identify at an early stage when what appears to be an argument is not really an argument at all, but rather a form of political performance art or a protestation of identity, such that it might be better avoided. They can also help us overcome our cultural obsession with the 'bottom line', or immediate practical outcome of the discussion, and help us capture the value and wisdom in the rest of our debates, which frequently gets left behind. Finally, they give us a tentative road map on how to educate a new generation, and how to keep educating ourselves and refining our own skills, for the sake of argument – in the best sense of the word.

A different kind of book

This book is hard to categorise. It draws on ancient insights, largely from the world of the Talmud, but it is by no means a compendium of rabbinic wisdom. It references research and best practices from the world of social psychology, but it is not an academic survey. And it offers advice and practices from the fields of negotiation theory and conflict resolution, but it is not a 'How to' handbook for negotiators. Nor, I should admit, does its author fit into a neat category. I am far from being a rabbinic authority, a social psychologist, or an authority on conflict resolution. But the challenge that is presented by the toxicity of our arguments today is itself a multidisciplinary challenge: it draws on ancient loyalties, preys on our psychological blind spots, and plays itself out in tribal and sectoral powerplays. So perhaps the perspective of a diplomat who has found himself in many difficult conversations and negotiations, and who has a love and fascination with his own, Jewish, tradition of constructive argument, may have something to offer.

With this in mind, I have tried to distil the wisdom in my own tradition, to test it against contemporary social and psychological insights, and to draw on my own practical experiences as a negotiator and mediator to see how it fares in practice in some of our hardest conversations.

My hope is that the result offers an insight into a sensibility and set of practices which can help others in navigating their own fraught debates, and that the exercise itself may encourage readers of other faiths and traditions to look at their own with an open eye for intuitions and tools that can enrich their own difficult conversations.

Arguing in three dimensions

The book opens with three chapters that set out the fundamental approach to thinking about argument in the Jewish tradition, breaking it down into three conceptual underpinnings, each of which is very different to our general way of thinking today.

First we will look at a radical reimagining of the idea of *truth*. Here we focus on the vertical dynamic, the tension between the conviction that there is a universal and absolute truth in a world above us, and a recognition that as individuals our grasp of this absolute truth is necessarily partial and incomplete. We will see how to develop confident humility, being humble about our certainties but confident in our capabilities, and we will consider the ways in which this reframing can help us re-examine our core convictions.

Second, we will move from a vertical axis to a horizontal one, with a reconceiving of the idea of *difference*, and the relationship between our own core convictions and those we are engaging with. Here too, a radical rethinking encourages us to develop a perspective in which differing truths can coexist, and to foster interpersonal practices of collaborative truth seeking.

Thirdly we will bring the horizontal and vertical axes together, with a concept that became known as *Argument for the sake of heaven*, a recognition that our path towards truth is integrally entwined in our engagement with others. To this end, we need to learn how to cultivate and capture not agreement but dissent, and how to build relationships and identities resilient enough to withstand difference and be strengthened by it.

After establishing these underlying concepts, in the chapters which follow we will look at the tangible tools and practices that have arisen from these approaches and which are critical to any genuine dialogue. We will start with practices that look inwards, at our own identities and influences. We will then turn to practices that shape the interaction between ourselves and our counterparts, strengthening both our arguments and our relationships. We will go on to look at the vital but imperfect tools that are the only way we have to convey our ideas, and think about how to become more effective listeners and communicators. And finally, we will consider how these insights can be used to nurture and sustain societies of effective arguers.

In the concluding section, we will think more broadly about what it means to live in difference, not as a fallback option when other avenues have failed, but as a positive choice, and the criteria for success that may tell us whether our arguments have truly been 'for the sake of heaven'.

But first, in a brief prologue, we will ask: why should a set of ideas developed in a distant land nearly two millennia ago be relevant to the challenges we face today? You can feel free to skip this historic detour if you like. In case you choose to do so, I'll just note that the answer I suggest is that these radical ideas, which saved a civilisation then, were born against the background of a social crisis strikingly similar to the one we face today.

Prologue

From Crisis to Conversation

> Never let a good crisis go to waste.
> Winston Churchill

I once invited some Christian friends to join me in synagogue. As we left, I had a sense that their daughter, a precocious nine-year-old, was a little disappointed. I asked her what she thought of the proceedings. 'It was all very interesting,' she said hesitantly, 'but where was the grand service of the Temple – the ceremonies of the High Priest and the singing of the Levites' choir?'

She was right to be puzzled. In fact, if she was looking for the temple rituals she had learned about in Sunday school, she would be more likely to find them in the services of the Catholic Church, or even in the ceremonials surrounding the British monarchy, whose coronation service includes rites anointing with oil and a changing of vestments taken directly from the service of the priests of ancient Israel.

But for the Jews, the modern Israelites, the religious tradition underwent a radical transformation, a fundamental reimagining of the core of the faith. This dramatic upheaval, which ultimately ensured the survival of the Jewish people, was born not in times of calm but in crisis. To understand the Jewish approach to dealing with difference and argument, we need to understand the trauma from which it arose.

Ancient Israel, around 70 CE

The people of Israel were confronting the greatest crisis they had faced in their history. Since the conquest of the land by the Roman general Pompey in 64–61 BCE, the Israelites had been subject to a new ruler – Rome. Jewish rebellions against the brutality of the so-called Pax Romana had been ruthlessly quelled by Roman forces, killing tens of thousands and making many more homeless. When those displaced people took refuge in Jerusalem, the Romans besieged the city and then sacked it. Now the Temple itself, the historic centre of Jewish faith and communal life, lay in ashes. As the trail of refugees left the ruined city, it seemed that hope had been banished too. The trauma was unspeakable. Homeless and spiritually adrift, the Israelites found themselves facing an acute crisis on three levels: spiritual, theological and social.

On the spiritual level, with the loss of the Temple, the priest-hood and the prophets before them, the people had nowhere to turn for guidance, nor any way to atone for their sins. From the theological point of view, the apocalypse they had witnessed presented a critical challenge to their faith. How could God have so abandoned his chosen people? But most serious of all, and exacerbated by the spiritual and theological challenges, was the social crisis. The Jewish people was breaking apart. Even while the Temple was still standing there had been friction between rival Jewish sects. Now, with the Temple's destruction and the people's exile, these disputes threatened to destroy any sense of cohesion and peoplehood that remained.

Exiled, broken, fragmented, it seemed that the people of Israel were poised to disappear into the pages of history, like so many other peoples before them. But they refused to go away. Instead, whether by accident or design, in the centuries that followed, one Jewish sect would reinvent their faith and communal life in a way that would enable them to survive and even thrive over the course of centuries spent in exile, in a way that no people had ever done before.

During the centuries that followed this exile, the life of the ancient Israelites would change beyond all recognition. Audacious innovation would reinvent the core structures of the faith. Without a physical centre in Jerusalem, Jewish religious life would become portable, built around the synagogue and the study house. Prayer and good deeds would become a substitute for Temple sacrifices. And, without priests to intercede for the people, every individual would effectively become their own High Priest, responsible for their own repentance and atonement.

But perhaps the most radical innovation was a daring attempt to address the dangers of sectarianism and prevent total fragmentation. The stroke of genius was to present difference, even fundamental divides, as a positive value – in today's terminology, not a bug but a feature. Argument, which had always been considered a danger and threat to social cohesion, would now come to be seen as something to be cherished, and dissent not as treachery but an asset to be welcomed. The rabbis would develop a new conception of truth, as something that could not be known authoritatively by any single individual or sect, but as something to be divined through collaborative effort.

No longer would leadership fall to the Priests and Levites by virtue of their lineage, but rather to the brightest scholars by virtue of their learning and wisdom. With the individual as the new High Priest, and collaborative study and argument the new model of revelation, over time the Beit Midrash or study hall would become the new Temple. As Rabbi Jonathan Sacks describes it:

> How do you create fraternity in a people as fractious as the Jews? The rabbis' answer lay in translating conflict into argument, and making argument itself the pulse of intellectual life. Having inherited a world in which, through internal conflict, Jews had brought disaster on themselves, the rabbis took disagreement and relocated it within the house of study.[1]

At a time when the Jewish people was at its most fragile and fragmented, the rabbis' radical reformulation of the essence of faith successfully preserved the cohesiveness and continuity of the community. To this end they reimagined the nature of that community. The tumultuous history of the time had taught them that community born of agreement is fragile. But community united by its commitment to joining in the same raucous conversation as each other would prove real and lasting.

A sense of how radical this reformation was, and how critical to Jewish survival, can be gained from looking at other Jewish sects that adopted different approaches and subsequently disappeared into history.

The Sadducees, the most aristocratic Jewish sect of the Second Temple period, made little effort to adapt to the post-destruction environment. Far from welcoming a plurality of views, they remained entrenched in the confidence of their own opinions (the very name 'Sadducees' comes from the root *sadak* – to be right). The Talmud recounts that the Sadducees even established days of celebration to mark their victories in arguments against their rivals the Pharisees. Seeing besting others in argument as a cause for celebration, and presumably, by contrast, seeing losing an argument as a cause for mourning, are not the foundations of an agile 'growth mindset', and today, not only is there no trace of their days of celebration but barely any record of their teachings survives.

Another group, the ascetic Essenes, seem to have been a breakaway sect from the Sadducees, though there was no love lost between them, with the Essenes repeatedly describing the Sadducees as 'wicked' and 'deserving to perish'. Not lacking in spiritual confidence, the Essenes saw themselves as a divinely appointed elect, the 'Sons of Light', who would, in an apocalyptic forty-year war, defeat the 'Sons of Darkness'. Sadly, the forces of darkness seem to have been more resilient than the Essenes, who would also have been almost entirely lost to history were it not for the remarkable discovery of the Dead Sea scrolls in the middle of the twentieth century.

In contrast to the Sadducees and the Essenes, the rabbis embraced disagreement, ensuring that it was their raucous tradition, and not the single-minded certainty of their counterparts, that would survive. In doing so they also gave birth to a new way of thinking about truth, difference and dissent which would accompany Jewish life from here on: argument for the sake of heaven.

Enter the Talmud

The text that embodies this approach is known as the Talmud. It is, slightly confusingly, a written account of an oral tradition. According to Jewish tradition, the written Torah that was received on Mount Sinai was accompanied by an oral Torah which served to amplify the written text and help apply it in different generations. This tradition was passed down by word of mouth for close to a thousand years. Around 200 CE, worried that this tradition would be lost, the sage Judah HaNasi wrote it down.

By this time, however, there were many differing versions of the tradition, so the creation of a single authoritative account was out of the question. Instead Judah HaNasi offered something radically different, bringing together the traditions not as a verbatim report, but rather *as an argument*. Crucially, instead of rejecting dissenting views to produce a unified position, he collected all the different opinions and presented them as debates. This account of the debates of the earliest rabbis is called the Mishnah. Over the following centuries this compilation served as material for further debates between scholars, known as the Gemara. These too were brought together, and the resulting compilation of Mishnah and Gemara, amounting, in the standard edition, to some forty volumes, is known as the Talmud. (In fact there are two different versions of the Talmud: the Babylonian, written in Aramaic, and the Jerusalem Talmud, in Hebrew. The first, the Babylonian Talmud, is the more widely studied.)

Although presented as a continuation of the oral tradition, the move from authority to argument reflected a fundamental theological change. No longer was the truth to be received as a divine dictate; rather it was to be carefully derived through a process of human debate. More than codifying law, the Talmud, in the words of scholar Moshe Halbertal, 'codified controversy'. An extraordinary passage in the Talmud gives a sense of this seismic shift. The Talmud recounts a rabbinic dispute over a new type of oven, specifically over the question as to whether or not it was susceptible to ritual impurity. One rabbi, Eliezer ben Hyrcanus, argues that the oven is ritually pure, while all the other rabbis insist that it is impure. When Rabbi Eliezer sees that his arguments have failed to convince his colleagues, he cries out, 'If the law is in accordance with my opinion, this carob tree will prove it.' At this point, miraculously, the carob tree leaps out of the ground. The other rabbis dismiss this proof, insisting that the law cannot be derived from a dancing carob tree. Rabbi Eliezer cries out, 'If the law is in accordance with my opinion, this stream will prove it.' The stream begins to flow backwards, but again the other rabbis reject miracles as a proof in matters of law. Rabbi Eliezer cries out, 'Let the walls of the study hall prove I am right.' The walls of the study hall begin to shake, but again the proof is rejected. Finally, in desperation, Rabbi Eliezer cries out, 'If the law is in accordance with my opinion, let Heaven itself prove it.' At that moment a heavenly voice is heard, saying, 'Why are you arguing with Rabbi Eliezer, as the law is in accordance with his opinion?' One might have thought that this would end the debate conclusively, but the rabbis respond by quoting the biblical verse 'The Torah is not in heaven' (Deuteronomy 30:12). The Talmud concludes the account by describing the heavenly response to this incident, stating that God himself laughed and said: 'My children have triumphed over Me; My children have triumphed over Me.'[2]

A librarian would be hard pressed to decide on which shelf the volumes of the Talmud should be placed. It defies simple categorisation. It is law, to be sure, but also philosophy, folklore, practical advice and a miscellany of other things besides. Jumping from subject to subject like a stream of consciousness, or perhaps a conversation between old friends, there is something surprisingly modern about its fluidity. It has been compared to the internet, and indeed with no authorial voice it is more like Wikipedia than other classic tomes. And it is this text, together with its subsequent commentaries and debates, even more than the Bible itself, that is the basis of most traditional Jewish study.

A page of the Babylonian Talmud in its classic format. The central text sets out the debates of the sages of the Mishnah and the Gemara, while around this are the debates and challenges raised by scholars over the past millennia

While the intricate logic of Talmudic debates is challenging, in Jewish life Talmud study is not restricted to an elite. For example, a volume of Talmud from the early twentieth century was discovered in Ukraine bearing the inscription 'This Talmud belongs to the study group of the society of woodchoppers of Berditchev'. One hundred years ago an initiative was launched for people to study one two-sided page of Talmud a day. Today many hundreds of thousands of people, not simply scholars, do just that, a study cycle taking a little over seven years. My father-in-law is currently in his fifth seven-year cycle of studying the entirety of the Talmud.

A page of Talmud includes the text of the Mishnah and Gemara in the centre of the page, and around them, like the rings of an ancient tree, commentaries from different countries and generations debating across space and time. My childhood Talmud teacher would say that the thin white margin around the page was the most important part, left for us to add our own voices and interpretations.

But the Talmud is more than a book. It represents a particular way of thinking, radical in its own time, and often surprisingly so even today. While the issues it discusses often seem remote and antiquated, the way in which these discussions take place is fresh and vivid. It suggests that many of our fraught debates today could perhaps be handled differently and more effectively.

A note on missing voices

The more I study the Talmud, the more remarkable to me is the vibrancy of its characters, and the relevance of its concerns, even across a chasm of one-and-a-half millennia. But at the same time, in many ways the Talmud is also – how could it not be? – a product of its own era. It contains passages of folklore that seem superstitious, and home remedies that seem quaint and quirky. And also, reflective of its era, it consists of almost exclusively male voices. There are, to be sure, occasional women of stature. Bruria and Yalta are two notable women scholars who give the male sages as good as they get, with learning and with wit. And there are other women who are mentioned, but whose voices we do not hear, like the women's group of 'moonlight spinners' who would meet at night and share whispered insights about their society as they spun wool beneath the moon. But for the most part, women's voices are absent.

Today, however, there is a vibrant and growing world of women's Talmud study and their voices and interpretations are belatedly being added to the corpus. I've often wondered how modern women Talmud scholars relate to the sages of the past, particularly when on occasion those sages make statements that reflect male attitudes of the time. One interesting approach is offered by writer and Talmud scholar Ilana Kurshan in her poetic and personal account of her journeys in the Talmud and in life, *If All the Seas Were Ink*. She describes how, shortly after her divorce, in the course of her daily Talmud study, she came across one sage's assertion that a woman would prefer to be married than to be alone even if 'her husband is the size of an ant'. Her reaction was surprisingly forgiving:

> It soon became clear to me that by the Talmud's standards I am a man rather than a woman – if 'man' is a spending, self-sufficient adult . . . the Talmud did not offend me because I was defying its classifications through my very engagement with the text.[3]

The story has a romantic addendum: among the scholars in the daily Talmud class where she was studying, Ilana met her future husband.

All of this is to say that the Talmud is in many ways a reflection of its own times, but in some ways that makes it even more relevant to our own. For those were times when the sages were applying creative genius to challenges strikingly similar to ours.

Fast forward

Two millennia later. Loss of social centres of gravity, lack of trust in authority, increasing friction and hostility between different groups and tribes. In the social and political crises that many Western societies are facing today we find echoes of the crisis in ancient Israel. We may not think in terms of temples and priests, but the trauma, the experience of losing a social centre of gravity and shared cultural space, and the resulting sense of society breaking apart into ideological factions with little effective communication and cooperation between them, reflect a similarly disorienting upheaval.

We may not have literally lost a generation of prophets and priests to Rome's violent suppression of revolt, but we have seen a dramatic loss of confidence in authority and in established knowledge. Both in Europe and the United States, surveys show a continuing decline in trust in political leaders, public institutions and the media. The most recent findings of the Edelman Trust Barometer, which has monitored public trust globally for over two decades, found that close to half of respondents saw government and media as divisive forces in society. The authors noted with concern:

> We find a world ensnared in a vicious cycle of distrust, fueled by a growing lack of faith in media and government. Through disinformation and division, these two institutions are feeding the cycle and exploiting it for commercial and political gain.[4]

Technology has exacerbated the trend. Our parents or grandparents had a single television news programme to choose from, which meant that everyone was exposed to the same information and each media outlet felt a responsibility to present a balanced consensus position. Today we have effectively moved from broadcasting to narrowcasting, with a plethora of channels available, algorithmically curated to our personal preferences and biases. While the staggering variety of offerings available to us means that in theory we have access to a broader range of views and ideas than ever before, in practice our own predilection for the confirmation of our biases means that we are increasingly living within the disconnected comfort of our own echo chambers.

Alongside this diminishing trust in authority and a growing insulation from differing viewpoints, we are witnessing a troubling decline in communal life and social capital. If in ancient times the destruction of the Temple deprived the people of a critical spiritual and social centre, today other vital places of connection and interaction are fading fast. In 2000, Robert Putnam charted the devastating effects of the decline in communal life in his landmark book *Bowling Alone*.[5] The book took its title from data showing that while more people than ever were going ten pin bowling, fewer than ever were doing so as part of a team. For Putnam this became a metaphor for growing social disconnect and lack of communal resilience. Further research since the book's publication has only served to strengthen these findings and highlight an epidemic of social disconnect and loneliness.

With shrinking common space and increasingly self-selecting sources of information, it is not surprising that societies are becoming increasingly fractious and tribal, and that important and necessary conversations are becoming rarer and more difficult. The irony is that at a time when it seems that such conversations should be easier – technology makes it seamless and effortless to engage with anyone, anywhere, and increasingly effectively even across language barriers – and a time, too, when they are becoming increasingly important in the face of critical common challenges including climate change and the impact of technological advances such as AI, we seem to have unlearned the core skills of talking effectively and productively about the things that matter most.

Can the ideas and practices developed to deal with the crisis in ancient Israel help us recover these skills? Micah Goodman, an Israeli philosopher and writer who has written extensively about the impact of social media on society at large, argues forcefully that they can. Likening the development of the smartphone and iPad to other disruptive technological advances throughout history, he notes that, for all their benefits, these advances have always taken a toll by reducing our own personal capacities. The great leap that came when cavemen developed the axe meant that over generations their own jaw-bite weakened. With the invention of clocks, people's inherent sense of the passage of time diminished. Goodman observes that now that GPS systems in cars are ubiquitous, the result, according to the latest research, is a deadening of our own natural sense of direction. He sees mobile technology in general as bringing about a similar trade-off: we see enormous benefits in terms of access to information, but consequently suffer a significant dilution of our intrinsic abilities, including the capacity to listen to ideas with which we disagree.

In considering this troubling trade-off, he notes that in other cases where we have paid a price for technological advance we have developed 'compensatory cultures'. For example, the culture of regular exercise compensates for the reduction in natural exercise that has arisen from our widespread use of cars and public transport. But what would a 'compensatory culture' to restore and preserve the cognitive abilities that our reliance on screens is weakening look like? The answer Goodman suggests is the Talmud: 'Our listening muscles, the ones that are atrophying because of digital technology, can be reawakened by drawing inspiration from and perhaps even reviving the ancient spirit of the Talmud.'[6]

The Talmud's approach to disagreement and debate is vitally relevant today. Whatever their position, the rabbis believed they shared a common purpose that made their collective inquiry worth pursuing. They sought neither to win nor to avoid an argument, but to elevate it into a search for greater wisdom and enlightenment. As such, they were not afraid of sharp disagreement but actively welcomed it, knowing that it would broaden their personal worlds and enrich their common tradition. They argued not with bad faith, but with respect for their interlocutor, even in the face of unbridgeable divides. Today, we need to adopt this ethos.

Remembering the crisis faced by the Israelites two millennia ago is both sobering and encouraging. The sobering message is that, without a proactive and audacious response, the Jewish people, like many others in that era of upheaval, would have disappeared into oblivion. Internal rifts and an inability to communicate are not just a social challenge; they present an existential danger. The more positive lesson is that challenges like those we confront today have been faced before. Courageous and radical rethinking enabled a devastated civilisation to survive and flourish.

In the chapters that follow we will see how many of the tools and practices that arose out of that crisis can help us address the critical issues that divide us today, whether political conflicts, or debates over such emotive issues as vaccination or abortion. But before addressing the tools themselves, we should consider the radical core principles that lie at the root of these practices. The first of these relates to a small matter called Truth.

Principles

Rethinking Truth, Difference and Argument

Chapter 1

Rethinking Truth: Truth Above and Truths Below

> Few things have done more harm than the belief on the part of individuals or groups that they are in sole possession of the truth.
>
> Isaiah Berlin

'Have you ever transmitted state secrets to an enemy country?' 'No.' My throat felt strangely dry and my voice trembled slightly. Would that show up on the polygraph machine? The rubber cuff on my arm felt tight, the sensor band scratched my chest, and beneath the clips on my fingers I could feel my pulse quickening. 'Have you been approached by an agent of an Arab country with which Israel does not have relations?' 'No.' Again, that dry tremble in the throat. My head knew the test was standard procedure for anyone involved in a sensitive mission like the one I was being assigned to, but my sweat glands didn't seem to have received the memo. Although I had been told not to, I stole a glance at the row of needles scratching their spindly lines on the roll of graph paper.

'Have you ever travelled to an Arab country with which we have no relations?' 'No.' The polygraph operator's face remained immobile. A long pause as the needles scratched, the only sound in the bare basement room. Then the questions continued.

Finally the operator raised his head and gave a hint of a smile as he disconnected me from the machine. 'Everything OK?' I asked. 'NDI,' he answered. No Deception Indicated. 'You're good to go.'

'But you did lie,' my wife said when I recounted the experience to her that evening. 'What do you mean?' 'You said you never went to any Arab countries we didn't have relations with. What about that hush-hush mission to the Gulf states a few years ago?'

I stopped short. When I was asked about travel to Arab states, I had automatically taken the question to be about trips made without the knowledge of the government. I had totally forgotten that I had in fact been sent to some of these countries by the government itself. During a promising period in the 1990s peace process we had identified the possibility of deepening relations with a number of Gulf states, and I had been sent on a below-the-radar mission to explore the possibilities. But this had completely slipped my mind.

'I'm sure that's not what they meant,' I answered a little too insistently. 'I really did tell the truth.' My wife looked doubtful. 'It depends what you mean by the truth,' she said.

A good place to start. What do we mean by truth?

The dangers of truth

In the 1970s the BBC produced a magnificent television series, *The Ascent of Man*. Designed as a companion production to its epic series *Civilization*, which focused on the history of Western art and culture, *The Ascent of Man* addressed the development of scientific thinking and progress. The writer and presenter was the Polish-Jewish scientist and polymath Jacob Bronowski.

In one of the final episodes, Bronowski addressed the limits of scientific certainty. He described the pathbreaking discovery by the German physicist Werner Heisenberg that no events, even at the atomic level, can be described with total confidence, a theory that became known as the Uncertainty Principle. Bronowski noted that, at the very time Heisenberg was refining his theory, clouds of certainty and intolerance were gathering in Hitler's Germany. Bronowski ended the programme with a heart-rending scene filmed at Auschwitz concentration camp. Knee-deep in an ash-filled lake in front of the crematoria, he looked at the camera and said: 'It was not done by gas. It was done by arrogance. It was done by dogma ... When people believe they have absolute knowledge, this is how they behave.' Bronowski concluded with the words of Oliver Cromwell, writing to the General Assembly of the Kirk of Scotland in 1650: 'I beseech you, in the bowels of Christ, think it possible you may be mistaken.'[1]

The conviction that truth can be known with certainty, and that we can know it to the exclusion of others, lies at the root of some of the greatest tragedies in history, from inquisitions and crusades to the great atrocities of fascism and communism, and also many of our own most difficult arguments and conversations.

If we are honest, we are all of us wrong on occasion, probably more often than we'd like to admit. Rabbi David Wolpe points out that there are more ways to get an answer wrong than to get it right, so it is fair to assume that we are more often wrong than right.[2] But the courage to recognise the failings of one's position, especially publicly, is extraordinarily rare. Think, for example, of the countless hours of 'talking heads' television programmes you have watched. How often have you heard someone admit to being persuaded by a point made by the other side? Or even to having moderated their own opinions? The predominant paradigm is of a battle in which any admission of change or reflection will be seen as a cowardly retreat and only give succour to the forces of the other side. Often it seems that we are more afraid of admitting that we were wrong than of actually being wrong.

While we may not be experts at persuading others, we all seem to have a talent for persuading ourselves. So much so that those instances in which people genuinely re-examine their core opinions, and think it possible that they may be mistaken, are rare and striking indeed.

The courage to change

The environmental activists among the audience at the Oxford Farming Conference in 2013 smiled in anticipation as Mark Lynas took the stage. A leading environmental campaigner and leader of a group called Earth First!, he was a strident crusader against the forces of industrialism, which he saw as conspiring to bring about environmental apocalypse. Convinced that big corporations were deliberately manipulating the world's food supply through genetic modification so that they could take over the world's food chain for profit, Lynas had become a prominent leader in the anti-GM movement. Soon the movement turned to action and Lynas was involved in a series of 'decontamination actions', leading expeditions to destroy experimental GM crops and organising sit-ins at GM corporations.

So the environmental activists in the audience had good reason to anticipate the kind of full-frontal attack on GM that Lynas had become famous for. Instead, they saw him stand at the podium and begin his speech as follows:

> My lords, ladies and gentlemen. I want to start with some apologies, which I believe are most appropriate to this audience. For the record, here and upfront, I want to apologise for having spent several years ripping up GM crops. I'm also sorry that I helped to start the anti-GM movement back in the 1990s and that I thereby assisted in demonising an important technological option which can and should be used to benefit the environment. As an environmentalist, and someone who believes that everyone in this world has a right to a healthy and nutritious diet of their choosing, I could not have chosen a more counter-productive path and I now regret it completely.

What the activists did not know was that Lynas had had doubts for some time, which started when he began to write a book about the consequences of human-made climate change. 'I didn't want my book to be just a series of anecdotes,' he explained, 'so I began researching the science.' Eventually he realised that he couldn't be pro-science on the climate and not look into the scientific data on food production too. When he did so, the science painted a picture far more complicated than the one he had bought into. Not only did he discover that the arguments he had been making – and teaching others to make – were not backed up by the evidence. In reality, the data pointed to the fact

that biological solutions, like GM, could play a key role in reducing chemical use in food production.

Reading (or watching) that speech,[3] one can only be moved by
the depth of courage that Lynas demonstrated. Today Lynas is
still living with the consequences of that admission, and remains
the target of hostility among many of his former allies. But it is
not courage alone that is on display. It is courage married to intellectual modesty and openness.

How can we cultivate this frame of mind, in our organisations,
in our children and in ourselves? Faced with this challenge two
millennia ago, the rabbis had a powerful insight. To change our
certitude in our perception of the truth, they realised, we need to
change our understanding of the idea of Truth itself.

Truth above, truths below

Alongside the upheaval and exile they faced two millennia ago,
the Jewish people was also in danger of disintegration as a result
of rifts between rival groups, each holding fast to their own truths.
The rabbis' response was to suggest a radical reframing of the
idea of truth and certainty. This framing, which underpins the
rabbinic approach to argument, can be summarised as 'Truth
above, but truths below'.

In Jewish thought, Truth – in the abstract – is revered as the
highest of values. From their earliest years, Jewish children are
instilled with a passion and awe for the concept of truth. When
introduced to the mysterious magic of the Hebrew language they
learn that *emet*, the word for truth, consists of the first, middle
and last letter of the *aleph bet*; and it combines the words *em* and
met, from mother's womb to the last dying breath. In the closing
words of the Shema, the holiest of prayers, God is described as
Truth. If, for the Greeks, what was beautiful was true, then for
Jews, what is true is beautiful.

This is Truth above. Truth below, in this imperfect world, is
another matter. Truth as an ideal is uplifting and inspiring, but in

practice the conviction that one is in possession of absolute verity can – and in history repeatedly does – lead to intolerance and persecution. But the alternative, absolute relativism, invites the mirror danger: a world in which all is permitted. Is there a way to navigate these rival differences, to avoid the dangers of uncompromising conviction on the one hand, and valueless relativism on the other?

In response there developed an unusual conception of Truth that seeks to walk this narrow but critically important path. It was illustrated by rabbi and philosopher Jonathan Sacks when he was invited to speak at a memorial service for philosopher Isaiah Berlin. He chose to relate to the concerns that Berlin had expressed about the dangers of claims to absolute truth: 'Few things have done more harm,' Berlin had written, 'than the belief on the part of individuals or groups that they are in sole possession of the truth.'

Sacks maintained that Berlin was right to be concerned that the conviction that one has access to absolute truth does indeed bring with it the dangers of hubris and intolerance. Then, however, demonstrating the unusual balancing act with regard to Truth encapsulated in Jewish tradition, Sacks quoted a surprising legend from the rabbinic Midrash. The legend recounts that, when God was creating the world, the Angel of Truth begged God not to create humankind. Humans will be full of deceit, Truth said. Imperfect humanity cannot live side by side with pristine truth. In the legend, God agrees with Truth – there is indeed a mismatch. But He chooses to side with humankind. Rather than reject humankind, God hurls Truth to the earth, where Truth splits into millions of shards. The Midrash concludes with the heavenly angels in dismay. What will You do without the holy seal of Truth? they ask. God answers by quoting a verse from Psalms: 'Truth will grow up from the ground.'[4] No longer an authoritative verity that descends from on high, Truth becomes instead an understanding that emerges organically from below.

Sacks cited this passage to make the point that there is indeed truth in heaven – in the Platonic ideal – but that here in our complex and imperfect world, there is not one Truth but truths, fragments that need to be brought together. The fact that truth is seen only partially and imperfectly is inherent to the human condition. 'The divine word comes from heaven,' he said, 'but it is interpreted on earth. Divine light is refracted through human understanding; we can glimpse a part but not the whole.'⁵

Language itself unavoidably places cultural limitations on our ability to comprehend a universal truth. There is no way we can speak, communicate or even think without placing ourselves within the constraints of a particular language, its contours shaped by generations of speakers, storytellers, artists and visionaries who came before us. This can lead to diametrically different approaches. Consider the German and Hebrew words for 'key'. In German, the word *Schlüssel* comes from the verb *Schliessen*, 'to close'. In Hebrew the word *mafteach* comes from *liftoach*, 'to open'. Two different ways of seeing the world, one seeing it as about order and containment, the other looking for ways to go beyond boundaries and open things up. Organic, animate and responsive to its environment, language indeed is life.

The notion that we can remain unflinching in our conviction that there is, in fact, an absolute truth, but at the same time must accept that our grasp of it is necessarily limited, echoes through Jewish tradition. Even the biblical prophets, a rabbinic legend teaches, only received divine revelation 'through a cloudy lens'.⁶

This approach explains a mystery in the heart of Jewish sanctity. In the centre of the Tabernacle of ancient Israel, the Tent of Meeting, in the very Holy of Holies, stood the Ark of the Covenant. Within the Ark were kept the tablets of stone, on which were engraved the Ten Commandments. Beside them in the Ark were kept the fragments of the original set of tablets which had been smashed by Moses when he descended the mountain the first time and saw the golden calf. Why was Moses commanded to keep these broken fragments alongside the whole tablets in the Ark? Generations of Bible commentators have offered a multiplicity of reasons, but it seems to me that they were simply too dangerous not to be locked safely away. If they were not closely guarded, the separate pieces might have been grabbed by different sections of the community, and each brandished as holy and absolute truth in its own right. Instead, they were to be placed in the holy Ark, next to the complete tablets, an eternal reminder that truth is not to be found in any one fragment that we might hold, but only in the whole, when we bring all the pieces together.

The fragment we hold

This reframing of the concept of truth is empowering and humbling in equal measure. On the one hand, it assures us that we are indeed custodians of truth, holding fragments of holy revelation, sparks of the divine understanding. On the other, it reminds us that while we may hold truth, we do not hold *the* truth. To get closer to *the* truth, as we shall see, requires a process of reaching out and engaging with others.

This framing doesn't ask us to give up on truth, but to have a certain humility about our version of it. A young man I was privileged to know, Benji Telushkin, was a remarkable student of Jewish studies, whose thoughtful writings were published after his untimely death. He found this idea reflected in the Garden of Eden in a way I had never noticed. In an essay he wrote at the age of fifteen he observed:

> Adam and Eve only took a bite from the Tree of knowledge of Good and Evil, they never ate the whole fruit. With Adam and Eve's limited consumption of the tree's fruit, came fractional knowledge . . . We, the descendants of Adam and Eve, did not eat all of the fruit, so therefore we do not know a big part of the universal truth. We fill in the blanks with our private agenda. This makes objective truth nearly impossible to achieve or to recognize . . .[7]

We are indeed custodians of truth, but not of the whole of the truth. There are fragments of the tablets, or parts of the apple, that are not in our grasp. While we may never attain the whole, we can constantly strive to gain a fuller picture. The truth that we cherish is in fact a thesis, one that we should be ready to re-examine and even change if necessary.

Consider the Talmudic story of Shimon HaAssamoni, who had to face the harsh fact that the truth that underpinned his life's work was built on shaky foundations. Shimon HaAssamoni is described as a dedicated scholar of the Hebrew text of the Bible. In particular, he was fascinated by a tiny word that recurs in the text. A characteristic of Hebrew is that the definite direct object is preceded by the word *et*. Generally, it is considered that this tiny word has no role in the text other than to distinguish the subject from the object, for otherwise, in the curious grammar of Hebrew, there would be no way to tell apart 'the boy ate the dog' from 'the dog ate the boy'. Shimon HaAssamoni, however, was convinced that, as a sacred text, every word in the Bible had special meaning, and set out to derive the added significance of every occurrence of the word *et* in the Hebrew Bible – some 1,420 occurrences! It seems that this painstaking exercise was proceeding well until he came to the verse 'You shall be in awe of [*et*] the Lord your God' (Deuteronomy 10:20). At this point he gave up on the exercise. How could anything be added to the Almighty God? The Talmud describes the astonishment of his students at his decision to give up his life's work, asking him: 'What will be with all the *et*s that you interpreted until now?' His answer is a model of intellectual integrity: 'Just as I received reward for the elucidation, so I shall receive reward for my renunciation.'[8] The message is clear: our ability to rethink our conclusions is just as impressive and worthy as the intellectual effort that helped us reach them in the first place.

Confident humility

Close to two thousand years separate Shimon HaAssamoni's renunciation of his life's scholarship and Mark Lynas's admission that the scientific evidence didn't support his core convictions about GM. But the two are kindred spirits, representing as they do a rare amalgam of intellectual modesty and personal courage – or, as one writer has termed it, 'confident humility'.

This term 'confident humility' is proposed by organisational psychologist Adam Grant in his book *Think Again*. He argues that, alongside the analytical skills we are traditionally taught, we need to acquire another set of cognitive skills that might matter even more: the ability to rethink and unlearn. To this end, he suggests, we need to develop a mind-frame of confident humility. He explains that both confidence and humility tend to be misunderstood. Regarding humility, he notes: 'Humility is often misunderstood. It's not a matter of having low self-confidence. One of the Latin roots of *humility* means 'from the earth'. It's about being grounded, recognizing that we're flawed and fallible.'

How striking that humility means 'from the earth', an interesting echo of the rabbis' vision of fragments of truth emerging from the soil. But humility alone is not enough. It might simply cower us into silence. So it must be matched with confidence. But as Grant points out, confidence is also often misunderstood:

Confidence is a measure of how much you believe in yourself. Evidence shows that's distinct from how much you believe in your methods. You can be confident in your ability to achieve a goal in the future while maintaining the humility to question whether you have the right tools in the present; that's the sweet spot of confidence . . . We become blinded by arrogance when we are utterly convinced of our strengths and our strategies. We get paralyzed by doubt when we lack conviction in both . . . what we want to attain is confident humility.[9]

In the frame of mind that Grant proposes, we remain confident in our ability to pursue the truth. Our humility relates to the judgements that we have reached at any given moment, which we are encouraged to see as hypotheses and not conclusions.

44

In our Difficult Conversations laboratories, participants are invited to share a moment in which they had reconsidered a core belief or assumption. Often these will relate to misjudgements of other people, and occasionally to fundamental changes of ideological position. What is always interesting to me is that for the most part, the process of genuine rethinking requires a catalyst, some significant event to shake us out of our certainties.

For James O'Brien, a popular British radio talk show host who enjoyed a reputation for his combative and sometimes brutal exchanges with his callers, the catalyst was a family crisis. With a daily radio show with over a million listeners, he might well have continued on his combative path indefinitely, were it not for an upheaval within his private life. When someone he deeply loved became seriously ill, he realised with a jolt that he was 'wildly ill-equipped to provide the help and support that was both my desire and my duty'.[10]

In becoming a better arguer, he realised, he had become less of a human being. Notwithstanding his fear that he might 'therapise himself out of a successful broadcast career' he underwent a process of therapy and self-examination, which he charts in his book *How Not to be Wrong*. He came to understand that his abrasive 'fight or flight' mentality had its roots in a troubled childhood, which included repeated beatings at an appalling British boarding school and which led him to subscribe to the notion that the best form of defence is attack. As a result, he admits, 'I found it impossible to retreat from any position, even if I'd only arrived at it five minutes previously.'[11] But not even the most committed Knight of the Round Table, as he puts it, would have wanted to spend his entire life in fifty kilos of full armour. Slowly he came to recognise that the rigidity of his positions was less a sign of strength than one of weakness and insecurity. He began to wonder 'whether some of the opprobrium we reserve for people who change their minds about politics and politicians springs from a suppressed knowledge that our own convictions are built on altogether flimsier foundations than we care to admit'.[12]

Hiding our doubts often seems an easier course than changing our views. An apocryphal story is told of a visiting lecturer at Cambridge University who left his lecture notes behind on the podium. The students were amused to see his handwritten note alongside one passage in his lecture: 'Raise voice, argument weak!'

O'Brien's journey from certainty to questioning led to a fundamental rethinking of his positions on issues as varied as police powers of stop and search, obesity and corporal punishment, concluding: 'There's no point having a mind if you never change it.'

When I was invited to join a team preparing an online course on contentious issues dividing Israeli society, the content of the course was hammered out in a lively steering committee comprising leading academics from across the political and ideological spectrum. Observing these debates, I noticed that one participant in particular, an eminent legal scholar, the late Ruth Gavison, seemed to carry notable weight and was listened to with especial interest and respect. The reason, it occurred to me, was that while the other committee members were also deeply intelligent and similarly eminent, she had a rare gift of considering every question that came up from first principles and without preconceptions. The result was that, unlike most other members of the committee, you never knew what position she would take, and were frequently surprised. It may be worth asking ourselves in a quiet moment: are our own positions and opinions disappointingly predictable, or have we retained the ability to think afresh and surprise others – and ourselves?

The sterility of certainty

'Doubt is not a pleasant condition,' wrote Voltaire, 'but certainty is a ridiculous one.' Certainty is not only ridiculous in its confidence and hubris; it is also barren and unproductive. It fails to question either others or itself; it fails to engage. It lacks what the poet John Keats termed 'negative capability', the creative capacity to live in 'uncertainties, mysteries, doubts'. This is beautifully expressed by the Israeli poet Yehuda Amichai:

The Place Where We Are Right
From the place where we are right
flowers will never grow
in the spring.

The place where we are right
is hard and trampled
like a yard.

But doubts and loves
dig up the world
like a mole, a plough,
and a whisper will be heard in the place
where the ruined house once stood.[13]

This is the starting point of the rabbis' reimagination of argument. Truth is not a battle to be waged or a crusade to be fought. Rather, in the image echoed by Amichai, it's a field to be ploughed and carefully tended. Our hesitations and uncertainties are not signs of weakness or a failure of conviction. To the contrary, it is certainty that is a sterile soil, incapable of giving birth to new ideas and creative expression. Genuine fertility can only come in a place of 'doubts and loves'. In such a field, nurtured with confident humility, truth may yet grow up from the ground.

Chapter 2

Rethinking Difference: Your Truth and Mine

When two people always agree, one of them is unnecessary.

William Wrigley, Jr

In the musical *Fiddler on the Roof*, two villagers bring a quarrel to the rabbi of Anatevka. The first villager presents his case. 'You're right,' says the rabbi. The second then presents his opposing case. 'You're also right,' the rabbi says. 'But Rabbi,' exclaims Tevye the milkman, 'they can't both be right!' 'You know,' says the rabbi, 'you are also right!'

The rabbinic conception of truth, as we have seen, relates to a vertical axis – a single absolute truth above and many fragmentary truths, or understandings of truth, below. In addition, the rabbis suggested another, horizontal, axis. Here, the relationship isn't between our understanding of truth and a higher truth, but between our 'truth' and the 'truths' of others. On this axis, there is not a binary choice between right and wrong in each instance, but rather, as the rabbi of Anatevka suggested, two opposing but potentially valid truths.

Consider the Talmud's description of a lengthy dispute between the schools of the sages Hillel and Shammai:

> For three years the schools of Hillel and Shammai were engaged in debate, with one side saying 'The law is like us', and the other saying 'The law is like us', until a heavenly voice emerged and proclaimed: 'Both sides' opinions are the words of the living God. But the law is according to the school of Hillel.'[1]

Notice that we are not told what this lengthy argument was about. This is because the Talmud is making a point about arguments in

48

general. There is a paradigm in which contradictory positions can coexist. Even in a debate between opposites, the spirit of the living God can be found on both sides. But as much as we may aspire to such a non-binary perspective, that is not the reality that we live in. Even the heavenly voice, after declaring that both sides have divine legitimacy, adds the seemingly contradictory caveat: 'But the law is according to the school of Hillel.'

There may be a higher world in which parallel rulings can coexist, but not ours. In our world we need practical courses of action. This is the paradox of Judaism's framing of truth. Truth above is singular and unified, but truth below is fragmented and multiple. In our limited realm we can only live according to one practical ruling at a time. But there is, we are assured, a non-binary vantage point where both can exist in parallel.

The conviction that competing and apparently inconsistent truths can, from a different viewpoint, be reconciled, was also conveyed by the rabbis in legends relating to the two tablets containing the Ten Commandments, surely the place where one would have most expected to find unbending certainty. The rabbinic legends recount a number of miraculous features of the tablets. One was that the letters of the Ten Commandments were chiselled all the way through the stones to the other side. This alone would be miraculous enough, since some of the Hebrew letters, like the English letters O and Q, contain closed circles that would require the stone within to float in mid-air. But for the rabbis the truly miraculous aspect of the writing was that it could be read equally well from both sides. Even in relation to the most fundamental tenets of faith, there are different ways in which things can be read, different perspectives that could potentially be reconciled.

A curious Talmudic story tries to offer a glimpse at how this kind of reconciliation might look in practice.[2] Two rabbis, Evyatar and Yonatan, are engaged in a debate over an episode described in the book of Judges, known as the story of the Levite's concubine. Their debate was specifically over the arcane issue of whether it was

49

a hair or a fly that ruined his bowl of soup and caused the Levite in the story to become enraged. While the debate over this literally hair-splitting issue is still in progress, the Talmud recounts that one of the rabbis, Evyatar, comes across Elijah the prophet, who is visiting earth from heaven. He asks him: 'What is the Holy One, Blessed be He, doing now?' Elijah replies, 'He is studying the episode of the Levite's concubine.' Evyatar seizes the moment to ask Elijah: 'And what is God's position on our argument?' Elijah replies: 'God is saying the following: "Evyatar, my son, argues this opinion, and Yonatan, my son, argues that opinion!"'

We might think that Evyatar would be flattered that his opinion, along with Yonatan's, is being cited by God. But, in fact, he is appalled, because he assumes that in the heavens above there is only the Truth, a single correct answer. He shares his frustration with Elijah: 'God forbid, is there such uncertainty in Heaven?' Doesn't God know what happened? Why does He mention both opinions? Elijah replies that there is no uncertainty. Rather: 'Both these and those are the words of the living God. The incident occurred in the following manner: there was a fly and then there was a hair.' Both opinions are true, and both are necessary to the story.

While the case in hand is simplistic, the message is profound. There *is* a single Truth on high, but from that vantage point it includes both, apparently contradictory, narratives. In fact, Elijah continues, not only *can* both narratives be true, but both *must* be true. Both were necessary for the story to happen, but only from the vantage point of heaven is this resolution visible. Can we here on earth aspire to this perspective?

The unity of opposites

One more recent rabbinic thinker who gave considerable thought to developing a perspective expansive enough to encompass opposing positions was Abraham Isaac Kook. In his early twentieth-century philosophical work 'Orot Hakodesh' ('Lights of Holiness'), he argues that truth is to be found in all ideas and ideologies – all flow from the source of wisdom and all are systematically connected. He invites us to imagine a different perspective, *achdut hahafachim* – the 'unity of opposites', in which all opinions are organically and harmoniously entwined. Drawing on the traditional image of the Torah as a 'Tree of Life', Kook gives a beautiful analogy. The spaces between our opinions and those of others are not areas of difference. Rather, they are like the spaces between saplings in the soil. What may look like distance is actually the space needed to give each independent sapling the room which will provide the light and nutrients required in order to develop fully. Kook's image echoes a statement about friendship by the philosopher Walter Benjamin: 'It does not abolish the distance between human beings but brings that distance to life.'[3]

The image of very differing positions as saplings that emerge from common soil finds contemporary expression in the work of social psychologist Jonathan Haidt. In *The Righteous Mind* he addresses the gulf of understanding between many conservatives and liberals. He makes the case that liberals and conservatives tend to draw their worldviews from a common soil, or shared set of values, with the differences in outlook deriving from the different weights accorded to the different values, like recipes with different quantities of the same ingredients. Liberals, he argues, tend to accentuate the values of fairness and preventing harm, while conservatives temper these with more traditional ideals of loyalty, authority and sanctity. He brings compelling evidence to show that while the weight we each give to these values may differ, to some degree they are all values we can and do respect. These are all necessary values in society, he argues, so the perspectives and positions to which they give birth are 'like Yin and Yang in Chinese philosophy, complementary and interdependent'. Echoing Kook, Haidt paints his own picture of *achdut hahafachim*, the unity of opposites: 'Night and day are not enemies, nor are hot and cold, summer and winter, male and female. We need both, often in a shifting or alternating balance.'[4]

This approach to difference is more radical than it seems at first. It is not a call for tolerance, but for partnership. The point is not to say that you have your way of viewing and I have mine, like the optical illusion of the young lady and the old woman, but rather to insist that we *need* to engage with others if we are to have any chance of advancing our understanding. If we are on a genuine journey towards truth, we cannot go alone.

The myth of the lone genius

The rabbinic tradition has at its heart a conviction that the search for truth must be a collaborative exercise: 'Form many groups and study Torah, for Torah is only acquired through study in a group,' advises the Talmud.[5]

This notion that the search for truth and understanding has to be collaborative stands roundly at odds with a deeply engrained Western conception – that of the solitary genius. Captured figuratively by Rodin's famous sculpture *The Thinker*, the view that profound insight is achieved by intense thought in moments of quiet contemplation is a persistent theme in the Western intellectual tradition. Whether it is Archimedes alone in his bath, or Newton sitting quietly beneath his apple tree, the dominant images and stories of human genius in Western thought tend to buttress the idea that the resources for achieving wisdom are to be found within ourselves.

In *Powers of Two: Finding the Essence of Innovation in Creative Pairs*, writer and arts critic Joshua Wolf Shenk challenges this conception. 'For centuries,' he notes, 'the myth of the lone genius has towered over us like a Colossus. The idea that new, beautiful, world-changing things come from within great minds is now so common that we don't even consider it an idea.'[6] Shenk argues that the myth of the lone genius 'emerged in the enlightenment, grew popular in the romantic era, and took its final shape in the contemporary United States'. It has been echoed and amplified by a culture that emphasises the role of the sole genius, 'the ones who made the Sistine Chapel or Hamlet, the light bulb or the iPod' in the spirit of Thomas Carlyle's declaration in the 1840s: 'The history of the world is but the biography of great men [and women].'

Shenk offers some interesting theories as to how exactly this myth took such deep root. He conjectures that we, the public, as consumers of art or literature, have contributed to the resilience of this myth ourselves, since we prefer to imagine ourselves in direct communication with an author or artist, rather than as an outsider eavesdropping on a creative dialogue between others. He also surmises that the Cold War may have played a role, with the United States being reluctant to attribute benefits to collectivist approaches and so insisting on the primacy of individualist creativity.

Whatever its origins, though, Shenk insists that the myth of the solitary genius is precisely that, a myth, 'predicated on an even more fundamental myth of the enclosed, autonomous self for whom social experience is secondary'.[7] Instead, as a truer way to understand the nature of creativity, he offers the model of the creative pair.

In a broad historical survey, Shenk not only looks at classic examples of creative pairings in science and art (the Wright brothers, Marie and Pierre Curie, Steve Jobs and Steve Wozniak and so on) but also reassesses figures who have found their place in our collective imagination as creative loners. On closer inspection he discovers that invariably these individuals too were inspired, challenged or otherwise received critical intellectual support from close partners or colleagues. In the arts, for example, Vincent van Gogh's brother Theo turns out to have been not only a manager and financial backer, but a true intellectual and creative partner, while Picasso and Matisse spurred each other on and inspired each other with collegial rivalry. Writers such as Thomas Wolfe and F. Scott Fitzgerald were nurtured and their publications profoundly shaped by editors whose roles went far beyond simply editing their manuscripts. Even Einstein, argues Shenk, depended on his colleague Michele Besso, who enabled him, as he said, to 'suddenly comprehend the matter'; while the leading investment analyst Warren Buffett often paid tribute to his more reticent but essential colleague, Charlie Munger: 'Charlie does the talking, I just move my lips.'

For all the attraction of the solitary thinker motif, argues Shenk, creative dialogue is where the business of insight and discovery is more likely to happen. This is a deeply rabbinic insight and, as we will see, it lies at the heart of a number of core practices that the rabbinic tradition developed, such as the *havruta* study partnerships that are central to the learning process.

Beyond being a pedagogical technique, the *havruta* methodology reflects the conviction that the search for knowledge is of necessity a collaborative enterprise. As a result, argument is not a clash of rival and disparate truths. Rather, it is a fiery crucible for the creation of something new.

Shenk gives a striking example from the modern age: the cooperative rivalry between musicians John Lennon and Paul McCartney. Their very different styles were critical to the musical synergy that gave the Beatles their unique voice, but the creative energy did not end there. Alongside their cooperation there was a strong internal rivalry. One of the arenas in which this played out was in the singles they produced, which were issued with one song on each side. All records had an A-side and a B-side, so that listeners would know which side to play first. The competition between the two, as to whose composition would be placed on the A-side, pushed each to their creative limits. As their producer and arranger George Martin described it, they were like two guys tugging on a rope – smiling, but each pulling with all their might. The competition came to a crux when each produced their own musical masterpiece for the same single – most memorably with 'Strawberry Fields Forever' and 'Penny Lane'. In a powerful symbolic representation of the power of adversarial collaboration, they released what they called a 'double A-side' single.

I suspect that if the rabbis of old had had the chance to hear the Beatles, they would have loved the notion of a double A-side single, capturing as it does the unique value of the creative clash. As it was, they called it something else: argument for the sake of heaven.

Chapter 3

Rethinking Argument: The Truth Between Us

As long as we think of disagreement as that which divides us, we shall dislike it; when we think of it as that which unites us, we shall cherish it.

Mary Parker Follett

A rabbinic tale tells of a student who had a question that troubled him deeply. He went to all the rabbis and teachers in his village and none could answer it. One of them told him that the only person who could answer such a difficult question was a great sage in a town many days' travel away. He tried to forget the question, but it would not let him rest. Finally, he made the journey to the distant town. He entered the sage's room and asked him the question. 'That is truly a great question,' said the sage. 'But tell me. Are you really prepared to give it away . . . for a mere answer!?'[1]

We are schooled to think of an argument as a problem to be solved. In Jewish tradition though, differences and questions are not simply equations in search of a solution, but rather engines to inspire and spur on creative thought. Indeed, in the realm of ideas the real value is to be found not where we agree but where we differ.

The notion that value is to be found in difference rather than agreement is a fundamental idea in modern negotiation theory. Negotiation analysts often divide the issues up for discussion on the table into *distributive* and *integrative*. Distributive issues are those where both parties want the same limited resource, so that a tug of war ensues. A common example is the price of an item: the seller wants it as high and the buyer as low as possible. There is no room for value creation, only value claiming. *Integrative* issues, on the other hand, arise from a difference in perspectives and priorities. Here, by *integrating* the different elements at play, there may be room for expanding the pie. The classic example given is of a parent who sees two children fighting over an orange. To make peace between them, the parent cuts the orange in two and gives one half to each child. But watching the children afterwards, the parent notices that one takes the flesh of the orange to make juice and throws the peel away, while the other takes the peel to make marmalade, casting the flesh aside. In fact, the parent realises that had they been sensitive to the difference of interests between the two sides, each child could have got not half of what they wanted, but all of it.

As simplistic as this example sounds, our negotiations in the Middle East give some practical examples of precisely this idea. One is to be found in the 1979 peace treaty between Israel and Egypt. At the time of the peace talks, Israel was in control of the Sinai desert, which it had captured in the Six Day War of 1967. Egypt demanded its return. With both sides insisting that they should be given the Sinai as part of any agreement, the dispute seemed intractable. But on closer examination it became clear that there was an essential difference between the stated positions of the two sides and their true core interests. For Egypt the critical interest was being able to declare sovereignty over the area, while for Israel the interest was ensuring that the territory could not be used to launch future attacks. The resulting agreement recognised Egyptian sovereignty but included security provisions, including demilitarised zones and the presence of multinational forces, to prevent hostile action.

A similar approach would later be used to resolve a dispute over border farming areas between Israel and Jordan. The agreement that was reached acknowledged Jordan's sovereignty but permitted Israeli farmers to continue to cultivate the areas in question. Had there not been a difference in terms of interest between the sides, no agreement could have been reached. As Mark Twain quipped, 'It were best that we not all think alike, it is difference of opinion that makes for horse races.'[2]

Truth and friction

While this 'win-win' school of negotiation achieved popularity in the 1980s, with classic texts such as *Getting to Yes*, the principle of digging down into our differences to find the potential for resolution goes back much further. Mary Parker Follett, a pioneering social worker and organisational consultant in the early twentieth century, was one of the first to suggest that the differences between us may be resources that can be made to work for us. She urged:

> I should like to ask you to agree for the moment to think of conflict as neither good nor bad; to consider it without ethical prejudgment; to think of it not as warfare, but as the appearance of difference, difference of opinions, of interests. For that is what conflict means – difference . . . As conflict is here in the world, as we cannot avoid it, we should, I think, use it. Instead of condemning it, we should set it to work for us . . . Why not? What does the mechanical engineer do with friction? Of course, his chief job is to eliminate friction, but it is true that he also capitalizes friction.[3]

Writing in a time of rapid industrialisation, Follett gives us a powerful image of friction as the resistance without which mechanical engines cannot run. So too, in our arguments, it is the spark-inducing clashes between our differences that spur innovation. It is precisely such creative clashes that led the Beatles to create the double A-side single, and the rabbis to reframe intense debates and disputes as arguments for the sake of heaven.

As we have seen, the rabbis offered a radical reimagining of the concepts of truth and difference. With regard to truth, they proposed a vertical axis. At the upper end was Truth, absolute and pristine. Below were truths, our fragmentary glimpses that are necessarily partial and incomplete. With regard to difference, on the horizontal axis, they proposed that even contradictory positions, if viewed from the right perspective, could be not just legitimate but could actually combine to offer deeper and fuller understanding.

The rabbis' conception of a good argument, one that is guided by the right motivation, and conducted in the right way, brings together these horizontal and vertical dimensions. The path to understanding truth, our vertical aspiration, runs through the horizontal dynamic of interpersonal dialogue. The search for truth is an inherently human exercise; our interactions with each other are intrinsically entwined with the divine. It is a model that seeks to navigate the tension between hubris and hopelessness: truth is not within us; it is between us. It is not 'we' – either you or me, the antagonists in the debate – who are 'for the sake of heaven', but *the argument itself* is for the sake of heaven. It is a ladder that we create together in order that we may climb to higher levels of understanding.

If the model of Rodin's *Thinker* became a symbol of the myth of the solitary genius, perhaps another Rodin sculpture, *The Cathedral*, captures the essence of this approach. Two hands, barely touching, create a sacred space between them. It is not the hands that are sacred in their own right, either singly or in combination; they are simply the scaffolding. But without them – both of them – the holy space within could not exist.

The search for truth – a moral journey

It's told that Mahatma Gandhi was once asked by a mother to speak to her son. 'The doctor says he must stop having sweet things or his health will suffer. Perhaps if you tell him, he will listen to you.' Gandhi told her to come back with her son a week later. One week later when she returned with her son Gandhi looked at the boy and said: 'Stop eating sweet things.' The mother looked at him in surprise. 'Couldn't you have said that a week ago?' Gandhi replied: 'But a week ago I was still eating sweet things myself.'

At the root of the concept of argument for the sake of heaven is the understanding that, while the truth is not to be found by simply looking within ourselves, it also cannot be discovered without us. The conviction that the truth cannot be divined outside of an inter-personal relationship has a fundamental implication. The search for truth is not simply an intellectual, but also a moral, endeavour. We may not be, as we might like to think, self-contained reposit-ories of truth, but we have the capacity to be channels for truth. As such, working on our moral selves and developing positive charac-ter traits can help clear the pipes through which insight and under-standing can enter the world. To engage effectively in the process of truth-seeking, we must, like Gandhi, work not only on the quality of our arguments but also on the quality of our selves.

Some scholars have suggested that recognition of this moral dimension is a defining characteristic of the Jewish approach to argument. Howard Kaminsky, Jewish scholar and mediator, in an extensive survey comparing general contemporary conflict resolu-tion techniques and traditional Jewish approaches, notes: 'I don't believe that I have ever seen in intermediary conflict literature a discussion about the importance of having pure, noble, or holy motivations as one finds in traditional Jewish approaches.'[4]

In the Jewish tradition, intellectual and moral qualities are inseparable. The Mishnaic compilation 'Pirkei Avot', 'The Ethics of the Fathers', lists forty-eight essential practices for acquiring Torah. Many of these are established habits of good study: clear thinking, precision, concentration, attentive listening, fine argumentation and so on. But interspersed among these, with no sense that there is any category difference between them, are qualities that we would not expect to find in a list of purely academic credentials, including: humility, joy, generosity, being someone who rejoices in their portion, and being someone who cites their authorities and gives credit to the person who taught them.

The twelfth-century sage Maimonides, in the introduction to his great philosophical work *The Guide to the Perplexed*, gives advice to the reader on how to embark on intellectual study. He begins by stressing the need to master the relevant fields of science and academic knowledge. But then he goes on to add that one should also 'thoroughly refine one's moral character and subdue one's passions and desires in order to guard against fallacies'.

The truth between us

In 1923 the Jewish philosopher Martin Buber published *I and Thou*, in which he argued that human life finds meaning in relationships and that ultimately it is our relationships with each other that bring us into relationship with God. In the book Buber gave a name to the space between us – *das Zwischenmenschlich* – the zone of 'inbetweenness'. It is in this in-between zone that the horizontal and vertical zones come together.

The Bible itself hints at the unique holiness of this horizontal place of meeting in describing the dedication of the Tabernacle in the wilderness. After weeks of preparation, Moses enters the Holy of Holies to hear the voice of God. Strikingly, as described in the book of Numbers, the divine voice emerges not from the Ark itself, which contained the holy tablets, but from the carved statues of angels on its lid, or more precisely, from the space between them: 'When Moses entered the tent of meeting to speak with the LORD, he heard the voice speaking to him from between the two cherubim above the atonement cover on the ark of the covenant law. In this way the LORD spoke to him.'[5]

It is a theologically radical image. In the heart of the holy Tabernacle stood the chamber of the Holy of Holies, and within that the holy Ark of the Covenant. When Moses enters this holiest of places he finds not truth or certainty, but a conversation, perhaps even a debate. In later centuries the rabbis would suggest that the angels on the Ark were not simply angels; they were a *havruta*, a study partnership, engaged in argument for the sake of heaven.

Arguments built to last

What does an argument for the sake of heaven, one that is genuinely motivated by a search for truth, look like in practice? And what about an argument that isn't? The Mishnah gives an example of each: 'What was an argument for the sake of heaven? That of Hillel and Shammai. What was an argument that was not for the sake of heaven? That of Korah and his followers.'[6]

The paradigm of a genuine argument for truth presented by the Mishnah is of the classic pairing of the disputing Talmudic sages Hillel and Shammai. Set against them, as the paradigm of the opposite, is Korah who, the Bible recounts, led a leadership rebellion against his cousin Moses in the wilderness.

Notice that the Mishnah seems to avoid a direct parallel between the two cases. Against the example of Hillel and Shammai, the classic pair of halachic disputants in the Talmud, we would expect the Mishnah to refer to Korah and also to Moses, against whom Korah led his rebellion. The argument in question, however, is not described as being with Moses, but simply as the argument of 'Korah and his followers'. Why should this be? The rabbis suggest that this was not really a conflict, certainly not one with Moses. Indeed the framing of the dispute only as concerning Korah and his followers carries with it a subtle hint that had he succeeded in his coup, he would soon have been at odds with his own camp. The Bible describes Korah as framing his objections to Moses' leadership on grounds of principle. However, the rabbis insist that, like many arguments in our time, Korah's rebellion is not about what he claims it to be about. There is no search for truth here, but rather a masquerade, concealing personal greed and ambition. The problem is not so much that Korah's argument is not truly for the sake of heaven, but that it is not an argument at all.

The so-called 'argument' of Korah is reminiscent of international negotiations in which the parties go through the motions of negotiation for public display, but with no real interest in progressing the matters at hand. There have certainly been times in the history of the Middle East peace process when the parties, on both sides, were more interested in being seen to be taking part in the process than they were in making the tough choices necessary to reach peace. Lee Blessing's 1988 play *A Walk in the Woods* presents the breakout conversations between two Cold War arms limitation negotiators, one Soviet and one American, in the woods outside Geneva, where the talks are taking place. The Soviet diplomat is hardened and cynical and holds out little prospect of progress. The American negotiator, by contrast, is young and idealistic and unstinting in his efforts to come up with new and creative solutions. A critical turning point in the play is when the idealistic American negotiator returns to Washington for instructions and is told by the President, 'Don't try so hard.' He realises that this is not in fact a genuine negotiation; he is playing a part in a political showcase. This is not unusual in diplomatic life. A well-known saying among diplomats is: 'You can change my opinion, but you can't change my instructions!'

As we engage in debate, therefore, the Mishnah suggests that we should ask ourselves what our motivations really are. Are we like Korah, only wanting our own way so that any argument that is brought, however cogent or persuasive, is simply window-dressing for a predetermined agenda? Or are we engaged in true dialogue towards the best solution, without a fixed agenda, where, as much as we believe in the truth of our case, we recognise that there may also be elements of truth and value in the case of the other side? This, the rabbis tell us, was the nature of the debates between Hillel and Shammai – not a public display, but a genuine search for truth.

The overriding wish to prevail, to achieve victory, is anathema to a genuine search for truth. In the words of the Hassidic master Nachman of Breslav: 'The notion of victory cannot countenance the truth, for even if someone sees the truth, they will reject it out of a desire for victory.'[7] But paradoxically, those, like Hillel and Shammai, who seek not victory but truth, are, in a way, assured of victory. As Jonathan Sacks notes: 'If I argue for the sake of truth, then if I win, I win. But if I lose, I also win, because being defeated by the truth is the only defeat that is also a victory. I am enlarged. I learn something I did not know before.'[8]

In portraying the two models of argument, the Mishnah comments that the first paradigm, the argument for the sake of heaven, 'will endure', but the second 'will not endure'. This formulation is puzzling, suggesting that the argument will continue indefinitely when we normally assume that arguments are there precisely to be resolved. But it makes sense when we recognise that an argument is not a problem to be solved but an engine of creative thought, a means to generate new ideas and sparks of truth.

The limits of legitimacy – the seventy-first face of wisdom

Before we turn from these rabbinic principles regarding truth, difference and argument, to the tangible practices that seek to reflect and embed them in our own arguments and difficult conversations, a word of caution may be in order. The approach we have looked at urges us to be humble with regard to our own positions, and open to recognising the legitimacy to be found within opposing views. Since truth is to be found through a collaborative exercise, we need to be open to new and surprising ideas, even – or perhaps especially – when they seem to run counter to our own deeply held convictions.

Before we get too comfortable in this particular conviction, though, we should consider whether in this also we may be mistaken. Do all positions and ideas deserve a hearing? Are there opinions that are so objectionable on the one hand, or ridiculous on the other, that they fall outside the parameters of legitimate debate? Is there a danger, as one American professor warned his students, of being so openminded that your brains fall out?

In Jewish terms one might frame the question slightly differently. A tradition teaches that there are seventy faces to the Torah: that is, a multiplicity of interpretations and positions that all have their own validity. But the insistence that there can be seventy valid positions doesn't rule out the possibility of a seventy-first face, a position that is invalid. How can we determine whether a position is one of the seventy legitimate ones, or a seventy-first that should be discarded?

The thrust of the traditional Jewish framings we have looked at is clear: when in doubt, hear them out. To use a phrase coined by American academic and activist Loretta J. Ross, it urges 'calling in' rather than 'calling out'. As Ross explains the difference: 'Calling out assumes the worst. Calling in involves conversation, compassion and context.'[9]

A Talmudic story takes this approach to almost comical extremes. A student approaches the great sage Judah HaNasi, and asks him about the laws of phylacteries (the boxed scrolls traditionally bound on one's arm and forehead during morning prayers). If a person is born with two heads, asks the student, on which of the two heads should the phylacteries be placed? Judah HaNasi has no patience for these absurd hypotheticals. 'Get out of here,' he tells the student. 'Or better yet, excommunicate yourself!' But before the student can respond, the Talmud recounts, another person enters with their own question for the rabbi: 'I have just had a firstborn baby with two heads. When I fulfil the commandment of making the traditional payment for the redemption of this firstborn child, do I pay for one child or for two?'[10] Without knowing it, the newcomer is chiding the sage, reminding him, in the words of Hamlet, that 'there are more things in heaven and earth than are dreamt of in your philosophy'.

In traditional Jewish thinking, closed minds are far more of a danger than open ones. There have been cases of excommunication in the course of Jewish history, most famously the expulsion of the seventeenth-century philosopher Baruch Spinoza from the Amsterdam Jewish community for what were seen as his heretical writings. But such exclusion is almost universally regarded as an exceptional measure, and one to be discouraged. Maimonides, in his codification of Jewish law, advises strongly against excommunication and indeed in listing the possible grounds for excommunication concludes with the 'crime' of declaring an unjustified excommunication – a stern warning that when we try to ostracise or silence others we may find ourselves silenced in turn.

Underpinning this approach is the understanding that things which seem outrageous and unacceptable may indeed be so, but not necessarily at all times and in all contexts. Jewish tradition preserves and cherishes minority opinions, the rejected viewpoints, because there may come a new day or a different situation in which that opinion will need to be relied upon. Many differences can be resolved, or at least mitigated, if we apply what Jonathan Sacks has termed the 'chronological imagination'. Over the course of Jewish history some debates between different sects have been so furious that they have led to excommunication and even the burning of books belonging to the other side. This is one reason why entering a Jewish library today is such a moving experience. On the shelves, the books of the different factions now sit peaceably side by side, together adding to the repository of Jewish knowledge. In the eighteenth century, for example, the followers of the brilliant rationalist sage the Vilna Gaon roundly attacked the radically spiritual teachings of the Baal Shem Tov, the founder of the Hassidic movement, leading to book-burning and violence. But 300 years later the books of their followers sit together on the shelves in dialogue.

There is, to be sure, a fundamental difference between dissent in the realm of ideas, and statements likely to lead to a clear and present danger, as we see in the classic objection against shouting

'Fire!' in a crowded theatre. In the Jewish tradition, this distinction finds expression in the character of the Zaken Mamre, literally 'a rebellious elder', but in practice a scholar who presents radically anti-establishment positions. Even where he wages a direct attack on the rulings of the court, the Jewish tradition avers, the maverick is committing no offence and should be free to express and teach his positions. Only when he specifically calls on people to defy the rule of law does he cross the line from the exchange of ideas to sedition.

Beyond cases of fomenting unrest and upheaval, the one instance in which Jewish tradition does have sympathy for declaring positions out of bounds is when the person proposing that position does not accept the rules of the discussion. In other words, the objection is founded not in the content of the position but in a rejection of the process of debate.

Another humorous Talmudic incident makes the case. The rabbis of the Talmud are discussing in what cases someone is obliged to make the effort to find the owner of lost property. One case relates to a fledgling dove, too young to fly, that one finds hopping on the ground. Can you keep it, or are you obliged to look for its owner? The Talmud answers that if there is a dovecote within fifty cubits (some seventy-five feet) of where the bird is found, one should assume that the dove hopped from there and give it back to the owner of the dovecote. If it is further than fifty cubits, the finder can keep it. At this point a mischievous rabbi called Yirmiya enters the discussion and asks: 'But what is the case if one leg of the dove chick is inside the fifty-cubit limit, and the other leg is outside – what is the ruling then?' It was for this impudent question, the Talmud notes sardonically, that Yirmiya was removed from the study hall.[11]

The truth is that the Talmud is full of arcane hypothetical situations. Why was Yirmiya's question so objectionable? It seems that the rabbis' outrage related not to content but to process. Any debate has to be conducted according to agreed rules. In this case, all must accept that some standard will have to be established.

One can always continue splitting hairs but ultimately, for an agreed social system to hold, at some point the hair-splitting has to end. Had the sages fine-tuned their ruling and specified which leg of the chick was the relevant one, Yirmiya would still, one feels sure, have found a way to identify the bizarre hypothetical case in which that particular foot straddled the line. It seems that he was undermining, not the specific ruling, but the very basis of discussion – the acknowledgement that some parameter would have to be agreed. If there is no agreement at this basic level, then there is no way, the rabbis are suggesting, to have any kind of constructive debate.

The contemporary writer Ian Leslie makes a similar point in his book *Conflicted*:

> Productive disagreement is all very well, but the truth is that some people don't deserve it. Yes, we can learn from our opponents, but not all of them have something to teach us . . . But it's difficult to identify who those people are in advance.
>
> I don't think we can say that some people are impossible to engage with on the basis of the views they hold. What I do believe though, is that some people are impossible to engage with because of *the way they disagree*. There are those who are relentlessly close-minded, aggressive and mean spirited, who always assume bad faith, who always grandstand and never listen . . . people who might pretend to disagree productively, only to suck you into futile battles.[12]

As Leslie notes, it is often difficult to identify people who are open to a genuine debate in advance, not least because they frequently don't admit it to themselves. One simple litmus test that can be helpful is to ask participants in a debate to offer a brief summary of the argument of the opposition. People who are irrevocably entrenched in their own position find it surprisingly difficult to do this, though it's an elementary aspect of having a constructive conversation. One medieval tradition advises that you are perfectly entitled to disagree with someone once you can state their case to their own satisfaction.

Making a distinction between content and process can be helpful to us in dealing with some of today's most contentious debates. In recent years the debates between pro- and anti-vaccine advocates have become highly charged, especially when, during the Covid outbreak, anti-vaccine activists were seen as endangering not only themselves but also society at large. Similarly debates over Brexit, gun control or the environment are stoked by bold assurances that 'our' side is protecting livelihoods, personal safety and the globe itself, while 'their' side is set on destroying them.

How can we defuse at least some of the tension in these debates? One way, in line with the rabbis' approach, would be to focus, in the first instance at least, not on the substance of the debate, but on the process. Both sides should be invited to present openly. What are the grounds for your opinion? Can you think of any kind of evidence that might be relevant to changing your view? Somebody who declares that no evidence whatsoever could persuade them to change their mind is effectively rejecting the process of debate and discussion is likely to be futile.

In one of his first speeches to the Synod of the Church of England, Archbishop Justin Welby addressed the highly contentious debate within the Church of England over same-sex marriage. He began his speech by holding up an ancient plumb line, a pendulum-like tool used to measure whether a building is standing straight, that had been discovered during a renovation behind a wall at his Lambeth Palace residence. He used it as a striking image to urge Synod members to think about whether their own house was standing straight, and to invite them to consider the process, or the 'how', of the disagreements they were having:

We must not be ashamed of the fact that we are a Church that has its arguments in public, loudly. It is healthy and good. The

plumb line doesn't judge disagreement. But it does hold me and
each of us to account for how we disagree.[13]

If one side to a debate says that nothing they hear could make
them change their mind, there is no mileage in continuing the
discussion. They do not hold to an opinion so much as cling to an
article of faith. A quotation attributed to Jonathan Swift cautions:
'It is useless to attempt to reason a man out of a thing he was
never reasoned into.'

In the world of peace negotiations, it is often said that peace is
made between enemies. That might be true, but not entirely. In
fact, peace can only be made between enemies who are at least
open to making peace with each other. Implacable enemies are
unlikely to reach peace. So too implacable disputants.

In short, as Korah demonstrated in his protest against Moses,
not every interaction that claims to be an argument for the sake of
truth really is one. The best approach seems to be to take a
moment to consider, as we enter a debate, whether our counterpart actually buys into the process, and if they have a genuine
willingness to change their view in the light of what they hear.
And then, even more importantly, to take another moment to ask
ourselves: in all honesty, do we?

Postscript: For anyone worried about the impudent Rabbi Yirmiya
who was expelled from the study hall for his hair-splitting questions, the Talmud, some 150 pages after the account of his expulsion, records a surprising addendum. Sometime later, we are told,
the rabbis were stuck with a different problem, a knotty question
of divorce law that required analysis of precisely the hair-splitting
type that Yirmiya was so good at, and they summoned him back.[14]
Even on issues of process, it seems, we should be careful not to
judge too quickly.

Practices

Tested Tools for Divisive Times

Identity: Start Out by Looking In

Participants often turn up to the opening session of our Difficult Conversations labs with their sleeves rolled up, metaphorically or literally, impatient to get into the cut and thrust of a full-blown argument. They are distinctly disappointed when they learn that for the first few sessions we will not be dealing with the other side of the debate at all.

Every argument has two sides, so fifty per cent of it is on our own side of the table. It makes sense for us to start with ourselves. At the very least, if we are hoping to persuade our counterparts to rethink their own convictions and certainties, we should begin by examining our own. This means thinking honestly, and perhaps painfully, about the role of our own identities and loyalties in shaping our opinions.

Among the practices that can help us to do tthis are: actually *strengthening* our identities to ensure they are resilient and independent; having the courage to own up to our influences; and learning to separate the arguments made from the arguers presenting them.

Chapter 4

Developing a Robust Identity

We don't see things as they are; we see them as we are.

Anaïs Nin, *Seduction of the Minotaur*

A friend tells me that when he was young, he would be taken to visit his elderly grandmother, a Holocaust survivor, for lunch. On the way, his mother told him he should never refuse his grandmother's offer of a second helping of chicken soup. When he asked why, his mother replied: 'She's not really asking you whether you want more soup. She is asking whether you love her.'

One of the characteristics of difficult conversations, indeed one of the things that makes them so difficult, is that they are rarely (only) about what they claim to be about. As with the grandmother's soup, beneath the surface lie unspoken needs and insecurities. These can turn discussion of an apparently simple issue into a minefield of sensitivities. As much as we like to think of ourselves as rational actors, we are never truly independent and self-sufficient. Into the realm of debate and argument we bring our personal histories, our traumas and our tribal influences. We should take a moment to recognise that the most complex, and most frequently ignored, aspect of any difficult conversation may be ourselves.

I spent a decade as a negotiator representing Israel in Middle East peace talks, during which time this became increasingly clear to me. In literature on negotiation theory, it is often pointed out that every large-scale negotiation is really several negotiations in one. The first, the most obvious, is what is termed the negotiation '*across* the table' – the classic tug of war between the two opposing sides.

But if we look more closely at the teams seated along the two sides of the table, we will see that each of the negotiators within the respective teams represents a different and sometimes competing set of interests. In an international peace negotiation, for example, a team may comprise a representative from the Ministry of Defence, who is concerned about what effect an agreement will have on the security situation; a representative of the Ministry of Finance, who is concerned about the financial implications; and a delegate from the Foreign Ministry, who is charged with monitoring and safeguarding international interests. So, in addition to the tension *across* the table, there is a separate tug of war among these different, sometimes conflicting, interests within the team. This dynamic is known as the negotiation '*along* the table'.

Beyond these two dynamics, there is a third arena of negotiation. Especially as the two sides begin to come closer to an agreement, the negotiators have to 'sell' the deal to the parties that sent them – their leaders or their constituencies. This is generally known as the negotiation '*behind* the table'. (When I teach negotiation seminars in the Middle East, battle-weary negotiators familiar with the shady dealings that often go on behind closed doors like to point out, only partly in jest, that another prevalent dynamic is the negotiation '*under* the table'!)

Many years in highly charged negotiation rooms, with countless frustrations and occasional moments of progress, led me to understand that in addition to these classic negotiation dynamics – *across*, *along* and *behind* the table – there is another, equally significant, albeit hidden, dynamic at play. It takes place *within* each of the negotiators in the room: a negotiation between the past and the future. It is the tension between our loyalty to our grandparents, to all those who have preceded us, suffered for us, perhaps even died for us, on the one hand; and to our grandchildren, to future generations, to the possibility of a better future, on the other. The challenge of peace negotiations is to amplify the voices of the future, of the grandchildren, so that they are as compelling as the voices and loyalties that reach out to us from our past.

This is an extraordinarily difficult challenge. It requires honest self-awareness and courage. Above all, it calls on us to recognise that we are not the dispassionate, purely rational actors we might claim to be, but rather we are the sum of the experiences, emotions and loyalties which have shaped us, and which, as much as we may think we enter the room alone, are present in full force alongside us.

Of course, not every difficult conversation is an international negotiation. None the less, in any significant and highly charged conversation, similar dynamics are at play. With this in mind, a group of professors at Harvard's Program on Negotiation directed their attention to the challenges of undertaking fraught and potentially hurtful dialogue. In the resulting book, *Difficult Conversations*, they suggested that most truly difficult conversations actually break down into three different conversations, layered one on top of the other.

- The first layer, the one closest to the surface, they called the 'What happened?' conversation. This is the discussion about the facts of the case.
- The second, deeper layer is the 'Feelings' conversation. What does each side feel? Are these feelings acknowledged?
- The deepest and most intractable level is the 'Identity' conversation. How does this disagreement impact on our self-image and our self-esteem? [1]

The genesis of a sibling rivalry

There is a striking echo of these separate layers of difficult conversation in the book of Genesis, in relation to the archetypal conflict of Jewish history, the rivalry that began with the brothers Esau and Jacob. How did this rivalry begin? In fact, the Bible gives not one but three separate accounts, each of which suggests a different level of difficult conversation.

At the simplest level, the Bible describes Esau as despising Jacob because he stole from him. Twice Jacob uses trickery to take privileges rightly belonging to his older brother: first, when he takes advantage of Esau's hunger on returning from hunting to extort his birthright in return for a bowl of pottage, and later, when he masquerades as Esau in order to receive the firstborn's blessings from their blind father Isaac. This makes up the 'What happened?' layer in the challenging relationship between them.

In passing, we might note that Esau's ravenous vulnerability at a critical moment reminds us of another potential element that can aggravate our difficult conversations, and one we should be mindful of ourselves. I certainly have a tendency to become irritable and impulsive when I've missed a meal. During the time I worked as Israeli ambassador to the UK, my team knew that working irregular hours, an emergency supply of chocolate bars was a good strategy to keep me on an even keel. When I returned to Israel one of my team presented me with a red fire-alarm box and a small hammer. Inside were some KitKats and the notice: 'In case of emergency: break glass!'

At the deeper, emotional level, the Bible tells us a story of parental favouritism. From the twins' earliest years it is clear that the blind and passive Isaac loves the active hunter Esau, while his wife Rebecca prefers the home-loving Jacob, creating an emotional rivalry that will accompany the boys throughout their lives. The sense of rejection and resentment that ensues creates the 'Feelings' conversation.

The third element to the story of the twins' rivalry takes place before they are even born. Rebecca, troubled by the painful rumbling in her womb, goes to a soothsayer, who gives her a prophecy. Two nations will emerge from you, he says, and the older will serve the younger. These expectations of the boys' future destiny constitute the 'Identity' conversation. (In fact the soothsayer's prophecy is curiously ambiguous. The Hebrew phrase *rav ya'avod tsair* is best translated as 'the older shall the younger serve', open not only to the interpretation that the older will serve the younger, but also to the precisely opposite interpretation that the younger will serve the older. Both sons are free to choose the interpretation that accords with their own ambitions, with tragic results.)

The Bible, like the authors of *Difficult Conversations*, reminds us that, when we enter into an argument, we are not alone. We are accompanied by our own emotional baggage, by expectations we have internalised from our parents, and by sensitivities and loyalties imbibed from our tribe and our society. As bridge-building journalist Monica Guzman puts it: 'We don't see with our eyes, we see with our biographies.'[2]

A genuine argument for truth, as we have seen, takes place in the *zwischenmenschlich*, the space between us. It does not happen within us, but it cannot happen without us. Our identities, whether we like it or not, become a part of the conversation, along with our idiosyncrasies and the quirks that we bring with us, not forgetting our tribal and cultural loyalties and biases. How can we best address these, so as to reduce the 'interference' that can confuse our lines of communication?

Strengthening our identity

Paradoxically, one of the ways we can reduce the distorting impact of our identities in debate is not to weaken but in fact to strengthen them. The more insecure our identities are, the more likely we are to be dependent on defining ourselves in terms of 'the other'. Our own opinions, and our opposition to theirs, become inextricable parts of our internal scaffolding, limiting our capacity for growth and change. By contrast, the more that we can cultivate personal identities which are vibrant and independent, the more likely we are to be confident and able to reach out openly and honestly. As the Hassidic teacher Menachem Mendel of Kotzk taught:

> If I am I because I am I, and you are you because you are you, then I am I and you are you. But if I am I because you are you and you are you because I am I, then I am not I and you are not you.

It is through strengthening our independent identity that we actually free ourselves for greater openness in our interactions with others. This insight also finds expression in the Bible's account of Jacob's struggle with Esau. A recurrent theme throughout the three accounts of the origin of the conflict between the brothers is the repeated references to the names of the protagonists as a reflection of their identity. Jacob's name, Yaakov, meaning 'the heel-grabber', is given to him at birth because, in line with the soothsayer's prophecy, he is already reaching out to overtake his older brother. When he steals the blessings, he continues to define himself in terms of his brother, disguising himself as Esau being the only way he knows to try to acquire what he feels is rightly his. His meaning-laden name surfaces again and again throughout the passage. The blind Isaac worries that 'the voice is the voice of Jacob' (which of course it is) while, on discovering the ruse, the tricked Esau fumes: 'Isn't he rightly named Jacob? This is the second time he has taken advantage of me.'³

Two decades later, the estranged brothers are set to meet again. Esau, accompanied by an army of 400 men, appears set for battle. Jacob, for his part, having prepared his family for the showdown, is left alone. Late at night he has a mysterious night-time struggle with an angel or, in more psychological interpretations, his own inner self. Either way, it seems that before he can reconcile himself with Esau, Jacob has to confront his habitual tendency to define himself in opposition to his brother, and to find a new identity for himself.

When faced with a difficult conversation or a confrontation, we are generally so focused on thinking about the potential arguments of the other side that we do not give much thought to the dynamics at work within us. The lesson of Jacob's night of struggle is that we are well served to start out by looking in. As we teach participants in our Difficult Conversations laboratories, unless we know ourselves, the things that define us and our ability to change them, we are unlikely to be able to bring about change in others.

Indeed, after his night-long (perhaps we should say life-long) struggle, a new Jacob emerges, no longer defined by his conflict with Esau. 'Your name will no longer be Jacob, but Israel,' Jacob is told by his victorious adversary, as he is given a new name, Israel, that defines him by his struggle with God,[4] rather than in relation to his older brother. By adopting an identity that is not tied up with the conflict with his brother, Jacob is finally in a position to overcome his past and be reconciled to his sibling.

Often it is our opinions that are immutable and unchanging, while our identities are inherently affected by and intertwined with those of others. The Jewish framing of argument suggests that we should strive for the opposite: resilient, independent identities that allow us to see our opinions as hypotheses to be challenged and developed, rather than an immutable part of ourselves.

Chapter 5

Owning Up to Our Influences

Don't ask me who's influenced me. A lion is made up of all the lambs he's digested, and I've been reading all my life.

Giorgos Seferis

Amit Segal and Amnon Abramovich are two Israeli journalists from very different places on the political spectrum. Segal comes from a hilltop West Bank settlement and tends to the right, while Abramovich, raised on a socialist kibbutz, holds views to the left of the spectrum. The two are often found sparring on Israeli television. On one occasion Segal, in a moment of self-reflection, observed: 'If I had been raised on a socialist kibbutz as Amnon was, and he was raised in a West Bank settlement as I was, we would still be having the same arguments. We'd just each be on the other side!'

We do not enter our conversations alone. We bring with us the influences of our environment and our education. Of the newspapers we read, the programmes we watch, the friends we spend time with. As much as we feel that our approach is open and balanced, we are all, to a degree, the result of the myriad voices we have heard, and that we continue to hear every day. But if we cannot fully undo our inherent biases, then we can at least be open to admitting them.

One of the ways in which we can do this is by 'citing our sources'. This is not a call to change our opinions, but simply to be open about where they have come from. If, in a political debate, all the facts on one side have come via a particular news source, especially one that is allied strongly with a partisan position, then, in the interests of genuine truth-seeking, that should be declared. Not because the facts in themselves are necessarily wrong, but because there may be additional facts and perspectives that haven't been brought into consideration.

This principle should apply not only to the things we have read, but also to the things we have heard from others. Good practice in academia insists that written sources be credited, but the truth is that people may well be more profound influences on us than books. Author and journalist Jonathan Freedland quotes his teacher Zeev Mankowitz as observing: 'People don't believe in ideas, they believe in people who believe in ideas.'[1]

The practice of citing our sources raises the curtain on the people we have silently admitted into the debate alongside us. It confesses to our often limited range of influences and filters, the bubbles to which we may have restricted ourselves. As such, it calls on us to swallow our pride, and so it is not always easy. But without doubt it raises the quality of our debate.

So important did the rabbis consider the practice of crediting our sources, they claimed it had the potential to help hasten redemption. In support of this assertion, the rabbis offered a biblical proof to show that giving due credit actually saved the entire Jewish people. The text that they cited comes from the biblical book of Esther. Esther, it will be recalled, has been appointed Queen of the Persian Empire, when her uncle Mordecai tells her he has learned that two of the palace guards are plotting to kill the king. Esther goes to the king to warn him, sharing the intelligence, the Bible notes, 'in Mordecai's name'. Later in the story, the evil Haman hatches a plot against Mordecai and comes to the palace in the early hours to ask the king for permission to hang him. The king, it turns out, has been unable to sleep, and so has asked that the book of the chronicles of the kingdom be read to him. His servants, it so happens, have just read to him about this valiant deed of Mordecai. Haman's plans to paint Mordecai as a villain are frustrated, and with them his plot to destroy the Jews of Persia. Giving due credit, the rabbis suggest, may have positive effects on a scale that you can't even imagine.

There is, to be sure, a good argument for encouraging the spread of ideas without worrying too much about attribution. Thomas Jefferson wrote: 'He who receives an idea from me receives instruction himself without lessening mine; as he who lights his taper at mine receives light without darkening mine.' In the Talmud, when Rabbi Abbahu learns that someone has been teaching his insights without giving credit, he is similarly unperturbed: 'Either way, whether through him or through me, the word is being spread.'[2]

In Jewish tradition, we can see this Jefferson-like free and easy approach to his sources in the writings of twelfth-century sage Maimonides. Rabbi, philosopher, writer, doctor, he wrote seminal works of Jewish philosophy as well as a monumental code which brought together disparate bodies of Jewish law into a single accessible work. In striking contrast to previous compendia of law, including the Mishnah and the Talmud, Maimonides did not cite the sources of the opinions he quoted. It seems that he hoped that in so doing he would end arguments and create a single authoritative work. But it was not long before scholars were arguing over his own 'authoritative' text, and editions of his Mishnah Torah are now published with competing commentaries around the main text, just like the earlier Talmud. In Jewish tradition, we may not win the argument, but argument, it seems, always wins.

In his introduction to his commentary on the tractate 'The Ethics of the Fathers', Maimonides admits that he has taken his teachings from many wise sources, but that to attribute every quotation would, he insists in a phrase that seems to describe itself, 'necessitate useless prolixity'.

I was always somewhat sceptical of Maimonides' approach, and his motives (clearly not citing his sources would make it harder for others to question his findings), but I found myself having a little more sympathy some years ago when I was commissioned to write a drama series, *The Rebbe's Court*, for Israeli television. The series was set in the heart of a Hassidic community, led by a charismatic rebbe. To convey a sense of the wisdom of the rebbe, I scanned the writings of other (real) Hassidic leaders over the centuries and incorporated many of their sayings and insights into his lines. I found myself feeling a little uncomfortable. Could I really take insights and wise sayings of rabbis through the ages and put them in the mouth of my fictitious rabbi without attributing them? Where possible, I did have the rebbe cite the source but to do this on every occasion would have become cumbersome, or to use Maimonides' phrase, necessitated 'useless prolixity'. I suggested to the production company that we could include the names of the rabbis from whom I had quoted in the final credits, but they thought this ridiculous. A rabbi friend calmed my fears, giving two reasons. The first, he said, is that it is in the nature of a television drama that characters are composites, so viewers will not expect that any insights the characters express come only from them or from their scriptwriter's brain. Second, he considered that since one of the goals of the series was to encourage people to think more sympathetically about the wisdom of the Jewish tradition, the original sources of the quotations would almost certainly have been happy to make an anonymous contribution to this cause.

In the context of an argument, citing our sources can play a subtle but important role in the way we present our case. As Rabbi Joseph Telushkin points out, it helps keep our arguments free from personal ambition, as attributing our knowledge to others makes clear that our motive is to deepen understanding, not to impress with our own wisdom or cleverness.

It can also affect the way that we use what we quote from others. In its discussion of the obligation to attribute sources, the Jerusalem Talmud offers some advice. 'When quoting from someone else one should imagine that the original author or speaker is standing before you.'[3] The question is not only whether the quotation we are bringing is accurate, in the narrow sense of the term, but whether our use of it is fair and representative in a broader sense.

While there are unambiguous rules against copying the writings of others without permission, the moral rights of authors not to have their views twisted are far less clear. But the impact can be more lasting and more damaging than the costs of copyright infringement. Consider Anne Frank's *Diary of a Young Girl*, which was turned into a Broadway play. In her diary, the teenage Anne, writing in hiding from the Nazis, had a strong sense that there was something uniquely Jewish about the suffering she and her family were undergoing:

> It's God who has made us the way we are, but it's also God who will lift us up again. In the eyes of the world, we're doomed, but if after all this suffering, there are still Jews left, the Jewish people will be held up as an example. Who knows, maybe our religion will teach the world and all the people in it about goodness, and that's the reason, the only reason, we have to suffer. We can never be just Dutch, or just English, or whatever; we will always be Jews as well.

However, when playwrighting couple Frances Goodrich and Albert Hackett wrote their Broadway version of the diary in the 1950s, they clearly felt that Anne's particularistic sense of Jewish suffering did not fit with the more universalist ethos of the times. So instead, they had her say: 'We're not the only people that have had to suffer. There've always been people that've had to. Sometimes one race, sometimes another.'

There is a strong case to be made for a universalist perspective on prejudice and discrimination, but surely it is wrong to put this in the mouth of someone who has unequivocally expressed a very different position. All the more so when, tragically, they are not around to speak up for themselves. Perhaps, if the playwrights had followed the Talmud's advice and made the effort to see Anne's face before them as they wrote their script, they would have been more sensitive to the obligation to quote with integrity and respect.

When quoting someone in support of our case, we should have the honesty to ask ourselves whether, in light of our knowledge of the source, they would feel comfortable being recruited to our cause. Are we quoting them in context? Are we taking their world-view fully into account? If not (that is, if the person whose opinion we value enough to cite might think otherwise about how we are using that opinion) perhaps we ourselves should be open to reconsidering our position.

Before embarking on the collaborative exercise of engaging with others in a search for better understanding, we would do well to consider that we ourselves are, in fact, a composite work, the result of a particular set of influences that have combined to shape our outlook and our positions. Owning up to our influences is, in its most simple sense, acknowledging the moral debt that we owe to those we have learned from. But, more profoundly, it is a duty to our partners in a debate. If we are to work together on this project of seeing truth, let me share with you not only my opinions, but also the factors and individuals that have shaped them. This openness not only invites our partner to consider whether we have relied on these influences fairly, and what other influences we may have missed, but also may encourage them to respond in kind and share their formative influences with us.

Chapter 6

Separating the Argument from the Arguer

So that our arguments may live, we give them to someone else.

Bo Seo, *Good Arguments*

A revealing Jewish joke dates from the period of the emancipation, when restrictions on Jews' involvement in wider society were lifted across Europe. A Jew travels from his small Polish *shtetl* to the big city of Warsaw. When he returns, he tells his friend of the wonders he has seen: 'I met a Jew who had grown up in a Yeshiva and was a great Talmud scholar. I met a Jew who was an ardent atheist. I met a Jew who owned a large business. And I met a Jew who was an ardent communist.'

'So, what's so strange about that?' asks his friend. 'Warsaw is a big city. There must be a million Jews there.'

'You don't understand,' answered the first. 'It was the same Jew!'

Our identities are complicated and multi-layered. All of us contain distinct and even contradictory senses of ourselves. The same goes for organisations and, as I learned in my role as ambassador to the UK, even countries. My events diary often reflected contradictory images of the country I was representing. On the same evening I might rush from one event to another. At the first I would be encouraging philanthropists to support a young and embattled state of Israel, facing overwhelming challenges. A short drive later I would be pitching to a group of business investors, assuring them that Israel, the 'Start-up Nation', was a technological superpower. Not only individuals, but countries too, can suffer from an identity crisis.

However, recognising the tensions and contradictions within us may be an important key to empathy and understanding. The imagery used by the rabbis to convey the idea of an argument for the sake of heaven – the space between the cherubim on the Ark in the Temple, or the spaces for nurturing growth between saplings in a forest – focuses on the space outside ourselves, to suggest that we should look for truth in the spaces between us. But I believe there is an important corollary. If we are able to detach our identity from our positions, we can also find such spaces within ourselves, in the spaces between competing values, both of which we hold. We will see that a central practice of traditional Jewish study requires students to rehearse all the arguments on both sides of a debate, to identify as deeply as they can with the entirety of an issue in all of its differing perspectives. This has the potential subtly but significantly to change the nature of our interactions on contentious issues. We may disagree with the opposing view, even strongly. But it is not foreign to us. In fact, even as we argue we can recognise that we harbour an echo of that position within ourselves.

In his book *Think Again*, Adam Grant suggests that one way of cultivating the frame of mind that will enable us to detach our sense of self from the positions we hold, is to define our identity in terms of values rather than positions. 'It's easier to avoid getting stuck to your past beliefs if you don't become attached to them as part of your present self-concept,' he advises. He describes how he went in search of individuals with the ability to detach their sense of self from the ideas and opinions they hold, including Nobel Prize-winning scientists. One of these was Daniel Kahneman, the economic psychologist. When, in the course of their conversation, Grant pointed out that some of his findings had been contradicted by later evidence, Kahneman's eyes lit up. 'That was wonderful,' he said. 'I was wrong.' Kahneman was not unnerved by this challenge to his previous conclusions, but on the contrary welcomed it, because, as he explained, it meant that he was now 'less wrong than before'.[1]

Separating their *argument from* their *identity*

As we work to separate our own identities from the opinions we hold, we would do well to do the same in thinking about those against whom we are arguing. In the subtle reframing of the tradition, the path to truth runs through our fellow man or woman. But the man or woman is not themselves the message.

One of the leading rabbinic figures of the twentieth century was Menachem Mendel Schneerson, known as the Lubavitcher Rebbe. Although he was stringent in his commitment to orthodox law and practice, he managed to maintain close and affectionate relationships with many individuals with whom he disagreed deeply. When asked how he was able to remain on such good terms with people from whose opinions he differed so greatly, he noted: 'I don't speak about people, I speak about opinions.'[2]

Separating the argument from the arguer can help diffuse much of the emotional tension below the surface of our debate. Confusing the two, by contrast, can have catastrophic results. The danger inherent in identifying people with their positions is highlighted in the most tragic story of a study partnership told in the Talmud. Rabbi Yohanan, a leading scholar of his generation, befriended Resh Lakish, a well-known bandit. When Resh Lakish repented the two became close study partners. On one occasion, however, the two became involved in a heated debate. The specific question dealt with the ritual impurity of a weapon, and Resh Lakish took issue with his teacher–partner's position.

Annoyed at being publicly challenged by his student, Rabbi Yohanan made a hurtful *ad hominem* attack on Resh Lakish: 'You would know: a bandit knows his banditry!' Stung to the quick at this gratuitous reference to his past, Resh Lakish answered, 'What good have you done me by influencing me to repent?' In the tragic account of the Talmud Resh Lakish fell into a depression and died, and following this Rabbi Yohanan, inconsolable, died as well.

This tragic story stands as a lesson of the terrible price of confusing the person with their opinion, and of shifting the focus from the argument to the arguer. It also, we should note, stands in stark contrast to almost every other argument in the Talmud, in which disputants hold dramatically opposed viewpoints yet manage to engage constructively and with respect.

In the heat of the Talmudic debate, Rabbi Yohanan lost sight of the larger picture. The goal in the argument is not to win the dispute, but to make the argument itself, with all its sides and in all its aspects, as powerful and compelling as possible. In the beautiful reframing of the rabbis, it is not we who are acting 'for the sake of heaven', nor is it those who are arguing against us. It is the argument itself that is for the sake of heaven.

Why did Rabbi Yohanan resort to such a cruel personal attack? The Talmudic account gives few clues but one can imagine that Rabbi Yohanan, the leading scholar of his age, was affronted at being publicly challenged by his student. Perhaps it was precisely because Resh Lakish had been a bandit that his opinion on this weapon-related issue at hand was more informed, and Rabbi Yohanan felt the need to bolster his own status by reminding the public of Resh Lakish's lowly origins.

In any event, it is clear that Rabbi Yohanan's attack was in no way a substantive contribution to the debate. To the contrary, it is most often when a party to a dispute can think of no legitimate response that they resort to personal attacks. There may be situations in which reference to the behaviour of an opponent is relevant to a debate, for example when it is so at odds with the position being espoused that it suggests bad faith or hypocrisy, but for the most part a shift towards personal attacks represents an attempt to evade rather than advance substantive discussion. Margaret Thatcher, no stranger to receiving personal attacks, made the point: 'I always cheer up immensely if an attack is particularly wounding because I think, well, if they attack one personally, it means they have not a single political argument left.'[3]

As a society we pay a steep price for this kind of resort to irrelevant personal attacks, and on many levels. Beyond dumbing down the quality of our public discussion, such attacks may deter high quality individuals who might otherwise engage in public service from doing so. Indeed, the Bible contains a specific prohibition on making personal attacks on leaders in Exodus 22:28: 'Do not blaspheme God or curse the ruler of your people.' The fourteenth-century Italian rabbi, Menachem Recanati, explained that the reason is precisely that such attacks are likely to persuade potential candidates that leadership is a thankless task, and discourage talented people from taking positions of public service.

But the price for such attacks may be even higher. If the Talmud's account of personal attacks leading to death – of Resh Lakish and eventually Rabbi Yohanan as well – seems exaggerated, Israeli political history sadly tells us that the opposite is the case. While Israeli political debate is raucous and often impolite, and hurtful insults are frequently bandied about in the Knesset, the posters which circulated during demonstrations against the Oslo peace negotiations, depicting Prime Minister Yitzhak Rabin dressed in the uniform of an SS officer, reached a new low. The campaign of incitement and demonisation of which they were a part ultimately led to his murder.

Arguing through avatars

I was surprised to learn how technology too can play a role by creating a useful sense of distance between participants and their positions when I visited the Center for Educational Technology in Israel. I was interested in learning about their latest online educational techniques, one of which was a computerised learning program in which students were represented on the screen by avatars. The students' onscreen avatars interacted with each other as they wandered around a virtual museum discovering more about different periods in history.

Sharing the evaluations received from the pilot users of the program, the developers noted that the avatar approach had actually had a pedagogic benefit that they hadn't anticipated: it made it much easier for teachers to critique the performance of their students. If a teacher had directly criticised a student, saying for example that they had not participated sufficiently actively in the lesson, or that their contribution had not been so helpful, this would, in all likelihood, have generated a negative, even hostile, reaction. But when teachers told students they had noticed that their avatar had not been particularly active or cooperative, the sense of detachment between the student and their avatar meant that the students felt their personal identity had been less impinged upon, and reactions of resentment were defused to a great degree.

Talmud study is not unlike this online program. In place of the screen there is the text of the Talmud; in place of avatars, the rabbis that populate the discussion. As a result, students of the Talmud too enjoy a distance between themselves and the argument, which helps to free them from the intensity that arises when we identify too closely with a position in the debate. Here the debate takes place at one remove, on the page, and rather than being between me and you, it is between Hillel and Shammai, or Abbaye and Rava, in a way that allows us the room to express support for one side, even as we recognise we may have sympathy for the case of the other. Whether a page of Talmud or a virtual learning environment, these approaches invite us to try to treat our own positions as avatars. They are not us, but are more like feelers we put out, wandering around the museum of ideas, ready to report back and advance our search for truth.

There is, to be sure, a certain reassuring comfort in seeing our viewpoints as immutable. But admitting the space between ourselves and our positions acknowledges a truth that we rarely recognise: our relationship with our ideas is organic and changing. Depending on our mood, on the people we have just met and on the experiences we have just had, we may at times feel closer to these ideas in ourselves, or farther from them, even while they remain none the less part of our identity. The goal is not to sever our relationship with our cherished positions, even were such a thing possible, but perhaps to leave room to admit, as

Bertrand Russell noted, that: 'None of our beliefs are quite true; all have at least a penumbra of vagueness and error.'[4]

When we recognise that the attempt to come closer to truth is an inherently interpersonal exercise, we realise that our own identities, and those of our counterparts on the other side, will always be somewhere in the room. Our goal is not to detach ourselves from them: this would not only be impossible, but would actually remove a vital element of the variety and depth of our discussions. Instead we should strengthen our identities and admit our influences. Only then can we hope to have an argument that truly addresses our positions and not our insecurities.

Collaboration: Finding the Value in our Differences

If the search for truth is a collaborative exercise, the quality of our arguments is dependent on the quality of our relationships with our counterparts. The more resilient our relationships, the more honest and effective will be the process of debate between us.

At the heart of genuine collaboration is the recognition that our opponents in our debates are not really our adversaries. They are, rather, the partners we need to create the best shared argument possible.

Key practices that can help bring this dynamic into our debates and our decision-making are engaging in adversarial collaboration, strengthening the positions of our opponents, and ensuring that we give expression to quiet voices of dissent that might otherwise not be heard.

Chapter 7

Adversarial Collaboration

In Italy for thirty years under the Borgias, they had warfare, terror, murder, bloodshed. They produced Michelangelo, da Vinci, and the Renaissance. In Switzerland, they had brotherly love, five hundred years of democracy and peace, and what did they produce? The cuckoo clock.

Orson Welles as Harry Lime in *The Third Man*

My friend Giacomo is a Catholic priest. Some years ago he and I made a deal: we would each give the other a tour of the old city of Jerusalem, sharing our most holy and treasured sites. It was remarkable how, within this tiny area, two narratives and sets of associations could live unknowingly side by side. As someone once whispered to me, in negotiations over the future of Jerusalem: 'This place has too much history and not enough geography!'

Giacomo's tour took us to many beautiful places: serene gardens and hidden courtyards, monastic islands of reflection and contemplation. Mine took us to more lively areas. I ended our tour in the study hall of a Yeshiva. As we entered the *bet midrash*, Giacomo looked around the hall, taking in the high decibel arguments, the pairs of young students shouting at each other, gesticulating and banging on tables, in astonishment. 'What are they arguing about?' he asked me. 'Everything!' I answered. Yes, as rowdy as it seemed, this was Torah study. This was *havruta*.

Havruta, from the Hebrew word for 'friend', originally meant studying in any collective forum, but over the centuries the term came to refer specifically to a study partnership between two people. The Mishnah describes how the Torah was transmitted down the generations by pairs of scholars, and many Talmudic arguments take place between well-known partner–antagonists. And today the core unit of Talmudic study in a traditional Yeshiva is the study pair of students learning in partnership, or *havruta*.

I have already mentioned Joshua Wolf Shenk's book *Powers of Two*, in which Shenk argues that the business of insight and discovery is more likely to happen in creative dialogue than in solo pondering. In doing so, he supports the rabbinic contention that the search for knowledge is of necessity a collaborative enterprise. *Havruta* is one of the key ways in which this insight finds expression in Jewish study.

In a traditional Yeshiva setting, finding a suitable *havruta*, or study partner, is probably the most important step to learning effectively, even more than having a good teacher. The process of choosing your partner, and perhaps breaking up with them when things don't work out, is not unlike dating, and there is indeed a personal dimension to the relationship alongside the intellectual one. But though deep friendships may develop (I know *havruta* pairs who have studied together for forty or even fifty years), the goal is precisely not to have an immediate easy companionship, but to find a counterpart who will push back against us, and help us climb to new heights in learning and understanding.

The *havruta* approach has found enthusiastic support beyond the Jewish community. A surprising case is South Korea. After a book of lessons from the Talmud written by Marvin Tokayer, a rabbi posted to Japan, was translated into Korean in 1974, it became a runaway best-seller, with millions of Talmud books sold, including through the popular automatic book-vending machines they have there.[1]

Most South Koreans have never met a Jew, so the fascination seems unexpected, to say the least. In 2011, the South Korean ambassador to Israel at the time, Young-sam Ma, gave his explanation. 'Each Korean family has at least one copy of the Talmud,' he said. 'Korean mothers want to know how so many Jewish people became geniuses. Twenty-three per cent of Nobel Prize winners are Jewish people. Korean women want to know the secret.'[2]

Beyond the sale of books, this fascination with the Talmud has resulted in dozens of Talmudic academies, with branches in major cities throughout the country, catering to everyone from toddlers to adults. While some of the academies focus on stories from the Talmud, for the most part it is not the content that is Talmudic but the methodology. While the subjects taught in the academies differ, what they all have in common is that they study using the *havruta* approach.

The phenomenon has led to an interest in pedagogic research into the effectiveness of the *havruta* process. One such study pointed to a range of benefits resulting from these study partnerships: 'The *havruta* approach to learning and teaching encouraged more active learning; the students took more responsibility for their own learning. By focusing on allowing greater student autonomy, the teacher became more facilitative of the learning process.'[3] Educational psychologist David Johnson cites research that points to an even broader range of benefits of teaching through what he terms 'constructive controversy'. These include greater mastery and retention of material, deeper understanding and better decision-making.[4]

Clashing tools, sparking logs

Looking for a fitting analogy for the power of *havruta*, one rabbi in the Talmud draws on the book of Proverbs (27:17) to liken study partners to iron tools that sharpen each other. Another sees them as logs in a fire, which will go out if each sits alone, but which by rubbing against each other will allow the fire to grow.

The images of the Talmud have a strikingly modern resonance. In Shenk's survey of constructive partnerships he quotes one journalist who witnessed an argument between Google founders Sergey Brin and Larry Page within hours of their first meeting, describing his impression of 'two swords sharpening each other'. In a different context, the famous magical duo Penn and Teller described the constructive arguments between them as 'the kind of hatred that's like flint and steel'.

The two Talmudic analogies, sharpening swords and sparking logs, capture two different benefits of the *havruta* dynamic. The first focuses on the participants honing each other's intellects. The second analogy focuses less on the participants and more on the contribution they can make to universal knowledge, the warmth a fire gives to its surroundings, or the sparks of insight and creativity that are thrown out from clashing flints.

In both analogies, though, the value of the *havruta* lies not in agreement or similarity, but in difference. Without difference, without the meeting of disparate elements, there can be no sharpening, no generation of sparks.

A contemporary example of *havruta* is described by Nobel Prize laureate Daniel Kahneman in *Thinking, Fast and Slow*. Kahneman and his colleague Gary Klein had very different views on the psychology of decision-making. Klein, a leading figure in the school of naturalistic decision-making, was a strong opponent of Kahneman's approach, which focused on innate biases. Demonstrating a degree of curiosity and courage that enabled them to transcend their rivalries, the two agreed to engage in a series of joint research experiments to test their differing assumptions and more accurately map the boundary that separates intuition from its flaws. Kahneman gave the process they engaged in together the name 'adversarial collaboration', and this may indeed give us the most accurate translation of the term *havruta*. As Kahneman describes the experience:

> Over seven or eight years we had many discussions, resolved many disagreements, almost blew up more than once, wrote many drafts, became friends and eventually published a joint article with a title that tells the story: 'Conditions for intuitive expertise; a failure to disagree.'[5]

From straw-manning to steel-manning

A Jewish joke gives expression to the need for constructive tension – on the football field of all places. An elderly rabbi sees that his students are all fanatical football followers and asks them to take him to a match so he can see what all the fuss is about. After watching the match for half an hour, he turns to the students and says: 'I think I have the solution. Give *both* teams a ball!'

Simply having a study partner is not in itself sufficient. It can be as ineffective as a game with two teams on the pitch but both having their own ball. Only if each side is committed to trying to defeat the other can the game take place. And only if each study partner does their best to challenge their counterpart will their study be effective.

The point is reflected powerfully in the Talmud's description of the study partnerships of the sage Rabbi Yohanan. For many years Yohanan had studied in *havruta* with the reformed bandit Resh Lakish. After Resh Lakish's tragic death, the Talmud relates that Rabbi Yohanan's students try to bring him out of depression by looking for a substitute study partner. They settle on the scholar Rabbi Elazar ben Pedat. The Talmud recounts:

> Rabbi Elazar ben Pedat went and sat before Rabbi Yohanan. With regard to every matter that Rabbi Yohanan would say, Rabbi Elazar ben Pedat would say to him: There is a ruling that supports your opinion. Rabbi Yohanan said to him: Are you comparable to the son of Lakish? In my discussions with the son of Lakish, when I would state a matter, he would raise twenty-four difficulties against me in an attempt to disprove my claim, and I would answer him with twenty-four answers, and the *halakha* by itself would become broadened and clarified. And yet you say to me: There is a ruling which supports your opinion. Do I not know that what I say is good? Being rebutted by Resh Lakish served a purpose; your bringing proof to my statements does not.[6]

For Rabbi Yohanan, the yes-man approach of Rabbi Elazar was as useless as training with a weak sparring partner before a big fight. Without friction, in the *havruta* images of the Talmud, the tools would not be sharpened, the fire would not be fed.

A conversation recorded between the German Chancellor Otto von Bismarck and the British Prime Minister Benjamin Disraeli suggests that Disraeli saw the generation of opposing views as being very important, and also very Jewish. When Bismarck complained that his parliament quarrelled with him about everything, Disraeli is reported to have replied, 'If Britain's members of Parliament would not argue with me I would pay them to do so.' Bismarck asked Disraeli from where he had learned this unusual approach. Disraeli's reply: 'From the teachings of the Israelites, which are bursting with arguments.'[7]

Contemporary writers on management and constructive argument in the workplace have come to similar conclusions, encouraging us to challenge ourselves against the strongest version of the opposing argument, even if it seems detrimental to our own position. Conor Friedersdorf, writing in *The Atlantic*, notes the disservice we often do ourselves by 'straw-manning', deliberately taking issue with a weak representation of the opposing argument, perhaps by picking up on a poorly phrased point or taking the position to illogical extremes. If we truly wish to engage in the most honest and productive form of disagreement, rather than 'straw-manning' we should engage in 'steel-manning'. He quotes a blogpost by Chana Messinger. Steel-manning, she says, is 'the art of addressing the best form of the other person's argument', suggesting what this might mean in practice:

> This is the highest form of disagreement. If you know of a better counter to your own argument, say so. If you know of evidence that supports their side, bring it up. If their argument rests on an untrue piece of evidence, talk about the hypothetical case in which they were right . . . Because if you can't respond to that

better version, you've got some thinking to do, even if you are more right than the person you're arguing with.[8]

While our focus here is on deepening the quality of arguments, and not on scoring points, it's worth noting that strengthening the opposing argument can also help make our own case sound more persuasive. Two-time World Debating Champion Bo Seo described one of the surprising things he was taught as a school debater:

> Our coach, Simon, taught us to not only record but also *strengthen* the other side's arguments before responding to them. If the opponent had left out an example or a crucial line of reason, we had to supply it and say, 'Now, the opposition could have said . . .' This sounded to us like an own goal. However, Simon insisted that responding to the strongest possible opposing case maximises our chance of persuading the audience and, maybe, even our opponents. It forces us to lift our game and take the other side seriously. Whereas good speakers gloated about opponents' mistakes, great debaters rushed to repair them.[9]

One maxim in the Talmud uses a surprising metaphor to capture the spirit of adversarial collaboration: 'If prostitutes help each other out with their make-up, shouldn't scholars do the same [and help make each other's arguments stronger]?' Whatever the metaphor we choose to use, is it really possible to capture the spirit of this constructive rivalry outside the pages of the Talmud and the Yeshiva study hall? A number of modern examples suggest that we can.

A professional disprover

Alice Stewart, a British scientist in the 1950s, was convinced that X-rays done on pregnant women caused them harm and could even lead to their babies dying from childhood cancer. But she was aware that the medical establishment, which had adopted X-rays as standard practice, would be extremely reluctant to give her a fair hearing. Being one of the few women in the profession stacked the odds against her even more. Aware that establishment experts would use every possible argument against her, she recruited a colleague, George Kneale, a statistician, to help her prepare her case. She urged him to challenge her evidence with every possible argument so that she would be prepared for anything the other doctors might throw at her. When she answered his challenges, she insisted that he try to demolish these points too with any statistics at his disposal. Thanks to this insistent steel-manning, Alice Stewart was able to defy the odds, make her case and save the lives of thousands of infants. Asked about his contribution to this achievement, the bashful George Kneale answered modestly: 'My job is to disprove Dr Stewart's theories.'[10]

Kneale appreciated that the most significant contribution he could make to Stewart's case was to argue forcefully against her. To truly help those we care about, being on the other side may be the best way of being on their side. This is as true in our personal lives as in our professional lives. In the Garden of Eden, when God creates Eve as a partner for Adam, He describes her as *ezer-knegdo*. The traditional translation of the term, dating back to the King James Bible, is 'helpmeet', but this misses the tension and balance in the phrase. It's better translated as his 'helper-opposer'. That is the very model of a constructive relationship, and it is found right at the start of the human story. The British Chief Rabbi Ephraim Mirvis explains:

[The term] *Ezer-knegdo* suggests that ultimately if you truly love somebody you will offer constructive advice. Sometimes you'll be with them, sometimes you'll be against them and it will be palatable because you know the person loves you and it's coming from the right place.

The idea that opposing someone can be the best way of supporting them flows naturally from the idea that a genuine argument should be directed at building up the cause of truth, rather than breaking it down. For truly, in a genuine search for truth there are no sides. Or rather: we are both on the same side, the side that wishes our argument to be as well founded and as true as possible.

How would we adopt this approach in our own debates? When we look at the people with whom we develop and soundboard our ideas, have we truly found a *havruta* for ourselves, challenging us to sharpen and strengthen our positions? And are we truly serving as an *ezer-knegdo* to others, helper–opposers giving candid, constructive feedback to those around us? Can we begin to think of opponents a little differently, as people who may be on the other side of the debate, but who are actually helping us test our ideas and inch, together, a little closer to the truth?

Chapter 8

Nurturing Dissent

Has there ever been a society which has died of dissent? Several have died of conformity in our lifetime.

Jacob Bronowski

At an important meeting of the management of General Motors, Alfred P. Sloan, the company's legendary CEO in the first half of the twentieth century, opened the session saying: 'I take it we are all in agreement about the decision we have to make here.' When everyone nodded, he went on: 'Then I suggest we postpone further discussion of the matter till our next meeting, so that we have time to develop disagreement and really understand what the decision is about.'[1]

Counter-intuitive as it may sound to Western minds, schooled as we are in the myth of the solitary genius, Jewish tradition insists that in order to advance truth we need to nurture dissent. This conviction is reflected in the surprising extent to which the tradition celebrates dissenters and works to foster and capture the wisdom of dissenting approaches. The tradition even encourages the reciting of a blessing over differences of opinion. The Talmud teaches:

> One who sees multitudes of Israel recites: Blessed is He . . . Who knows all secrets. Why is this? He sees a whole nation whose minds are unlike each other and whose faces are unlike each other, and He who knows all secrets, God, knows what is in each of their hearts.[2]

Every different face is a vessel containing a different mind and point of view, and these, the Talmud suggests, are to be cherished and blessed. We would not wish to live in a world where faces are all alike, so neither should we aspire to uniformity of opinion.

Creating an environment that nurtures dissent requires more than celebrating difference in principle, however; it calls on us to celebrate the dissenters and to hold up as models those with the courage to stand against unquestioned wisdom.

Jewish sources reflect a strong tradition of admiration for dissenters and contrarians. Indeed, the Midrash suggests that Abraham was chosen by God precisely because he *was* a contrarian. It notes that the term *Ivri*, used to describe Abraham, and which became the origin of the term 'Hebrew' itself, literally means a 'side' and derives, we are told, from the fact that 'All the world was on one side and he, Abraham, was on the other side.'[3]

Models of dissent continue throughout the Bible, particularly among the prophets. The prophets were, each in their own way, courageous contrarians, speaking out against the people and their leaders. As Abraham Joshua Heschel, himself a prophetic voice against racism and discrimination in the United States, noted in an essay titled 'Dissent': 'The greatness of the prophets was in their ability to voice dissent and disagreement not only with the beliefs of their pagan neighbours, but also with the cherished values and habits of their own people.'[4]

In the case of Abraham, his most brazen expression of dissent is not against the nations of the world or against the Jewish people but against God himself. In Genesis 18:25, when he hears from God about the planned destruction of the cities of Sodom and Gomorrah, he doesn't hesitate to challenge the Almighty: 'Far be it from you to do such a thing – to kill the righteous with the wicked, treating the righteous and the wicked alike. Far be it from you! Will not the Judge of all the earth do right?' Jonathan Sacks observes that 'In any other faith, it seems to me, those words would be close to, maybe even tantamount to, blasphemy! And yet there they are at the core of Jewish faith, one of the great prophetic utterances in our literature.'[5] Perhaps the most surprising aspect of the account is not that Abraham challenges God, but that God *invites* the challenge, saying, 'Shall I hide from Abraham that which I am about to do?' God knew that Abraham would challenge him. But despite this, or rather precisely because of it, he invited Abraham's response.

The notion of arguing against God is theologically challenging, to say the least. But it is important in terms of creating a sensibility in which dissent is valued and supported. Perhaps someone raised on stories like this, where speaking out against authority is held up as a trait to be admired and modelled, will find it easier to raise their own voice, and the idea of speaking out against their boss or community leaders might seem a little less daunting.

Encouraging dissent

There is an important role for recognising and appreciating individual dissenters – those who have a particular gift for pointing out the problems in any given situation. But dissent also needs to be nurtured and encouraged at the organisational level. In particular, large organisations with powerful hierarchies have difficulty capturing the wisdom of more junior members of staff who are reluctant to come out against their superiors.

The Sanhedrin, the ancient Jewish court, struggled with this problem. One solution it adopted was the practice of starting deliberations by hearing the views of the most junior judges, the ones seated in the side benches, so that they would not be intimidated by having already heard the opinions of their more eminent colleagues.

The benefits of encouraging dissent, and the costs of silencing or ignoring it, have both been evident to Israelis in the field of defence. One of the Israeli Defence Force's most significant air operations in recent years was an attack that decommissioned a Syrian nuclear reactor in 2007. Describing the operation years later, the Commander of the Air Force, Eliezer Shkedi, shared that the approach he adopted to ensure that the attack would not escalate into a full-scale war actually came from a very junior officer in the Operations Division. 'He simply brought the best idea,' noted Shkedi, 'so we listened to him as if he were a Brigadier General.'[6]

By contrast, while the full details have yet to emerge, it seems that a number of junior intelligence officers, mostly women, had suspicions that a massacre was being planned prior to the terrible events of 7 October 2023, in which 1,200 Israelis were killed and more than 250 kidnapped. Their warnings, however, were disregarded and not passed on to the higher echelons, with tragic results.

Creating an environment that gives confidence to more junior members to voice dissent can mean the difference between life and death in civilian life as much as in military operations.

In an extensive analysis of the Korean Air disaster in 1997 that took the lives of 229 passengers and crew, Malcolm Gladwell points out that the deferential Korean culture made it difficult if not impossible for the Korean co-pilot to convey to the control tower the severity of their situation. This was not an isolated incident. As Gladwell points out:

> Korean Air had more plane crashes than almost any other airline in the world for a period at the end of the 1990s. What they were struggling with was a cultural legacy, that Korean culture is hierarchical. You are obliged to be deferential toward your elders and superiors in a way that would be unimaginable in the US.[7]

Gladwell describes how Korean Air's efforts to address this problem involved re-educating their crews, including insisting on communication in English, since they found that the Korean language was too imbued with respect and subservience. But English-speakers too can be vulnerable to the dangers of deference. The investigation board established to investigate the Columbia Space Shuttle disaster in 2003 reached a conclusion similar to that of the Korean investigation, as Cass R. Sunstein notes in *The Power of Dissent*:

The Columbia Accident Investigation Board emphasized the need for NASA to develop a distinctive kind of culture, one that discourages deference to leaders, sees dissent as an obligation, promotes independent analysis and insists on a wide range of voices. The broadest lesson is simple. Well-functioning organizations discourage conformity and encourage dissent – partly to protect the rights of dissenters but mostly to promote interests of their own.[8]

As a general rule, Israeli society is not characterised by subservience. Workers tend to call their bosses by their first names, and have little hesitation in suggesting that they may be mistaken. The frank and sometimes abrasive tone can be frustrating, so perhaps there is some comfort to be found in the thought that this same impudence may reflect the right kind of cultural DNA to make air crashes less likely!

So important is dissent, indeed, that where there is no difference of opinion, we may have to proactively generate some ourselves. We have noted that Hillel and Shammai were perpetual disputants, revered by the Mishnah as the archetype of arguers for the sake of heaven. It is worth noting, though, that this pairing did not come about by chance. It seems to have been organised deliberately to ensure that differences of opinion would continue to generate constructive debate.

Hillel and Shammai are described by the Mishnah as being the latest in a long line of pairs of community leaders – the President of the Sanhedrin and the Head of the Rabbinic Court in each generation. The Mishnah describes how, in each generation, the two office-holders took opposing positions on a longstanding dispute over the procedure for conducting the festival sacrifice. After five cycles of leadership pairings who had kept the disagreement alive from generation to generation, a new pair was appointed – the sage Hillel, and another sage by the name of Menachem. Little is recorded about this Menachem, except for the fact that he did not disagree with Hillel on this issue. With no disagreement, the Mishnah records, Menachem had to be replaced. His replacement was the more combative Shammai, who did indeed disagree and thus kept the debate alive.

Perhaps the most extreme expression of the imperative towards dissent in the Talmud is an unusual principle of Talmudic criminal law. According to the Talmud, if in a capital case all the judges are unanimous in seeking to convict, the defendant *must be acquitted*. The principle appears to challenge all logic. A defendant whom some judges think innocent might be sentenced to capital punishment, but not one who all agree is guilty. It seems that this principle was more relevant in theory than in practice; in all but the highest court there was a possibility of appeal, with the result that capital sentences were rarely, if ever, implemented. But the ruling underlines the conviction that for a legitimate deliberation to take place, the arguments on all sides must be voiced and every possible defence, however far-fetched, presented. Truth needs dissent, and successful conviction needs a robust defence.

The power of a single voice

A single voice of dissent holds out the possibility that minds might change. As portrayed dramatically in the famous play and movie *12 Angry Men*, a single dissenting juror might, with passion and patience, bring around his fellow jurymen and save the life of an innocent young man. Cass Sunstein, a US legal scholar who has written extensively about the importance of dissent, cites research that emphasises the point. In carefully designed group deliberations, it was clear that where a number of group members (actually plants) confidently supported a particular view, for example on the question matching the length of a line on a card to the correct one of three 'comparison lines', the group as a whole tended to follow its most confident members, even when the comparison was, on the face of it, demonstrably wrong. But the existence of a single voice of dissent dramatically reduced both conformity and error. His conclusion: 'The clear implication is that if a group is embarking on an unfortunate course of action, a single dissenter might be able to turn it around, by energising ambivalent group members who would otherwise follow the crowd.'[9]

For dissent to do its work in guiding our decision-making processes, though, it must be genuine. In recent years organisational psychologists have learned to be sceptical about processes which create the illusion of dissent, but which in practice contribute little to the quality of discussion.

One such study, conducted by Berkeley psychologist Charlan Nemeth, ran an interesting experiment in which she compared the impact of the presence of a genuine dissenter on a group discussion in which one participant was merely tasked temporarily with the role of playing devil's advocate. The decisive result was that authentic dissent led to far more productive discussions, generating more original ideas, than discussions with someone artificially manufacturing their disagreement. This, she suggests, may be because the group's awareness that the allocated devil's advocate was only playing a role led to complacency that the group had protected itself against narrow-mindedness.

In another study, Nemeth questioned the value of the popular 'brainstorming' model, which seeks to generate solutions by creating a non-judgemental environment under the mantra that there are 'no bad ideas'. She compared groups of brainstormers working to come up with ideas to solve a traffic congestion problem. Some groups were told to brainstorm in the traditional manner, without criticising each other's solutions. Others were permitted to debate and criticise. Surprisingly, the debaters actually generated more ideas, and more practical ones, than the indiscriminate brainstormers. Banishing disagreement was not as effective as encouraging it.

Capturing dissent

Creating an environment that celebrates and encourages genuine dissent is important, but not enough in itself. For us actually to reap the benefits of the thinking of all in the room, and not only of those whose arguments win the day, we need to find a way to ensure that opposing views, and the value within them, are preserved.

A remarkable characteristic of the Jewish oral tradition, as recorded in the Mishnah, is its insistence on recording dissenting opinions, even those which were never relied on in determining the law. Indeed, religious students of Talmud spend much of their time studying opinions that they are, in terms of the decided practice, forbidden to follow. And yet these outvoted dissenters also have their place, alongside the victors, in the tradition.

Why does the Mishnah take such pains to ensure that the rejected dissenting opinions are preserved? The Mishnah itself provides the answer.

> Why is mention made of the opinion of a single person in connection with that of many, when the final decision is invariably with the majority? In order that when a court should happen to approve of someone's opinion it might base its decision thereon, for no court may annul the decision of another court, unless it be superior to the latter both in erudition and number. If, however, it be superior only in one respect, in either erudition or number, it cannot annul; it must be superior in both.[10]

While it may not have won the day, the minority opinion speaks to a certain truth. In a different time, in a different context, it may even provide the basis for an alternative ruling. It too is a fragment of the tablets, preserved with reverence in the Ark of the tradition.

This Mishnah, discussing arguments, is itself, as might be expected, the subject of an argument, and it goes on to record a dissenting view. 'Rabbi Yehuda says the minority opinion is recorded so that if anyone says "But I have a tradition that rules a different way", they can be told it is recorded here in the name of this rabbi, and it has been rejected.' The minority view is recorded not to be legitimised, says Rabbi Yehuda, but rather to prove that it was considered and rejected. As my friend Tal Becker has pointed out, this presents us with a rather splendid paradox. Rabbi Yehuda, who argues that minority views are not to be relied on, is himself a minority opinion. If he is right, then he is wrong. And only if he is wrong might his argument be regarded as having truth! Whether right or wrong, though, his dissenting opinion is preserved in the Mishnah and the argument is destined to endure.

As Bari Weiss has noted:

> The Talmud is not a document of the majority opinion, the opinion that ended up winning the day. It's a document, also, of the minority. Of the critics. Of the gadflies ... Encoded in Judaism's DNA is the countercultural perspective we need. On hearing multiple perspectives, on reason over passion, and on a kind of intellectual humility that understands that sometimes the minority opinion turns out to be right.[11]

Ruth Bader Ginsberg, herself a regular dissenter on the US Supreme Court in her time, observed:

> Dissents speak to a future age. It's not simply to say, 'My colleagues are wrong and I would do it this way.' But the greatest dissents do become court opinions and gradually over time their views become the dominant view. So that's the dissenter's hope: that they are writing not for today, but for tomorrow.[12]

Recording contrary opinions has another important benefit. Dissent breeds dissent. A participant in a discussion, wavering over whether to voice an alternative opinion, can draw strength from the fact that others too have stood out against the crowd. As such, public dissent provides encouragement to original thinkers and helps reduce the dangers of groupthink.

Talmud study is a celebration of multiple, rival perspectives. Indeed, students of Talmud rarely study the bottom-line legal rulings, and the practical conclusions of the rabbinic debate are for the most part not stated in the Talmud. What they study is the argument itself. They will often test their knowledge of a tractate by trying to reconstruct its *shakla ve'tarya*. The phrase, literally referring to the to and fro of haggling in the marketplace, refers here to the chain of arguments and counterarguments, proofs and counterproofs, that make up the backbone of the tractate. The test of whether a student has learned a tractate well is not whether they know the legal rulings that were decided, but whether they can reconstruct the to and fro of the discussion, making sure that no key argument, logical step or piece of evidence has been omitted.

It is striking that in modern life we so rarely do this simple exercise. Considering how much time we spend debating our differences, and how significant are some of the decisions that we reach, we rarely step back to think about the process of debate and dialogue that leads to the final bottom line.

Daniel Kahneman has suggested a very similar discipline to help organisations improve their own decision-making, a practice that he calls a 'decision journal'. This is a record of 'the main arguments pro and con and what were the alternatives that were considered'.[13]

While generally social media doesn't seem to improve the quality of our debates, it can actually help in keeping track of the to and fro of our arguments. Broadcaster and former UK politician and diplomat Rory Stewart has admitted that he likes X, formerly Twitter, for precisely that reason:

I love arguing on Twitter. There's something very, very satisfying about the discipline of that word limit. You get to put out your argument and then somebody comes back and then you come back at them. And I love the clarity of that. It's a beautiful way of arguing, which wasn't available to us until Twitter was around.[14]

Whether face to face or online, keeping our eyes on the to and fro of the debate has other important benefits too. It can provide a protective brake against finding ourselves in endless circular squabbling, revisiting points that have been made repeatedly before. Additionally, in our recap we are required to overcome our confirmation bias, and give voice to points made, even if they don't happen to support our own position. In highly charged discussions, where passions and emotional stakes are high, this discipline can also help us find common ground. We might differ strongly on the issue under discussion, but perhaps we can concur on the *shakla ve'tarya;* that is, on how each side of the debate can be best presented.

There's one more advantage of the *shakla ve'tarya* exercise. It helps us internalise the debate. Requiring us to state the arguments for *both* sides helps reduce the degree to which we identify only with one side of an argument. While we may still have strong personal views and opinions, being required to give voice to opposing views means that we too become, in some way, invested in that other side's viewpoint. The argument ceases to be one of 'us and them', and becomes, to some degree, a debate within ourselves. As *New York Times* columnist David Brooks has noted, describing the bitter splits that have divided much of the United States in recent years: 'And here's the hard part of the war; it's not between one group of good people and another group of bad people. The war runs down the middle of every heart.'[15]

Shortly after I took up my diplomatic posting in London, I went to give blood at a donation centre near Oxford Circus. The blood drive was the result of a competition, called 'The Impossible Brief', devised by the advertising agency Saatchi and Saatchi to find ideas to help resolve the Israeli–Palestinian conflict. The powerfully simple idea which won the competition (out of more than a hundred entries) was that Israelis would donate blood that would be given to Palestinian patients, and Palestinians would donate to Israelis. The campaign was titled 'Blood Relations', with the tag line, 'Could you hurt someone who has your blood running through their veins?' The campaign was compelling in itself, but it serves as a metaphor too.

In situations of acute difference, finding common ground can mean not only finding a way of tolerating the voices of others, but also giving voice to the dissenting voice that we so often try to silence within ourselves. In our most difficult conversations, it is worth taking a pause to ask ourselves whether there is perhaps a trace of the opposing argument that we can identify, running through our own intellectual veins.

Many organisations claim that they value dissent, but in practice reward conformity and commitment to the status quo. To be effective, fostering dissent requires more than lip service. As we have seen, it calls on us to hold up genuine models of dissent to give courage to others, and the adoption of practices – like those of the Sanhedrin and at General Motors – to ensure that their voices are heard. Once we have put in these efforts, we would be foolish not to take steps to capture the insights that have been generated. Even if they are not relevant to our decision-making today, they make a critical contribution to better understanding in the future.

Chapter 9

Alternative Thinking

It ain't what you don't know that gets you into trouble, it's what you know for sure, that just ain't so.

Mark Twain

The terrible massacre of Israelis that took place on 7 October 2023 was the most tragic event in recent Israeli history. With the murder of over 1,200 and the kidnapping of 251, it led to a devastating war with many thousands of fatalities and casualties. Beyond the horrendous loss of life, the events were tragic in another way. The disastrous failure of intelligence that blinded Israel to the attack on 7 October was precisely a lesson that Israel had committed to learn from a similar disaster almost exactly fifty years before.

The Yom Kippur War of 1973 was the single greatest military disaster in Israel's history. The surprise attack by Egyptian and Syrian forces resulted in more than 2,600 dead and over 7,000 injured. The disaster was all the more traumatic coming just a few years after Israel's extraordinary victory in the Six Day War of 1967, which had given Israelis a misguided sense of invincibility.

The painful process of self-examination that followed the disaster revealed that it was above all a catastrophic failure of intelligence. A Commission of Inquiry found that almost the entire intelligence community had bought into what became known in Hebrew as the *conzeptia*, a fixed paradigm of thinking that proved to be tragically wrong. This paradigm held that Israel's deterrence was so strong that there was no real possibility of an armed attack by its neighbours. A feedback loop within the political and intelligence leadership reinforced this assumption. There were clear indications of war preparations by Israel's Arab neighbours but the dominant prism of the *conzeptia* swept these away. A leading newspaper censored its military correspondent's description of hostile troop movements as panic-mongering. As Zvi Zamir, Chief of Israel's Mossad intelligence agency, would later admit, 'Our intelligence process became a cross-fertilisation-breeding disaster.' In the aftermath of the inquiry, Israel resolved to make every effort not to fall foul of such devasting groupthink again.

One of the outcomes of the inquiry was that Israel's intelligence establishment decided to set up a special unit, a 'Red Team', armed with all the available intelligence and charged with the job of challenging the received wisdom. The name of the unit is taken directly from the Talmud: *ipcha mistabra* – literally, 'Perhaps it's the other way round'. To this day, not only this dedicated unit but every Israeli intelligence officer is authorised and even encouraged to point out blind spots and alternative interpretations that the received wisdom in that community may be missing. Tragically, as we have seen, this very principle was subject to a blind spot in the weeks leading up to the events of 7 October.

Challenging our assumptions

The phrase *ipcha mistabra* is used by the rabbis in the course of narrow Talmudic debates to question the logic at hand, but more broadly it reflects a sensibility that goes to the heart of Talmudic thinking. This is a sensibility that is always questioning our own assumptions, even questioning our own questions. If, for example, someone raises an argument based on an earlier rabbinic teaching, the Talmud will raise possible objections: Is that really the entire teaching? Have we understood the context correctly? Did the rabbi quoted really say that? Could he have subsequently changed his mind?

Only partly in jest, one scholar tried to encapsulate the difference between Greek logic and Talmudic logic. Greek logic, he noted, goes as follows: 'All ravens are black. That bird is a raven.

It follows that that bird is black.' Talmudic logic, he suggested, is rather different, going as follows: 'All ravens are black. That bird is a raven. It follows that *either* that bird is black, *or* it is a new kind of raven that we have never come across before!'

Nearly two millennia before the term 'confirmation bias' was coined by English psychologist Peter Wason in 1960, *ipcha mistabra* thinking was an attempt to counter this cognitive weakness. Confirmation bias is our unique human talent for picking up on evidence that supports our view and being blinkered from anything that contradicts it. This aspect of human nature has been recognised for centuries (400 years ago Francis Bacon noted that 'the human understanding when it has once adopted a position . . . draws all things to support and agree with it') but only in recent years has research captured the extent of our capacity for blindfolding ourselves against evidence that counters our preconceptions, and also the range of ways in which we do this, including how we select our evidence, interpret and recall it. One significant finding of this research is that the more years of education one has had, the *more likely* one is to be susceptible to confirmation bias, and to subconsciously edit the facts available to suit our preconceptions. Educators take note.

At the point of greatest certainty

A rabbinic legend about the birth of the prophet Samuel highlights the point that it is at our moments of greatest certainty that we need to question our most trusted convictions.

At the start of the story of Samuel, Hannah, who will become Samuel's mother, is childless and distraught. Desperate to have a child, she goes to the Temple in Jerusalem and pours her heart out in silent prayer. Watching her from afar is Eli, the High Priest. Seeing her lips move with passion, but hearing no sound coming out, Eli concludes that she must be drunk. 'How long will you make a drunken spectacle of yourself!' he berates her. 'Put away your liquor!' 'I haven't drunk anything,' answers Hannah. 'I am simply pouring out my soul before the Lord.' Eli realises that he has misjudged her, and adds his prayers to hers.

The rabbinic account is troubled by Eli's quick rush to (mis) judgement. How could he have been so decisive – and so wrong? It offers its answer in the form of an addition to the narrative. In this addition, Eli is confused by the sight of Hannah's passionate but silent prayer. To understand better he consults with the *Urim* and *Tummim*, the miraculous letters on the High Priest's breastplate. According to tradition, when asked a question by the High Priest, particular letters engraved on the breastplate would light up, and would combine to reveal the answer. When Eli asked the breastplate about Hannah's behaviour, certain letters – *heh*, *kaf*, *resh* and *shin* – lit up. Eli combined them to form the word meaning 'drunk' – *shin-kaf-resh-heh*, making the word *shikorah* – and so he berated her, confident that he was right in his assumption that she was intoxicated. But in fact, says the Midrash, Eli combined the letters incorrectly. He should have combined them with a slight change in the order to make the word meaning 'she is like Sarah' – *kaf-shin-resh-heh*, making the word *keSarah* – to indicate that she was really like the righteous matriarch, wife of Abraham, who was similarly childless and prayed devotedly for a child.

All this takes place in the heart of the Temple, with an oracle of absolute truth: the Talmud teaches that, unlike the prophets, the *Urim* and *Tummim* don't make mistakes. Yet the Midrashic legend insists that it is in this place of greatest certainty, when the lights on the breastplate are glowing at their brightest, that the danger of being wrong may in fact be at its greatest.

Embracing alternative thinking

At the time of the Ipcha Mistabra unit's establishment close to fifty years ago, encouraging internal challenge in this way was an unusual and radical practice. Today it has become far more widespread, not only in the intelligence community, but in other areas too. Investment houses, for example, frequently encourage internal teams to challenge their investment theses, though few go quite as far as Warren Buffett, who gave this advice on making investments: 'It appears to me that there is only one way to get a rational and balanced discussion. Directors should hire a second advisor to make the case against the acquisition, with its fee contingent on the deal *not* going through.'[1]

Social scientist Gary Klein has proposed a simple but powerful exercise to help introduce the spirit of alternative-view thinking in group settings: the 'premortem'[2]. Unlike a postmortem, which seeks to understand what went wrong after it is too late, the premortem seeks to anticipate blind spots and possible weaknesses when there is still time to change direction. In its simplest form, when a group of people are largely in agreement on a course of action, the exercise asks them to imagine that one year has passed and that in this imaginary future it is now clear beyond doubt that the course of action that was decided upon has proven to be a disastrous failure. Participants are invited to suggest what might have gone wrong. Suddenly the dynamic of the discussion changes; rather than focusing on why they should pursue this course of action, people are challenged to come up with reasons why they should not do so. Something subtle changes in the psychology of the meeting too. Far from being perceived as 'spoilers' frustrating an agreed plan, participants who identify hidden pitfalls are now seen as valued contributors to the exercise. A premortem is by no means guaranteed to identify every possible cause of failure in advance, but it is a helpful tool in capturing hesitations that might otherwise be swept under the boardroom carpet.

This is a powerful tool for decision-making within organisations. But individuals can benefit from it too. An exercise that I sometimes use in Difficult Conversations laboratories is to ask participants to write a page in an imaginary journal, imagining that they are two years into the future. As they look back, which of the assumptions they are holding on to today might turn out to be wrong?

Another very simple technique to encourage people to rethink their certainties, especially regarding their assessments of what they think will happen in the future, is to ask them to give a percentage assessment of the likelihood of their prediction coming to pass. Even if the percentage they give themselves is high, say in the 90s, they will also be opening themselves up to the possibility that there are alternative scenarios. It goes without saying that we should ask ourselves the same question regarding our own confident predictions.

As individuals, organisations and societies, we can adopt practices that will help reduce our tendency to bolster our own assumptions, causing us to realise that our own deeply held convictions may indeed be more partial and fragmented than we have always supposed. If we succeed in opening ourselves to this possibility, then we may even be ready for the next challenge: if our own cherished positions are less right than we thought, can we open ourselves to the possibility that those of our opponents might be less wrong?

Communication: Words Are All I Have

It is hard to communicate with words, but impossible to communicate without them. George Orwell advised that 'probably it is better to put off using words as long as possible and get one's meanings as clear as one can through pictures and sensations',[1] but we have yet to find the telepathic technology to put his recommendation into practice.

Perhaps the best that we can do is to enter into our most difficult conversations with an awareness that we are using imperfect tools, and to do all we can to make our channels of communication as clear from interference and static as possible. Better communication will lead to better arguments.

This means adopting practices that can sharpen our listening and our questioning, and broadening the range of our self-expression to include storytelling, humour and silence, in order to present our own case as fully and compellingly as possible.

Chapter 10

The Seeing Ear

Courage is what it takes to stand up and speak; courage is also what it takes to sit down and listen.

Winston Churchill

One of the challenges of being an Israeli diplomat, I've discovered, is that for many people you are representing not one country but two. The first is the modern state of Israel, a geopolitical entity with governmental policies and strategic interests like any other. But the other country is an aspirational vision of what the Holy Land could or should be, cherished within the hearts of many people, inspired by their faith or their historic imagination – the 'Israel within'. Often, when confronted with the reality of a modern state dealing with complex challenges and achieving varying degrees of success, observers can find their cherished hopes dashed – based as they are on the 'Israel within' – and feel a sense of frustration and even anger. I, as the most easily accessible expression of the state, often found myself on the receiving end of these sentiments.

Why, representatives of progressive Jewish movements would ask, was their movement not adequately recognised by the state? Why, campaigners for the rights of minorities wanted to know, was Israel not living up to the aspirations of its Declaration of Independence in relation to minority groups? Why, traditionalists would demand, was the Jewish state not being more faithful to its biblical mandates? And so on. Sometimes I would try to offer a substantive response, or at least provide some context, whether it be in terms of regional dynamics or coalition politics. But over time I found that often the most effective, and perhaps most meaningful, response was simply to reply: 'I hear what you say and will report it faithfully to Jerusalem.' The effect was extraordinarily powerful. My interlocutors didn't want an answer – certainly not my answer. They wanted to know they had been heard – by me, and by extension the government, to whom I duly reported their concerns.

I found something similar when I would visit university campuses, where debates on Israel and the Middle East were often at boiling point and civil discussion seemed impossible. One exercise that I discovered could be helpful was to invite students to write, on one side of a piece of paper, without judgement, the position of the other side as they understood it. Each student was then asked to give their summary to a student holding an opposing viewpoint, to be edited and corrected as they saw fit. Truth to tell, in many cases tensions were already so frayed that even engaging with this exercise was an impossible task. But where participants are prepared to set aside their own opinions sufficiently to take this simple step forward, to give ear and voice to an opposing viewpoint, and to be open and willing to hear where they might have misjudged or misinterpreted, it can be surprisingly effective in creating the beginnings of trust and genuine dialogue.

The ear and the eye

I will sometimes ask participants in negotiation training sessions what superpower they would most like to have to help them at the negotiation table. One of the most common suggestions is the ability to mind-read the thoughts of the other side. 'Well, actually, you already have a superpower that comes pretty close if you use it,' I'll tell them. 'It's called listening!'

Attentive listening is not generally regarded as a Jewish trait. I recently attended an international Jewish conference which was intended to build bridges between North American Jews and Israelis. A welcome attempt to bridge gaps, it took place under the slogan 'Let's talk!', but it might have been more successful had it been named 'Let's listen!' Still, while Jews are often perceived to be talkative (perhaps overly so), Jewish tradition places a strong emphasis on the act of listening.

One fundamental difference between the ancient Greek and ancient Jewish civilisations was the emphasis of the two societies on seeing and on hearing respectively. Greece had a profoundly visual culture. Its greatest achievements had to do with the eye, with seeing. It produced some of the greatest art, sculpture and architecture the world has ever seen. Judaism, by contrast, with its faith in an invisible God, tended to be suspicious of the visual. The very act of creating a graven image was prohibited, and the Bible warns against the eyes leading the heart astray. In the biblical account, God communicates in sounds, not sights. In reciting the central declaration of their faith, Jews cover their eyes and recite: *Shema Yisrael . . .*[1], exhorting: 'Hear, O Israel . . .'

Western society is still predominantly influenced by the Greek tradition in which knowing is seeing. As Jonathan Sacks observes, our vocabulary of understanding is primarily visual in nature. We speak of insight, foresight and hindsight. We offer observations, and illustrate and illuminate our points to support them. And when we understand something, we say, '*I see.*' In Jewish tradition, by contrast, the key metaphors of understanding are of hearing. The word *shema*, 'to hear', echoes throughout the dialogues of the Talmud: *Ta Shema*, 'Come and hear'; *Ka mashma lan*, 'It teaches us this'; *Shema mina*, 'Infer from this'; *Lo shemiyah lei*, 'He did not agree', and so on.

Listeners rule

One of the most powerful indications of the importance of listening in Jewish tradition is the insistence that arguments are won not by those who speak the best, but by those who listen better.

Earlier we looked at the passage in the Mishnah describing the long-running dispute between the School of Hillel and the School of Shammai. After years of debate a heavenly voice announced, 'Both sides' opinions are words of the living God.' But notwithstanding this declaration of the legitimacy of both sides' views, a practical ruling had to be made. In theory, both opinions might be valid, but in practice only one could be followed. So, as described in the passage, the heavenly voice declared: 'Both sides' opinions are the words of the living God ... But the law is in accordance with the School of Hillel.'

Why did the School of Hillel win the day? The reason cited by the Mishnah has nothing to do with force of intellect, but rather with the willingness of the School of Hillel to hear the views of others: 'They were accommodating and agreeable, would teach their own positions and those of the School of Shammai, even putting those of the School of Shammai first.'² Hillel's view takes precedence not because he makes the best argument, but because he is the best at listening to the arguments of others. Indeed, of all the sages in the Talmud, Hillel stands out as a model of engaged, even radical, listening.

In most cases, our first encounter with any of the rabbis in the Talmud is when they speak; that is, when their views are quoted. Our earliest encounter with Hillel, though, is not on an occasion when he speaks, but when he listens. The Talmud introduces us to Hillel as a poor woodchopper in Babylon. He would save half of his paltry earnings for his family, and use the other half to pay the entry fee for the study hall. One day he had not earned enough to pay to enter the study hall. Although the day was cold and snowy, his passion for learning was so great that he climbed on the roof to listen eagerly to the lessons through the skylight. Only when his body, covered with the falling snow, blocked the light from the skylight did the teachers look up and notice him, bringing him inside to warm up by the fire and commence his journey to become one of the Jewish world's greatest scholars.

Hillel acquired a reputation as a listener, and also as a man of enormous patience. So much so that the Talmud recounts a story of a man who makes a hefty bet that he can get Hillel to lose his temper. One Friday afternoon, when Hillel is bathing to prepare for the Sabbath, the man stands outside Hillel's house and shouts that he has an urgent question. Hillel emerges, wet from his bath, and invites him to ask his question. The man asks his question, 'Why are the heads of Babylonians round?' – which is not only infantile, but also insulting, since Hillel himself is a Babylonian. Still, Hillel answers with patience and respect. Again and again, the man returns to disturb Hillel with provocative questions ('Why are the eyes of this tribe bleary?', 'Why are the feet of that tribe flat?') and again and again Hillel, dripping from his bath, listens patiently and responds, until, with the Sabbath close approaching, the man says: 'I have many more questions to ask, but I am afraid lest you get angry.' At that point, the Talmud recounts, Hillel wraps himself in his bathrobe and sits down before him, saying: 'All of the questions that you have to ask, ask away.'

Hillel's posture – wrapping up, sitting down, leaning in as we might say, the equivalent today of turning off our mobile phone or asking an assistant to hold all calls – reminds us that true listening is no passive activity. The philosopher Roland Barthes distinguishes listening from hearing: hearing is a physiological phenomenon, listening is a psychological act. We are always hearing, but listening is a choice.

We tend to think of ourselves as good listeners, but in practice many of us rarely make the choice to lean in and truly engage. Jewish teacher and leadership coach Erica Brown recalls being interviewed by a community leader who asked her nothing about herself or her work. When, after half an hour of reciting his own jokes and anecdotes, she did finally get a chance to speak, he seemed distracted and looked around the room. Writes Erica: 'I asked him only one question: "Do you consider yourself a good listener?" He smiled broadly, looked straight at me, and replied, "People tell me that I'm a wonderful listener."'

Once in a rare while we may catch a glimpse of ourselves as others see us. I remember once calling one of my younger children, who was watching cartoons on the television, to come and join the family for supper. 'Not now,' he called back. 'I'm watching the news.' Ouch. A conversation with another of my children reminded me that, even when we think someone is listening, what they take from it is not always what we intend. My young son turned to me one day and said: 'You know when the Israelites were coming out of the wilderness, Moses really wanted to go with them into the land of Israel. He *really really* wanted to go into the land of Israel!' I was feeling proud of how strongly my son connected with the Bible story. Until he added: 'Well, that's how much I want a PlayStation!'

As much as we may admire the facility of leaning in to listen, we may still ask why, in these debates between Hillel and Shammai, Hillel's facility for listening should be the deciding factor in determining which side has made the better case. Contemporary scholar and biographer of the Talmudic Hillel Rabbi Joseph Telushkin suggests that the ability of Hillel's students to listen means that their arguments were better founded. By listening carefully, they exposed themselves to the logic of their opponents and the arguments against their own positions, and in doing so they had acquired greater intellectual depth and made their own case stronger. Telushkin suggests that all of us can adopt a more Hillel-like approach in our own lives, advising:

> Don't read only books and publications that agree with and reinforce your point of view . . . If you seldom hear, read, or listen to views that oppose your own, and if almost everyone you talk to sees the world just as you do, your thinking will grow flabby and intolerant.[4]

To Telushkin's advice, I would add that it makes sense to seek out the very best expression of opposing views that you can find. It is all too tempting to find extreme voices that we can easily ridicule and dismiss, allowing us to settle even more comfortably into our own convictions. I subscribe to a number of newsfeeds and podcasts that fall outside my ideological comfort zone. Frustrating as they may often be ('I'm actually paying to read this stuff,' I sometimes mutter), they very often challenge my thinking, and on occasion even change it.

Cultivating curiosity

How does one cultivate an attitude of active listening? One critical element seems to be curiosity. Recent years have seen a growth of scientific research in relation to the surprising power of curiosity to overcome prejudice and bias. As we noted previously in our discussion of confirmation bias, education and intelligence can't be relied on to counter our prejudices. To the contrary, they may only bolster our ability to be selective in our evidence, and to rationalise our rejection of facts that don't square nicely with our preconceptions. Studies have shown that individuals who are more informed on an issue, say for example climate change, tend to be more extreme than those who hold similar views but with less factual basis. This is a troubling realisation for anyone who believes that education carries an assurance of greater moderation and understanding, but the research does provide a glimmer of hope. Education per se may not help counter bias, but curiosity does.

In one study, a group of Yale academics and film makers, who were interested in studying potential audiences for scientific documentaries, assessed people's opinions on public issues which should be informed by science. They used two scales to measure the participants in the study. The first assessed their scientific background, and the second their degree of curiosity about scientific issues, as gauged by the extent and quality of the material they chose to read and watch on the subject. The participants with stronger scientific backgrounds, it turned out, were more entrenched in positions that aligned with their political outlook. On issues like global warming and fracking, liberal participants with a more scientific background were the most concerned about the health and safety risks, while conservatives with a more scientific background were the least concerned, confirming that higher levels of scientific education actually result in *greater* polarisation between the groups, not less. But looking at the other scale, it turned out that an ongoing sense of curiosity, as opposed to knowledge, had a different effect. While differences between political groups still remained, the more curious the participant, the more open they were to appreciating the concerns of the opposing viewpoint, and to exposing themselves to articles and opinions that contradicted their existing beliefs.

When we think of qualities that equip people for leadership, we don't tend to put curiosity high on the list. But the Bible suggests that it was in fact curiosity that marked Moses out as a leader. Tending his father-in-law's sheep in the deserts of Midian, he was struck by the sight of a bush that burned without being consumed. His statement that led him to his encounter with God and his mission to free his people, was not one of faith or political courage, but of curiosity: 'I will go over and see this strange sight – why the bush does not burn up.'

In the world of ideas too, more often than not it is simple curiosity rather than profound thinking that yields the important breakthroughs. As Isaac Asimov wrote: 'Great discoveries often begin not with "Eureka" but with "That's funny!" '[5]

Approach with awe

'The Ethics of the Fathers' is a compendium of rabbinic wisdom from the sages of the Mishnah. In one striking passage, the sage Ben Zoma offers a counterintuitive definition of the qualities of wisdom, strength, wealth and honour:

> Ben Zoma said: Who is wise? One who learns from every person . . . Who is mighty? One who subdues their [evil] inclination . . . Who is rich? One who rejoices in their lot . . . Who is honoured? One who honours their fellow human beings.[6]

Ben Zoma's message is that all too often the qualities that we tend to think have external measures, that are something outside ourselves, are really the result of what is to be found within. True strength is found in conquering ourselves, true wealth is found in our ability to feel satisfied with what we have, and true honour is to be found not in how we are treated but how we treat others. But perhaps the most surprising of Ben Zoma's definitions is of wisdom: 'Who is wise?' he asks. His answer: 'One who learns from every person.'

It is a radical answer, suggesting not merely that there are other people we can learn from, but that wisdom is to be found by listening to *every* person. From the apparent fool and bigot, to the annoying neighbour, and even the troublesome provocateur who repeatedly interrupted Hillel in his bath. As G.K. Chesterton once wrote, there is no such thing as an uninteresting person; there are only uninterested people.

New York Times columnist David Brooks captured this spirit in an article of advice on how to have better conversations. 'Approach with awe', he advised:

C.S. Lewis once wrote that if you'd never met a human and suddenly encountered one, you'd be inclined to worship this creature. Every human being is a miracle, and your superior in some way. The people who have great conversations walk into the room expecting to be delighted by you and make you feel the beam of their affection and respect. Lady Randolph Churchill once said that when sitting next to the statesman William Gladstone she thought him the cleverest person in England, but when she sat next to Benjamin Disraeli she thought she was the cleverest person in England.[7]

The physical posture of Hillel in his bath towel – wrapped and rapt, leaning in – is an outward expression of a mental attitude, one which requires effort to cultivate. It is an attitude that requires us to consciously quieten the voice inside us, and open ourselves to that of the other. Stephen Covey, author of the best-seller *7 Habits of Highly Effective People*, has noted: 'Most people don't listen with the intent to understand; they listen with the intent to reply.'[8] If we are honest with ourselves, the motives that encourage us to insert ourselves into a conversation often have little to do with advancing the quality of the dialogue and the opportunity for joint learning. Sometimes they are actually an attempt to pre-empt or divert the conversation away from directions that make us feel uncomfortable. On other occasions we may simply want to use the conversation as a grandstand for promoting ourselves, in the eyes – or rather ears – of our counterparts, or of other observers. It's been suggested that a useful acronym to keep in mind when you're talking to someone is 'WAIT', standing for 'Why Am I Talking?'

Communicating our listening

Listening, done well, is not a passive exercise. To be effective we must find a way of conveying to our counterpart that this is not a monologue but a dialogue. An analysis by Harvard academics based on 360-degree assessment of the listening behaviours of over 3,000 participants in a management development programme found that 'good listening is much more than being silent while the other person talks'. Summarising their findings in the *Harvard Business Review*, they noted:

> While many of us have thought of being a good listener being like a sponge that accurately absorbs what the other person is saying, instead, what these findings show is that good listeners are like trampolines. They are someone you can bounce ideas off of – and rather than absorbing your ideas and energy, they amplify, energize, and clarify your thinking. They make you feel better not merely passively absorbing, but by actively supporting. This lets you gain energy and height, just like someone jumping on a trampoline.[9]

Courses in effective listening suggest an array of techniques to communicate our interest, including murmurings of approval and nods of assent. TV reporters, I have found, are particularly adept at encouraging interviewees by making visual indications of interest (nodding, raising their eyebrows and so on) without making any noise that might interfere with the soundtrack of the interview. In regular conversation, such calculated gestures can seem artificial and may be unnecessary. Radio host Celeste Headlee notes: 'If you're really listening, you don't need to pretend to be listening.' One effective way of ensuring we are listening actively, and of showing that we are doing so, is reflecting back to our counterpart what we have heard them saying. This is a powerful way of increasing the trust needed for genuine dialogue, by giving the speaker the confidence they have been truly understood.

Aneurin 'Nye' Bevan was a Welsh Labour Party politician. He left school at fourteen to work as a coal miner. He became involved in local union politics and rose to become an MP and the youngest member of the cabinet. He overcame a childhood stammer to become an outstanding speaker, and with his sharp mind and persuasive Welsh accent was an exceptional orator. On one occasion, though, he proved not just the power of speaking, but of listening. In a contentious parliamentary debate Bevan found himself continually interrupted by the jeers and shouting of the opposition and unable to make his case. After repeatedly trying to make himself heard, he addressed the opposition directly: 'The honourable members of the opposition clearly have many points to make. I ask only that I be given ten minutes in order to state their case as I understand it. If, at the end of the period, they still consider that their case remains unrepresented I will yield the floor.' In the minutes that followed, Bevan presented the opposing case with clarity and with respect. At the conclusion of his presentation, even his opponents joined in the standing ovation, before allowing him to continue to make the argument for his own side.

The Bible recounts an instance of such reflecting back in the book of Kings. Solomon has just been given the gift of wisdom and the Bible proceeds to tell a story that demonstrates the new depths of his understanding. In this famous story, two women of low repute come before Solomon to judge their case. The story is usually cited as an example of Solomon's wisdom but when rereading it recently, something else struck me. As you read the account, with which you may be familiar, see if it strikes you too:

> The first woman said, 'Please, my Lord! This woman and I live in the same house; and I gave birth to a child while she was in the house. On the third day after I was delivered, this woman also gave birth to a child. We were alone; there was no one else with us in the house, just the two of us in the house. During the night this woman's child died, because she lay on it. She arose in the night and took my son from my side while your maidservant was asleep and laid him in her bosom; and she laid her dead son in my bosom. When I arose in the morning to nurse my son, there he was, dead; but when I looked at him closely in the morning, it was not the son I had borne.' The other woman spoke up, 'No, the live one is my son, and the dead one is yours!' But the first insisted, 'No, the dead boy is yours; mine is the live one!' And they went on arguing before the king. The king said, 'One says, "This is my son, the live one, and the dead one is yours"; and the other says, "No, the dead boy is yours, mine is the live one." So the king gave the order, 'Fetch me a sword.' A sword was brought before the king . . .[10]

The story continues with Solomon proposing to cut the baby in half so that the two women can share it. One woman supports the idea, while the other says she will give up the baby so that it will not be killed, whereupon Solomon declares her to be the true mother.[11] The aspect of the story that is usually emphasised is the psychological wisdom of Solomon in making a threat that reveals the inner motivations of the two women. But, demonstrating that texts need to be listened to as carefully as people, tucked away in the account is an arresting example of reflecting back. After hearing the two sides' presentation of their case, Solomon summarises the two versions: 'One says, "This is my son, the live one, and the dead one is yours"; and the other says, "No, the dead boy is yours, mine is the live one."'

Before passing judgement, indeed before saying anything else, Solomon indicates clearly to both sides that their voices have been heard. And in fact, as rabbinic commentators have pointed out, his perceptive summary holds the key to the problem's solution. One of the women places the emphasis on keeping the live child, the other on the other woman keeping the dead one. It seems that Solomon's great gift of wisdom may have been rooted in his ability to listen attentively and well.

Entering their world

In the most famous story relating to Hillel recounted in the Talmud, Hillel and Shammai are approached by a proselyte who demands to be taught the entire Torah while he stands on one leg. Shammai has no time for such games and shoos away the proselyte with a builder's measuring rod. Shammai's very name means 'surveyor' or 'measurer', and his approach is characterised by holding others to his own fixed standards. Hillel, on the other hand, is willing to step out from his own preconceived worldview and enter another's. He does not question the legitimacy of the one-leg test and answers the questioner: 'That which is hateful to you, do not do to another; that is the entire Torah. The rest is interpretation. Go study.' Hillel's answer does not begin from his own vantage point, with his own preconceived standards. Rather, the criterion he offers is entirely oriented towards his questioner: 'what is hateful to *you*'. Always a listener, Hillel evinces again his ability to enter the world of his conversation partner.

The ability to demonstrate radical empathy in this way is rare and deeply impressive. When I was attending sessions at the United Nations in New York, some of the legal advisers representing the different countries would often play a curious game. On any issue, before any country's representative spoke, they would try to guess exactly what position they would take. While the views of the respective countries on the major issues of the day are fairly well known, when it gets down to more intricate matters this is far harder to anticipate, especially when you are considering the more than 190 countries in the United Nations. But, by having listened carefully and empathetically to the views of each country in previous debates, a number of the legal advisers showed an extraordinary, Hillel-like capacity to enter into the minds of others and anticipate their positions.

E is for Empathy

Are you by nature a Shammai or a Hillel? It's far from definitive, but a one-minute ice-breaker exercise I sometimes use in teaching mediation can give a very quick indication of where one stands on the empathy scale. I ask the class to imagine that their forefinger is a crayon, and quickly, without thinking, to write the letter E on their own forehead.

Try it now, before reading on.

Now, ask yourself whether you wrote the letter E facing you; that is, as you would read it. Or did you write it facing outwards, as others would read it? If you wrote facing outwards that may suggest that you are inclined to place yourself in the shoes of others. If you wrote facing yourself, there may be some work to be done here.

Improving our ability to listen can be extremely difficult, not least because we tend to be sure that we are good listeners to start with. A simple way to start our journey to become better at it is to listen in pairs. It can be extraordinarily revealing to touch base with someone else who was privy to the conversation, and ask them: 'What were the main points that you thought X was making?' And second, 'What were they really saying?' The answers may surprise you.

For something that many of us are convinced comes naturally, listening effectively and well takes surprising effort. But we have some great models to guide us, from the leaning-in posture of the sage Hillel to the perceptive reflection of King Solomon. And if we are successful, we will ensure not only that we hear others better, but that our voice is heard better too.

Chapter 11

Better than an Answer

> As I have moved up in my career, I have discovered that it is more important for me to know how to ask questions. I can leave finding the answers to others.
>
> Dedi Perlmutter, entrepreneur and innovator

As a young child in Talmud class, my teacher would praise any student who could answer his questions. But the highest compliment my teacher could pay a student was to say that they had asked a *gevaldige kashe*, a wonderful question.

A good question is better than a good answer. In the context of conversations, it is one of the most powerful ways of communicating our engagement and concern more deeply than simply repeating what we have heard. David Brooks shares an example:

> I have a friend named Pete Wehner who is an amazing listener. I'll describe some problem to him and he'll ask me some questions. There comes a moment in the conversation, after he's asked four or five questions, when I expect him to start offering his opinion and recommendations. But then he surprises me and asks six or eight more questions, before eventually offering counsel or advice . . .[1]

But questions are not just an aid to relationship-building. In Jewish thinking, relentless questioning is the fount or source from which understanding flows. Linguistic scholar Rabbi Matityahu Glazerson notes that a connection between questioning and the flow of understanding is reflected in the Hebrew language, in which the basic interrogative word 'what' (in Hebrew *ma*) forms the core of the word for water, *ma-yim*. But not only in Hebrew. In fact, there is a curious similarity in many languages between the equivalent words to *ma* and *mayim*: *wass* and *wasser*, *what* and *water*, *quoi* and *aqua* . . .

Albert Einstein too saw questions as the critical gateway to knowledge: 'The important thing is not to stop questioning . . . Never lose a holy curiosity.' Einstein had doubts about whether the education system recognised the importance of questioning. 'It is a miracle that curiosity survives formal education,' he said. 'I never teach my pupils. I only attempt to provide the conditions in which they can learn.'

In this attempt Einstein was reflecting a longstanding Jewish approach to education, which places questions at the heart of the learning experience. The Seder night, the annual retelling of the story of the Exodus, which is such a feature of Jewish life, is a night of questioning. Many of the unusual customs of the Seder night – the unusual foods, the ceremonial dippings of vegetables – are, the rabbis tell us, there to pique the children's curiosity and provoke them to ask questions. And the Seder service itself cannot begin until a child has set the ball rolling by asking the four questions of the *Ma Nishtana*.

But questions are not only for children. The Mishnah instructs that if there are no children at the Seder the adults should each ask questions of each other, even if they are renowned scholars themselves.

A question of quality

Not all questions are equal, though. The Harvard researchers who studied the power of active listening that we referred to in the last chapter identified four different types of questions:

1. 'Simple' questions – 'How are you?'
2. 'Mirror' questions – 'I'm fine. How are you?'
3. 'Full-switch' questions – ones that change the topic entirely
4. 'Follow-up questions' – 'That's interesting. Why do you think that was?'[2]

Of these four types, it was the last, the follow-up questions, that seemed to have special powers of engagement. For one thing, they are genuine questions, not statements disguised as interrogatives ('Surely you don't really believe that?'). But on top of that, they convey a more profound level of listening and desire to know more and are likely to take the conversation further and deeper.

The questions of the Talmud are primarily follow-up questions of this kind. In Jewish life there are, to be sure, other kinds of questions. The usual Hebrew word for a question is *a she'ela*. Such questions tend to be narrowly focused and action-oriented, requesting rulings with regard to halachic practice ('I'm on medication, can I take it on Yom Kippur?', 'Is one permitted to smoke?'). But Talmudic questions are rarely this simple. They are invariably follow-up questions crafted to deepen engagement and further dialogue. A Talmudic question is rarely a *she'ela* but rather a *kushya*, literally meaning 'a difficulty' but better understood as an invitation to work together to resolve an issue. There are various types of such a challenge, ranging from internal inconsistencies or ambiguities to contradictions with other texts or statements made by other authorities, each type signposted by the interrogative word or phrase that introduces it.

What all these types of questions have in common is that they show respect for our counterpart, and a genuine interest in understanding their position more deeply. In short, all reflect a desire to create a learning conversation.

Trial lawyers are taught never to ask questions to which they do not already know the answer. But in a conversation designed to lead us to greater understanding we need to adopt the opposite approach. The most valuable questions are those that will open a door and reveal intellectual vistas we never could imagine. They never lose sight of the quest at the heart of the very word 'question'.

In this sense, Talmudic questions are less like the barbs that lawyers throw in cross examination and more like the questions that a careful doctor would ask in order to reach a diagnosis. A critical first step in addressing any issue in dispute is to clarify exactly where and how we differ.

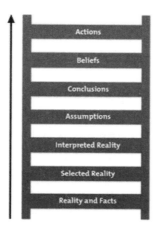

Contemporary business consultants have recognised the value in developing tools to identify exactly where in the chain of events from theory to practice a dispute is centred. One tool to this end is the 'Ladder of Inference' developed by Chris Argyris of Harvard Business School, popularised in the book *The Fifth Discipline*. The Ladder of Inference tracks the mental processes that take us from our understanding of reality, through our natural process of selection and interpretation of events, their translation into assumptions over time, and finally to our reliance on them to reach conclusions. This useful tool helps us identify at which rung on the ladder the respective participants differ. This in itself can help clarify potential directions for resolution. If we disagree on the facts, we might consider thinking about what it would take to reach a common factual basis. On the other hand, if we agree on the evidence but disagree further up the ladder, on our assumptions or conclusions, further factual exploration is unlikely to help; we would be better served to dig deeper into our process of interpretation.

In the Talmud, this kind of diagnostic process is a standard prelude to discussion and debate. Two common Talmudic interrogatories may serve as an example. *Be-mai peligei* – 'On what do they actually disagree?' – is a question used in cases where there is agreement on the practical result of a debate but a difference over the rationale that led to that conclusion. For example, the Talmud describes an argument between the sages Rava and Abaya on the question of whether a transaction which breaches a religious law, say a contract signed on the Sabbath, violating the day of rest, can none the less have legal validity. As the Talmud delves into a range of practical examples, it turns out that the two scholars actually agree on the practical result in every case. 'So on what do they disagree?' asks the Talmud. It answers that the agreement is on the question of principle: which of the two laws, the Sabbath or the binding nature of a contract, has primacy; which is the general rule, and which is the exception?

This type of question contrasts with a different one, *Mai nafka minnah* – 'What follows from it?' – which focuses not on the reasoning but on the practical consequences of a difference of opinion. For example, as we have seen, Jewish tradition places an emphasis on not claiming credit for the work of other writers. But is the reason for this obligation primarily to ensure that the original author gets the credit, or to prevent ourselves from seeming to be wider read or more learned than we really are? The *nafka minnah*, or practical difference between adopting these two reasons, could be that considering the latter requirement, making a general statement, 'These are not my own ideas', would suffice to meet the obligation. However, while this statement would prevent people from getting a false impression of our own erudition, it would not give due credit to the original author.

Though they do not use the Hebrew phrase, moral philosophy professors often consider *nafka minnah* type situations. The famous 'trolley car dilemma' is a vivid example: if a trolley car is about to run over five people, and diverting it to another track would kill a single person, should you divert the trolley? Your answer to the question points to a *nafka minnah*, identifying which particular philosophical approach you identify with. A utilitarian view, which seeks to maximise the good of the many at any cost, would argue for diverting the trolley, while a deontological position, which sees certain moral actions as obligatory irrespective of their consequences, would argue that one should not actively cause the death of another person.

Taken together, such questions help us locate the source of the disagreement, and place it at the relevant level within the decision-making process.

From theory to practice

Beyond helping to focus our efforts on the critical node of disagreement, the Talmudic principles of *Be-mai peligei* and *Mai nafka minnah* on the one hand, and the model of the Ladder of Inference on the other, share another important benefit. They serve to remind us that within any major area of disagreement there can, in fact, be many layers of agreement; we may differ on one rung of the ladder but agree on many others. The great American-Jewish leader the Lubavitcher Rebbe was once asked how he managed to maintain cordial relations with another community leader with whom he had a fundamental dispute. 'We disagree on one commandment [out of the 613 in the Torah]. But we agree on 612 others.'[3] Similarly, CNN political analyst Van Jones was surprised when, as a progressive young activist, he managed to find common ground with staunch conservative Newt Gingrich, until Gingrich advised him: 'Your "ninety percent enemy" can still be your "ten percent friend".'[4]

Drilling down to discover where the real points of difference lie can help shrink the areas of contention, and even find potential areas of collaboration. A number of sensitive diplomatic contexts have given me the opportunity to see this in practice.

Bridging troubled waters
I had the chance to test the power of the *Be-mai peligei* ('On what do we really differ?') type of approach when I was asked to

represent Israel before a United Nations inquiry to investigate the Gaza flotilla incident in 2010. This incident related to a flotilla of six boats sailing from Turkey in order to break the naval blockade on shipping to Gaza. Israel had established the blockade in order to prevent arms and ammunition reaching terrorist groups, following repeated attacks launched from Gaza. As the boats neared, Israel offered the flotilla organisers the option of delivering their cargo through the port of Ashdod, where it could be checked, and humanitarian aid would be transferred on to Gaza. But the flotilla continued towards the blockaded area of sea regardless. When further warnings to change course were ignored, Israeli naval commandos boarded the boats. Five of the six boats were redirected without incident, but on the sixth, the *Mavi Marmara*, the commandos were met with armed resistance. In the ensuing fighting, nine Turkish activists were killed and ten Israeli commandos were injured.

The incident drew widespread international condemnation and led to a serious deterioration in relations between Turkey and Israel. In an attempt to clarify what exactly had happened and to pave the way to a reconciliation between the two countries, UN Secretary General Ban Ki-moon established a Panel of Inquiry.

Turkey and Israel were both invited to send representatives to Geneva to present their understanding of the incident to the panel, and we began to think how best to present our case. In international tribunals of this nature, the behaviour of the parties usually follows a predictable pattern, with both sides grandstanding and harnessing whatever ammunition they can to hurl at the other side. The highly politicised atmosphere of many UN forums tends to encourage the adoption of extreme positions and highly charged rhetoric. In this case, however, the personal involvement of the Secretary General, and the appointment of Geoffrey Palmer, former Prime Minister of New Zealand and a respected legal academic, to chair the inquiry, suggested that there might be the possibility of a more productive dialogue.

As we prepared for the tribunal, we considered taking a *Be-mai peligei* approach. We broke down the issues in contention into different categories: the legality of the blockade, the intentions of the flotilla organisers, the lawfulness of the type and extent of force used and so on. Then, in relation to each issue, we asked ourselves, as honestly as we could, where Turkish and Israeli interpretations differed. What was surprising, considering the public tension surrounding the incident, was how many points of agreement there were, both on the facts of the case and on the legal principles that applied to them.

Our presentation reflected this understanding. After sharing our analysis of the breakdown of the issues at hand, we took each one and presented our understanding of where, on the Ladder of Inference, the differences lay and what, in our view, had led to these alternative interpretations.

In the event, this approach proved to be very helpful. The Palmer report, for the most part, adopted our analysis of the areas of agreement, and narrowed the debate to focused areas of disagreement. Here it found that the naval blockade imposed by Israel had been legal and there were 'serious questions about the conduct, true nature and objectives of the flotilla organizers'. At the same time, it concluded that in the circumstances, there had been instances in which the degree of force used had been excessive.[5]

By narrowing the areas of dispute in this way, and conveying to each side and its constituency of supporters that their perspective had been heard and noted, the way was paved for a process to restore relations between the two countries. This was not a simple process, and included carefully negotiated apologies and the payment of compensation. But it was made possible by an approach that sought to build on areas of agreement and narrow the areas of dispute – an exercise that requires us to ask the right kind of questions.

Be-mai peligei or 'Where do we differ?' questions help us train our focus on the specific area of disagreement. By contrast, *Mai nafka minnah* or 'What are the implications of our differences?' questions challenge us to think through what the practical ramifications of our dispute are – and may open up a way forward. On closer analysis we may find we are not as far apart as we thought, or that seemingly intractable problems can be circumvented in surprising ways. The power of the latter approach was made clear to me in a diplomatic situation no less sensitive than that of the Gaza flotilla: negotiations over the future of Jerusalem.

Jerusalem is a place of paramount significance to Jews, Christians and Muslims. Its status remains the most combustible issue in the Israeli–Palestinian conflict. Over the years, disputes and allegations in relation to Jerusalem have often led to violence. For this reason, in the 1990s, in the Oslo negotiation process, Israel and the Palestinians agreed that negotiations regarding the future of Jerusalem would be postponed for several years to a later phase of talks, and so would not have to be addressed in the earlier negotiations. However, when as part of these talks it became necessary to deal with the issue of elections for the Palestinian Authority, the Jerusalem question couldn't be entirely avoided. The agreed framework provided that Palestinians in East Jerusalem would be allowed to participate in the elections. But it was not clear what 'participation in the elections' actually meant. Did it mean that there would have to be polling stations located in East Jerusalem? Israel argued no – it had been agreed that the hot-button issue of Jerusalem would be addressed in the future, not now; until then, any Palestinians who wished to vote could travel outside Jerusalem and vote in the West Bank. The Palestinian negotiators, for their part, insisted that participating in the elections required the physical presence of polling stations in East Jerusalem.

This looked like a textbook example of an irreconcilable dispute. Either the polling stations would be in the city, or they would not be in the city. But a *Mai nafka minnah* approach helped the two sides understand that in practice the differences were not so wide. The Palestinian side had no real difficulty with Palestinian voters travelling a short distance to cast their ballots. The issue was primarily symbolic. They did not want to be seen in any way to have waived their demands in relation to Jerusalem.

This understanding paved the way for more creative thinking. It was agreed that most East Jerusalem voters would cast their ballots in polling stations in the West Bank, but in areas which had been considered part of Jerusalem under historic Jordanian rule. Still, the Palestinian side insisted that for symbolic reasons some voting had to take place within the city proper. To this end, it was agreed that elderly and infirm voters could vote in a number of post offices based in East Jerusalem. The Palestinian side could claim that this was actual voting in East Jerusalem, while Israel could claim that, because the process took place in a post office, this was effectively postal voting and the real act of electoral participation was happening elsewhere.

This apparent resolution was not, however, the end of the story. A dispute then arose over what the boxes to be stationed in the post offices should look like. Should the slit be in the side of the box, like on a post box, or in the top of the box, like a ballot box? Eventually, with election day fast approaching, the sides agreed to construct special boxes in which the slit was located in a corner edge which had been cut off at a forty-five-degree angle, so that one side could claim the slit was at the top, and the other that it was at the side.

It might seem strange, comical even, that seasoned diplomats should spend their time indulging in convoluted mind games of this sort, but on issues that strike close to the heart of their national identity, those deepest and most difficult of conversations, agreeing to create some room for alternative narratives may be an appropriate, perhaps the only, way to find resolution. Some have called this 'leaving space for the victory speech of the other side'. But these opportunities can only be identified if we ask the right kind of questions.

Grading questions, not answers

Negotiation expert William Ury describes the Strategic Arms Limitation Talks – or 'SALT' – that took place between US and Soviet negotiators in the 1970s. At one point the US negotiator burst out in frustration that his Soviet counterpart wasn't showing any flexibility at all. The Soviet negotiator replied: 'You keep asking me questions that I have an answer to. Why don't you ask me questions that I don't have answers to?'

We are educated in a system that focuses on grading our answers. But if we seek to have deeper, more constructive conversations, we should grade our questions too. Questions can be hammers to intimidate or whips to browbeat, and these can give us the satisfaction of seeming to make progress in advancing our cause. But such gains are too often illusory. For our best conversations, we should be aspiring to find questions that will act as keys to unlock doors of understanding that would otherwise have remain unopened.

Chapter 12

The Power of Storytelling

> The human mind is a story processor, not a logic processor.
>
> Jonathan Haidt

The Knesset, February 2013

It is the opening session of Israel's parliament. An unusual speech is about to be made. Ruth Calderon, a newly elected member of the Knesset on the list of the centrist Yesh Atid party, steps forward to give her maiden speech carrying a large volume of the Talmud, and – probably for the first time in the history of the Israeli parliament – she proceeds to teach a Talmud lesson from the podium.

More than a politician, Calderon is a scholar of the Talmud, but an uncommon one. She grew up in a wholly secular family and only as an adult did she discover a fascination with the Talmud and subsequently begin a movement to encourage secular Israelis to engage in traditional Jewish study. Watching her from the Speaker's chair with obvious scepticism is Yitzhak Vaknin, a representative of the ultraorthodox Shas party. The ultraorthodox are suspicious of Talmud study undertaken by non-practising Jews, all the more so when they are women. But Calderon, undaunted, begins her lesson.

She chooses to teach a troubling Talmudic story.[1] It tells of a scholar named Rehumei who studied in a distant academy, coming home to his wife only once a year, for Yom Kippur. But one Yom Kippur he was so deeply engrossed in the subject he was studying that he forgot to come home. When his devoted wife learned that her husband was not coming home, the Talmud says that 'she shed a tear and at that moment the roof that Rehumei was sitting on collapsed beneath him and he died'.

It would be a dark and disquieting story at any time, but at this moment it is even more charged. It is a powerful metaphor for a controversial issue in Israeli society, the fact that the majority of ultraorthodox men study in Yeshiva and consequently enjoy exemption from military service. Like Rehumei, their devotion to study separates them from their duty to the national home.

But Calderon has not come to score points. She invites her Knesset listeners to think about both sides of the story, as if on a split screen. On the one side Rehumei, engrossed in his learning on the study hall roof; on the other his neglected and tearful wife. Neither, she suggests, has a monopoly on the truth. Rehumei feels he is right to study; his wife feels she is right in wanting him at home with her. Calderon addresses the critical issue of army recruitment directly:

> Sometimes we, the secular Israelis, feel like the waiting woman, serving in the army, doing all the work while others sit on the roof and study Torah; sometimes those others feel that they bear the entire weight of tradition, Torah, and our culture, while we go to the beach and have a blast. Both I and my disputant feel solely responsible for the wellbeing of our national home. Until I understand this, I will not perceive the problem properly and will not be able to find a solution.

Calderon goes on to note that the scholar's name Rehumei in Aramaic means 'love'. 'Rehumei is derived from the word *rehem*, womb,' she explains, 'someone who knows how to include, how to completely accept, just as a woman's womb contains the baby.' The use of this term, she suggests, is 'a feminist gesture by the sages'.

At this point the Speaker of the session, the ultraorthodox Vaknin, interrupts. But his scepticism is gone. He is captivated. And he adds his own insight: 'The word "*rehem*" also has the numerical value of 248, the number of positive commandments in the Torah,' he says. Calderon is delighted. '*Yasher Koach*, may you have strength! Thank you for participating!' And Vaknin celebrates this moment of Talmudic *havruta* too. 'I think the idea she is saying is wonderful,' he says. MK Calderon ends by reciting an improvised prayer for success in her work as a public servant, and for keeping 'my integrity and innocence intact'. And the ultraorthodox Vaknin loudly answers, 'Amen!'

It is an extraordinary moment. Even by the standards of national parliaments the Knesset is characterised by its loud and raucous disputes, often accompanied by fierce personal attacks. Yet here, in discussion of one of the most sensitive issues in Israeli life, the Jewish character of the state and the sharing of public burdens among its different sectors, we witness not the hoisting of drawbridges and the sharpening of knives, but a moment of genuine empathy and mutual appreciation. This remarkable alchemy could not have been achieved through argument alone. It was only made possible by the power of a story.

Halakhah *and* Aggadah, *law and narrative*

In harnessing the power of storytelling, Ruth Calderon was channelling a longstanding Jewish tradition in which narrative is an essential complement to law, and a critical element in any debate or discussion.

For Jews, the Bible is the source of law, containing the 613 commandments that shape Jewish life. But the Bible is also a narrative, a story that has shaped Jewish identity no less than the commandments themselves. The relationship between narrative and law is complex; sometimes the two reinforce each other, but on occasion the biblical narrative acts as a critical commentary or counterargument to the black-on-white letter of the law. Under biblical law, for example, oldest sons receive preferential treatment, including receiving a double portion of inheritance. But in the narrative, almost all of Israel's leaders (Isaac, Jacob, Joseph, Moses, Saul and David, for a start) were younger sons whose older siblings were passed over, sending a message that the younger was not only not disadvantaged, but might even have been preferred. Similarly, biblical law (amended by later rabbinic edicts) permits men to take more than one wife. But in every case where the Bible describes a household with more than one wife (Jacob's wives Leah and Rachel, Elkana's wives Hannah and Penina, or Solomon's many wives) the narrative emphasises that this is a recipe for disaster and that only strife and acrimony will ensue.

The interplay between law and narrative plays out too in the cycle of the Jewish year. The festivals are circumscribed by stringent laws, but at their heart are stories. For days or even weeks before Passover, Jewish households are cleaning and searching for leaven, changing crockery, and preparing the various foods required by Jewish law for the ceremonial eating and dipping of the Seder night. But what has shaped the Jewish consciousness over the centuries more than these practices is the *Haggadah* – the story of the exodus from Egypt – that lies at the core of the Seder night ceremony. At the heart of our other festivals, too, we find stories that capture the essence of the day and convey it in ways that are deeper and more lasting than any legally mandated practice: the story of the impoverished convert Ruth brings the acceptance of the Torah and its humanity to life on the festival of Shavuot; the tale of Jonah who runs away from his mission to warn the sinners of Nineveh but finally comes to accept it charts a journey for our souls to follow on Yom Kippur; the courage of Esther sends a message on Purim that however dark the horizon, salvation can come in a moment; and so on.

But the integral entwining of law and narrative is at its deepest in the book that Ruth Calderon carried with her on to the Knesset podium, the Talmud.

Talmudic tales

For the contemporary reader, the Talmud is a strange and even intimidating work. We are educated in school systems with sharp divisions between subjects of study; in universities with clearly defined faculties and a chasm between the arts and sciences; and in libraries where knowledge is divided and shelved in neatly distinct categories. But the Talmud, at once ancient and yet somehow postmodern, defies subject categories and rejoices in connections and interconnections. Jonathan Rosen, in his lovely meditation on *The Talmud and the Internet*, likens it to the worldwide web:

> Though it may seem sacrilegious to say so, I can't help feeling that in certain respects the Internet has a lot in common with the Talmud. The Rabbis referred to the Talmud as a 'yam', a sea, and though one is hardly intended to 'surf' the Talmud, something more than oceanic metaphors links the two verbal universes. Vastness and an uncategorisable nature are in part what define them both.[2]

Broadly, within the web of the Talmud, we can identify two literary genres that ebb and flow together. The first, *Halakhah*, is the legal dimension, including both the bottom-line rulings and, more extensively, the detailed jurisprudence through which these rulings are derived. The second, *Aggadah*, is everything else – stories, interpretations, reflections, folklore and much more.

The Talmud itself offers an Aggadic allegory to highlight the indivisible nature of the marriage of law and narrative. It recounts the story of two students, one of whom insisted that his teacher teach only *Halakhah*, law, while the other demanded *Aggadah*, narrative. So insistent were the two students that, according to the Talmud, the moment the teacher began to teach the preference of one student, the other would disrupt the lesson. The teacher sought to calm them with a parable of a man with two wives, one young and one old. The young wife pulled out his white hairs, so that her husband would appear younger. The old wife pulled out his black hairs so that he would appear older. The teacher concluded, 'If I listen to you both, I'll end up completely bald!'[3]

As different as they are, *Halakhah* and *Aggadah*, law and narrative, are both essential. They nourish our understanding in different ways. As Jonathan Sacks describes it:

> The two literatures have a different feel about them. They reflect different sensibilities. *Halakhah* is detailed and demanding and uses sophisticated rules of jurisprudence. *Aggadah* is more intuitive and imaginative. One might almost call them the left and right hemispheres of the Jewish brain.[4]

One of the Jewish thinkers to delve most deeply into the nature of these two hemispheres of *Halakhah* and *Aggadah* was Abraham Joshua Heschel, Professor of Jewish ethics and mysticism at the Jewish Theological Seminary of America, and one of the outstanding Jewish philosophers and theologians of modern times. He described the allocation of labour between these two literary genres as follows:

> *Halakhah* deals with the law; *Aggadah* with the meaning of the law. *Halakhah* deals with subjects that can be expressed literally; *Aggadah* introduces us to a realm that lies beyond the range of expression.
> *Halakhah* teaches us how to perform common acts; *Aggadah* tells us how to participate in the eternal drama.
> *Halakhah* gives us knowledge; *Aggadah* gives us aspiration.
> *Halakhah* gives us the norms for action; *Aggadah*, the vision of the ends of living.
> *Halakhah* prescribes, *Aggadah* suggests; *Halakhah* decrees, *Aggadah* inspires; *Halakhha* is definite; *Aggadah* is allusive.
> There is no *Halakhah* without *Aggadah*, and no *Aggadah* without *Halakhah*. We must neither disparage the body nor sacrifice the spirit. The body is the discipline, the pattern, the law; the spirit is inner devotion, spontaneity, freedom . . . Our task is to learn how to maintain a harmony between the demands of *Halakhah* and the spirit of *Aggadah*.[5]

For all his insistence that there must be a balance between the two genres, one can sense that Heschel has a strong personal preference for the realm of aspiration rather than knowledge, inspiration rather than decrees, the joy of the spirit rather than the discipline of the body – that is, for *Aggadah* over *Halakhah*.

But if Heschel is the student who prefers his rabbi to teach *Aggadah*, the rival case is made by an unexpected disputant. Haim Nahman Bialik is regarded as Israel's first national poet and was himself a major scholar of *Aggadah*, compiling the most widely used collection of Aggadic legends. It is surprising, then, to find him in the corner of *Halakhah*, making a powerful case for its primacy. His argument seems an unexpected one: that the law is not dry and formulaic; its development is itself a creative process. In developing Jewish law, the rabbis may not be working in paint or stone, but they are artists, none the less, working on a much larger canvas, in the life of a people:

> [Halachic rulings] grow little by little, piece by piece, out of all the stream of human life and action, till in the end the fragments add up to a single total . . . *Halakhah* is the master-art that has shaped and trained a whole nation.[6]

He goes on to make an additional argument, noting that Talmudic law is actually itself made up of stories, or at least vignettes. And in truth, in presenting legal cases the Talmud does not present them in abstract and anonymous terms, but rather offers concrete scenarios that bring the situations to life: 'Two men take hold of a shawl', 'When the potter puts in his pots', 'When a man puts down his cask', thus creating what Bialik describes as 'a kaleidoscope of pictures, large and small, of actual Hebrew life over a period of a thousand years and more'.

In short, someone opening almost any Jewish text, from the Bible onwards, and most especially the Talmud, is likely to be surprised at the vibrant presence of story. Not only in the Aggadic portions, but, as Bialik points out, even in the legal debates, law is never far from narrative. For the Talmud, law is life, and life is stories.

Stories: solid, subversive, sustainable

The traditional Jewish instinct that learning and debate are enhanced by the inclusion of a narrative dimension is supported by a wealth of scientific research studies in recent decades which attest to the unique ability of stories to reach us in ways that other forms of argument cannot. In particular, they suggest that stories have a rare talent for being solid, subversive and sustainable.

Solid

'The human mind,' explains Jonathan Haidt, 'is a story processor, not a logic processor.' As much as we may wish to think of our intelligence as pure and abstract, it turns out that we are hardwired to connect to the concrete and the personal rather than the intangible and dispassionate. As Dan and Chip Heath, writing in *Made to Stick*, point out:

> Language is often abstract, but *life* is not abstract . . . Abstraction makes it harder to understand an idea and to remember it. The concretisation of ideas, turning them into something solid, makes them far easier to grasp.[7]

Consider this thought exercise, which I sometimes use in negotiation training seminars:

> You are in a bar and meet someone with an unusual deck of cards. Each of them has a letter on one side and a number on the other side. He places four such cards on the table, each showing one letter or number: A, D, 5 and 8. He now tells you that on every card that has a vowel on one side, there is an even number on the other side. Which cards would you have to turn over to know if this rule holds true?

Take a moment to think about the question. It can be surprisingly tricky. But now imagine a slightly different scenario. This time it is the bartender who asks the question.

> The bartender tells you that it is her job to ensure that there is no underage drinking of alcohol in the bar. Sitting along the bar at the moment are four people – one is drinking whisky; one is drinking cola; one, she knows, is sixteen; and one, she knows, is twenty-five. She asks you which people's age or drink she'd have to check.

The answer here is obvious: she needs to check the whisky drinker's age and the sixteen-year-old's drink. What's less obvious is the fact that it is essentially the same problem as before. It should now be clear that the two cards you should turn over are the ones showing A (which may have an odd number on the reverse) and 5 (which may have a vowel).

A well-crafted story, or a choice metaphor, can enable us to see with clarity something that we otherwise wouldn't, and subsequently to convey it to others. There is a story told of early Zionist leader and Israel's first President Chaim Weizmann, who was once asked by a member of the House of Lords: 'Why do you Jews insist on going to Palestine when there are so many undeveloped countries you could settle in more conveniently?' Weizmann answered: 'That is like my asking you why you drove twenty miles to visit your mother last Sunday when there are so many old ladies living on your street . . .'

In our peace negotiations, our Palestinian counterparts would often seek a metaphor to effectively convey their perspective. On one occasion they wished to share their sense of frustration at provisions which would permit an Israeli security presence to remain in areas officially transferred to Palestinian control. They told us the traditional story of 'Musa's hook'. Musa is a mischievous character who appears in numerous fables. In this one he sells his house, but on one condition. He can still have access to a hook on the wall of the house, to hang his coat on. The buyer thinks this is odd, but because the price is so good he agrees. The following day Musa appears, demanding to use his hook. The owner lets him, but very soon Musa is running in and out of the house to use his hook at all hours of the day and night. Finally, totally frustrated, the buyer gives up. He leaves the house and Musa moves back in. That, they told us, is how it felt when Israel demanded security access to areas under Palestinian control. In our subsequent negotiations the phrase 'Musa's hook' would often be invoked as a vivid and concrete expression of Palestinian concerns.

Subversive

There is a real power in narrative to break down stereotypes. I had an unusual personal experience of this when I was commissioned to write a TV series, *The Rebbe's Court*, set in the ultraorthodox Hassidic community. This community is a sector of Israeli society that mostly keeps itself closed off from other Israelis. As a result, secular Israelis know little about them, and tend to regard them with suspicion, if not resentment, since for the most part they do not serve in compulsory army duty. The idea of the series was to tell stories from inside the community, with an emotional dimension that would enable secular Israelis, with no connection to this world, to find themselves identifying and empathising with the characters. We knew we were making progress when we received an email from a secular viewer who confessed that on Yom Kippur she had found herself praying for one of the Hassidic characters in the show!

Sometime later, I discovered that the power of narrative worked in the other direction too. In one episode of the series, a secular detective pretending to be an ultraorthodox visitor is invited to a Shabbat meal at the rebbe's house. He is asked to sing one of the Sabbath tunes from his community and in desperation he sings the chorus of an Israeli pop song, 'Night train to Cairo', and the rebbe's followers all join in. At a wedding

I met an ultraorthodox rabbi who confided that in his community, having watched the series, they now sing that melody at their Shabbat meal!

Stories are slippery – in a good way. They are the most subtle and effective weapons at our disposal to infiltrate the barricades of logic we build to protect our cherished opinions. 'The best arguments in the world won't change a person's mind. The only thing that can do that is a good story.' So writes Richard Powers, the award-winning novelist, in his extraordinary environmental novel *The Overstory*, itself an intriguing model of how narrative can touch and motivate readers when bare arguments fall short.

James O'Brien, the fiercely combative radio host who rethought many of his certainties in the face of a family crisis, gives an example of how a simple personal story had the power to make him change his mind. Among the groups of people O'Brien would regularly make fun of on his show were people whose affection for their pets seemed, to him at least, to be greater than their affection for other people. He would bait dog-owners by asking how long they would have to lie dead on their sofa before their dog started eating them. One day, following one of these tirades, he received the following email:

Dear James
My wife of fifty-four years died in January and if it wasn't for the company of our two Dachshunds I know I could not have endured the pain of losing her. Your radio show has also been a great source of comfort and company to me over the last few months. Please think of me the next time you are discussing owners who perhaps seem excessively fond of their dogs.
Your sincerely
Dennis

This simple story moved O'Brien in a way that no logical argument could have done. 'I felt something shift inside me,' he wrote.[8]

Aristotle, in his famous educational curriculum, considered that the field of rhetoric required the teaching of three skills: Logos, Ethos and Pathos. Logos represents the logic of our argument, our debating points. Ethos relates to the credibility of the speaker, the reason why the audience should listen to them and give weight to their opinion. And Pathos represents the emotional force of our presentation, the element that doesn't appeal to our mind but tugs at our heartstrings.

Of Aristotle's three elements, for many of us Logos represents our comfort zone. If asked to prepare a persuasive speech, refining our intellectual arguments and seeking the evidence that bolsters them will be the aspect to which we tend to devote most of our attention. So it is frustrating, to say the least, to discover that research suggests that the intellectual dimension counts for less than ten per cent of the persuasive force of our case. Rather, if we want to change people's minds, this will be achieved through Ethos, our personal credibility, and, especially if we want to persuade people to act, through Pathos, the degree to which we can convey the emotional force of our argument. Logic may convince people to sit still, but to inspire action requires Pathos, a tangible human connection. 'If I look at the mass I will never act,' said Mother Teresa. 'If I look at the one, I will.'[9]

Logical arguments are hopeless at evoking Pathos. But stories as a distillation of lived experience, whether factual or fictional, are uniquely potent. They are one of the most effective ways of breaking down preconceptions and prejudices and generating empathy. One research study found that people who read at least one book every month, or people who watch TV for a couple of hours a day, tend to score higher on respecting other people's viewpoints. Another study, by a group of Italian psychologists, found that people who had read Harry Potter books were on average less prejudiced and more likely to have respect for people outside their own social groups, in particular immigrants and refugees.

The historian Lynn Hunt has argued persuasively that the development of the idea of human rights in the eighteenth century was prompted in part by the rise in popularity of the novel. For the first time people could be transported through fiction into the lives and perspectives of others, members of a different class or nationality or gender, and begin to understand and be led to feel the real effects of prejudice and discrimination. Noting the effectiveness of Charles Dickens' novels in raising awareness of the harsh reality of child labour and the lack of workers' rights, George Bernard Shaw held that *Great Expectations* was far more subversive of the economic order than *Das Kapital*.

Recent research in neuroscience offers some insights into why storytelling touches us so much more deeply than a logical argument. It turns out that it reaches far more of our brain. MRI scans of subjects listening to stories show that many different areas of the brain light up when someone is listening to a narrative – not only the networks involved in language processing, but other neural circuits, too, especially during the emotional parts of the story. Even more strikingly, according to research undertaken at Princeton University, as you hear a story unfold, your brain waves actually start to synchronise with those of the person telling the story. Stories, it seems, are the shortest distance between people.[10]

Finally, a word regarding Aristotle's other element of rhetoric, Ethos. The credibility that encourages people to place their reliance on us, and to trust what we say, is hard to manufacture. Whether it is an authoritative tone of voice, a distinguished bearing, or the knowledge of the speaker's impressive resumé of achievements – these are not things that can be easily obtained. Still, here too a story can be helpful. A story explaining how, or perhaps most powerfully why, we have changed our mind. Consider Mark Lynas, the environmental activist who led groups tearing up GM crops and then told the Oxford Farming Conference how he had come to the realisation that he had been mistaken. That was Ethos.

Sustainable

Not only do narratives appeal to our appetite for the specific and the concrete, and infiltrate our emotional defences, but they have surprising longevity, remaining with us long after other types of content have been forgotten. I was particularly fond of one of my primary school teachers. I have no doubt that she taught me many useful things, but what remains with me decades later are the colourful stories of her childhood accompanying her father in his travels among the jungle tribes in Africa.

Dan and Chip Heath, in *Made to Stick*, make the point with Aesop's fable 'The Fox and the Grapes'. The story of a fox who persuades himself that the grapes he cannot reach are in fact worthless (giving rise to the phrase 'sour grapes') appears in many cultures and languages. Its longevity, they explain, is precisely because it is a story:

> [The fable] would not have survived for more than 2,500 years if it didn't reflect some profound truth about human nature. But there are many profound truths that have not seeped into the day-to-day languages and thinking of dozens of cultures . . . The concrete images evoked by the fable allow its message to persist. One suspects that the life span of Aesop's ideas would have been shorter if they'd been encoded as *Aesop's Helpful Suggestions*: 'Don't be such a bitter jerk when you fail.'[11]

Stories are sustainable too, not just in the sense that they last, but in that they often sustain us when little else will. Indeed, one particular story may well hold the secret of Jewish survival. While Moses is credited with having written down the stories of the Bible, the Jewish people's greatest storyteller was arguably the scribe Ezra. After the Israelites' first exile from their land, they returned to Jerusalem to find decay, despair and hopelessness. Ezra erected a large wooden stage and began reading to the gathered crowds the original story of their peoplehood. As Will Storr describes it in *The Science of Storytelling*: 'The story had an astonishingly galvanising effect on this tribe of exiles . . . It filled the exiles with a sense of meaning, righteousness and destiny.'[12]

One notable aspect of the way Ezra told the story was to prove critical to the survival of the Jewish people: the conviction that the tragedy that had befallen them was not a random event but a result of the people's own wrongdoing. Perhaps counterintuitively, this story of personal blame was not dispiriting but empowering. To a people that had been nurtured in slavery, spoon-fed in the wilderness, then watched their monarchy and leadership disintegrate, it carried with it a promise that they might none the less play a part in their own destiny. The American Jewish leader and rabbi Abba Hillel Silver, in his book *Where Judaism Differed*, noted that this conviction was very different from that of most peoples of the ancient world. For them, the theological logic was clear: if you were beaten in battle, it was a sign that your opponent's god was more powerful, so you would abandon yours and become a follower of theirs. But the Jewish story said something radically different. If we are defeated, that doesn't say anything about our God's lack of commitment to us; rather, it says something about our lack of commitment to him. As a result, exactly at the point that the faith of other peoples would be weakened, the faith and commitment of the Jewish people was strengthened.

For a people that had internalised a sense of helplessness and rejection, this new narrative thrust promised that they were not forgotten, and could yet be masters of their own destiny. It took the power of a good story to overcome another story. The late rabbi and peace activist Menachem Froman likewise used a story to reframe an issue, in this case the conflict between Israelis and Palestinians. He told of two neighbours arguing over a plot of land, and the land whispering to them both: 'I don't belong to you, you both belong to me.'

Chip and Dan Heath quote another example of the power of one story to overcome another. In the 1980s, Texas had a serious litter problem. The cleanup was costing $25 million per year and rising. None of the anti-litter campaigns that Texas had used (such as 'Please don't litter' signs, or bins marked 'Pitch In') even made a dent in the problem. The message they gave, that littering was impolite and antisocial, didn't begin to speak to the typical litterer, who was most likely to be an eighteen- to thirty-five-year-old male, driving a rugged pick-up. They needed a different story. It came in a series of television commercials all featuring macho Texas heroes, such as football and baseball players from the state of Texas. In one of the early commercials, a well-known Dallas Cowboys football player crushes a littered can with his fists and looks at the camera with a message for the guy who threw it: 'Don't mess with Texas!' 'Don't mess with Texas' isn't just a slogan, it's a story. It says that littering isn't antisocial, it's anti-Texan; it's not who we are. And it worked: within one year, littering had dropped by nearly thirty per cent.

Taking stories on the road

What might it mean to incorporate the narrative dimension into our discussions and debates? In my own diplomatic service, I've repeatedly been witness to the power of stories to go where other forms of expression cannot reach.

Discussions of Israel and the Middle East inevitably touch on deeply felt convictions and tribal loyalties, often creating an impenetrable wall of preconceptions, the solid bricks cemented fast by the mortar of identity. More often than not, trying to break down this wall and open up genuine discussion by marshalling statistics and facts is a fruitless effort. In situations like this, stories have a unique ability to penetrate the fortress of people's minds.

As a diplomat, I became a purveyor of stories in a way I had not quite expected. When I needed to give presents, rather than wine or chocolates I would always give books, especially contemporary Israeli novels that highlighted the human, unexpected, even quirky dimensions of Israeli life. In my public talks, too, I would try to include stories and quotes from literature to make my points, and was delighted when, on occasion, I was invited to speak specifically about Israeli literature, or the images of Israel in English literature. These lectures inevitably led to much richer, more nuanced discussions than the more traditional diplomatic presentations.

Consider a discussion about the establishment of the state of Israel in 1948. A presentation of the facts, whether of the UN's partition resolution of Palestine or Israel's war of independence, is likely to lead to a well-trodden recital of the established positions on both sides of the debate. But a story has the power to take the listeners elsewhere and open up emotional dimensions that they may be able to identify with, even if their political positions remain poles apart. Novelist Amos Oz gives an evocative description of the founding of Israel in his autobiography, *Tales of Love and Darkness*. His painfully introverted father responds to the radio broadcast of the UN partition vote by giving 'a long naked shout like before words were invented', then lifts the young Amos on his shoulders to wander through the dancing-filled streets. Much later, his father, fully clothed, climbs into his bed next to him, and, for the first time, whispers to him of the persecution he endured as a young child in Europe, and assures him that no longer will he be bullied just because he is a Jew. Then, writes Oz:

> I reached out sleepily to touch his face, just below his high fore-head, and all of a sudden, instead of his glasses my fingers met tears. Never in my life, before or after that night, not even when my mother died, did I see my father cry. And in fact I didn't see him cry that night either: it was too dark. Only my left hand saw.[13]

With younger audiences, I learned that rather than regaling them with a history of the Middle East, sharing stories would be more engaging and lasting. A story does not need to be lengthy; legend has it that Ernest Hemingway won a bet that he couldn't write a story in only six words with the moving two-sentence story, 'For sale: baby shoes. Never worn.' With this in mind, when meeting youngsters I would take with me a small box of objects, each of which illustrated a story about Israeli life. A packet of Bamba, the unusual Israeli puffed peanut snack, which has been found to inoculate Israeli kids from peanut allergies and which serves as a metaphor for a society that encourages its children to take risks and develop resilience. An airway resuscitation tube, as a reminder of my IDF combat medic course in which I was sworn to treat all injured on the battlefield equally, and the dilemmas that arise in the height of conflict. A model of an EL AL plane, as a reminder of the time I was on an EL AL flight with a passenger who complained that his seat was wobbly, until the stewardess explained that the seats had all been removed the night before so as to maximise capacity when rescuing Ethiopian Jews and flying them to safety in Israel, and had been hurriedly put back in place that morning. And so on.

If I make an effort to bring stories into discussions, it is in large part because I have seen how deeply they are able to affect my own thinking. In the Israeli–Palestinian negotiations I was involved with, for example, discussions of Israel's security measures often trod a predictably unproductive course. The Israeli side is well rehearsed at providing statistics of attempted terrorist attacks to highlight the need for its restrictions. But hearing at first hand from your Palestinian counterpart about the impact of crossing points and entry permits on the daily life of individuals has the power to provide a different perspective.

I spent a number of years as a consultant to Israel's philanthropic and third sector and became interested in the challenges facing the Arab residents of East Jerusalem. In this part of the capital, which came under Israeli control in 1967, there are a host of serious challenges, including inadequate provision of basic services and lack of opportunity for young people. Although I had studied the reports that set out the grim situation in statistics, it was only when a Palestinian friend, a resident of East Jerusalem, shared with me the draft of his autobiographical novel that the reality hit home. His account of his childhood – funny, poignant, at points heart-breaking – did more to develop my understanding and provoke empathy than any number of dry reports. In part motivated by this awareness, I established a forum of foundations committed to working to address the discrepancies between East and West Jerusalem. Pathos and storytelling helped move me to action.

The binary channels in which we conduct our discussions tend to corral us into an arm-wrestling dynamic. In practice, there is always more common ground than we are led to believe. I have found this to be true even in the most fraught situations.

When I was called on to serve as a government spokesperson I was frequently interviewed just at the height of conflict situations. The tenseness and complexity of the situation would be aggravated by the fact that such real-time interviews take place when facts are still obscured by the fog of war, in the face of a flood of unsupported allegations on social media, and coloured by the tendency of radio and TV interviewers to bring their own binary frames to their coverage. In such situations, and when I had a moment for introspection between interviews, I set myself a personal challenge. I would think of two people I know: the first a very thoughtful Palestinian counterpart, with whom I became friendly in the course of our negotiations, and who has shared with me some of the painful challenges of life in the Palestinian areas, and the other a good Israeli friend whose teenage daughter was murdered in a Palestinian terrorist bomb attack. I asked myself: is it possible to conduct the interview in a way that is not a betrayal of either of my friends' stories? To my surprise, it has generally been less difficult than I expected. While the formal positions of the two sides don't suggest a lot of common ground, the humanity reflected in their narratives creates a genuine space for empathy.

We are the story

Solid, subversive, sustainable: stories are among the most effective tools we have to infiltrate the barricades of logic and reach the heart of our counterparts. When so many of our debates are conducted in a single register, cornering us into opposing positions, narrative, which operates on many levels of experience and nuance, opens up the possibility of recognising that, while we may differ on one level, there are other levels on which we are not at odds but may find a deep alignment. This is even more powerful when the stories that we share are our own.

Ruth Calderon's speech to the Knesset was so powerful because it was, in fact, not one story, but two. The first was a Talmudic legend, which demonstrated how our shared ancient texts can provide a vocabulary for some of our hardest conversations. But the second was more important still. She framed the ancient story within her own: the story of a secular Israeli who had grown to feel that she had been deprived of her heritage and who set out to reclaim it on her own terms. 'I did not inherit a set of Talmud from my grandfather. I was not acquainted with the Mishnah, the Talmud, the Kabbalah or Hassidism,' she began, adding: 'When I first encountered the Talmud and became completely enamoured with its language, its humour, its profound thinking, its modes of discussion and the practicality, humanity and maturity that emerge from its lines, I sensed that I had found the love of my life, what I had been lacking.'

Calderon did not purport to make her argument in purely neutral, objective terms. She was, she freely admitted, a product of her childhood and her environment. By embracing these influences, and sharing them openly, her argument became not weaker but stronger.

Across the Red Line is an unusual BBC Radio programme in which individuals holding deeply divergent points of view on public and policy questions engage, with the help of conflict resolution experts and psychologists, to try to reach a deeper and more empathetic understanding of the issue and their differences. After each has stated their case in a traditional across-the-table format, the participants are encouraged to move from the table to sit next to each other on a couch, where they take part in a series of exercises, including more deeply questioning and then restating the other's point of view. Perhaps the most significant stage of the process, however, is when each tells the 'story' of what shaped their original thinking on the issue. Even on issues where the opinions held are diametrically opposed, the stories themselves can surprise with their potential to reveal common ground.

In one episode, two women leaders – one a feminist activist, the other a successful business executive – were debating whether 'victim culture' was a help or a hindrance to the advancement of women. For the activist, women's solidarity was key to any hope of progress, while for the CEO, successful women executives had far more in common with other business executives than with other women. Only when each told their personal story did something other than the clash of their positions become apparent. Both women, it turned out, had grown up in similar working-class backgrounds and had been motivated to overcome their disadvantages. Both had realised that this was not something they could do alone; they required the support of a mass movement. It was here that they differed, with the first allying herself to the women's movement, and the second to the wider struggle for working-class advancement. Their policy positions remained at odds, but at least they were able to recognise that at another level they had a surprising amount in common.

Telling our own stories requires courage. It calls on us to recognise that our opinions are not immutable and objective, but rather have been shaped by our life experiences. Sharing these experiences is a gesture of honesty and openness to our counterparts. Yes, these are my opinions, we are saying, but here too are the influences that helped produce them. Perhaps, it suggests, if I had

had different stories, different influences, perhaps even yours, I might think differently.

Opening ourselves in this way expresses a kind of vulnerability. John Steinbeck described it movingly as a plea to others to identify with and ease our loneliness.

> We are lonesome animals. We spend all of our life trying to be less lonesome. One of our ancient methods is to tell a story begging the listener to say – and to feel – 'Yes, that is the way it is, or at least that is the way I feel it.'[14]

Sharing our stories is a way of opening our heart. And it is one of the best ways we have of opening the hearts of others.

Chapter 13

Connecting Ideas to Reality

If you don't try to really pin down what somebody's saying, you get a very lazy form of thought, and a lazy form of thought, in the end, is a version of lying.

Rory Stewart

One morning I was leaving my house early for the airport, to fly out to a round of Israeli–Palestinian negotiations. Seeing me leaving with my suitcase, one of my young sons asked me: 'Where are you going?' 'To the negotiations,' I answered. He looked thoughtful and then asked: 'What are you trying to achieve?' 'Peace,' I replied. He looked at me dubiously, then smiled before insisting, 'No, seriously . . .'

I've mentioned this incident to international mediators involved in our conflict to urge them to speak about peace in a way that resonates with Israelis and Palestinians. Simply painting a utopian picture of an ultimate resolution, a picturesque signing ceremony on the White House lawn, fails to have credibility with the people of the region – my son included – since it doesn't connect to the reality as they experience it. Believable peace is hard, complicated and imperfect. If you want your arguments to be credible, they have to resonate with the lived reality. While the Talmud does have its occasional moments of esoteric wondering, with contemplations about the meaning of dreams and the end of days, for the most part it shies away from abstractions. Its discussions are almost always rooted in concrete, tangible examples so that the real-world implications are never far from mind. A discussion about returning lost property will never refer to an abstract 'item', but will present a concrete example. As the discussion continues, the tangible example used will change according to the particular circumstance under discussion. Considering the various principles at play in the obligation to return lost property the object in the Talmudic discussion will seamlessly morph from a bunch of figs to a loaf of bread or a pottery jug, or from a lost object to a stolen one, each item and situation having different characteristics, but all subtly reminding the arguers that the discussion is not purely theoretical but rooted in the real world.

Keeping our discussions tethered to real-world examples continually tests our ideas against reality. Richard Feynman, the Nobel Prize-winning physicist, described a very similar technique that as a young man he would use in order to follow complicated mathematical theories.

> I had a scheme, which I still use today when somebody is explaining something I'm trying to understand: I keep making up examples. For instance, the mathematicians would come in with a terrific theorem, and they're all excited. As they're telling me the condition of the theorem, I construct something which fits all the conditions [like a set of balls]. Then the balls turn colors, grow hairs, or whatever, in my head as they put more conditions on.[1]

Not only does tethering our exploration to real-world examples clarify our thinking. It also reminds us that the goal of our debates is to guide us in relation to real-world situations, thus helping prevent us from following abstract ideas to intellectually logical but practically absurd conclusions.

When I first became involved in the Israeli–Palestinian peace negotiations, I read as many books about the history of the conflict and the myriad attempts to resolve it as I could get my hands on. As an international lawyer, I was disappointed, to say the least, that the positions reflected in the books written by international lawyers on both sides tended – not always, but surprisingly often – to be more extreme and less accommodating than those written by negotiators and practitioners. It seemed that the process of espousing legal principles enabled the authors to climb ladders of analysis that led them up and away from the realities and human dilemmas of the situation on the ground. I was reminded of the warning one of my early legal mentors had given me: lawyers should try to be people too.

Talmudic thinking pushes back against the notion that abstract theoretical thinking is one of the highest forms of analysis, uncluttered by the muddiness of the real world. To the contrary, in Jewish thinking, knowledge that is tried and tested in the real world is on a far higher level.

The point is made in the striking story of the sage Shimon bar Yochai and his son Elazar.[2] According to the Talmud, on hearing that the Roman emperor of the time was looking to kill him, Shimon and his son Elazar fled and hid in a cave where they spent the next twelve years studying together. Learning that the emperor had died, they emerged from the cave. But they had reached such heights of intensity in their learning that when they saw people engaged in their regular worldly tasks like reaping and sowing rather than engaging in the life of the spirit, the intensity of their gazes set everything that they looked at on fire. On seeing this, the Talmud recounts, a heavenly voice declared: 'Have you come out to destroy my world? Go back into your cave!' Shimon and Elazar returned to the cave and studied for a further twelve months. When they came out again, they had learned to look at the world outside without destroying it. Higher than their theoretical knowledge, developed in total seclusion, was a level of understanding that enabled them to re-engage with reality. In raising a younger generation with the skills to engage in constructive debate, we would be well served to inculcate this sense that the highest type of knowledge is one which constantly tests itself against the reality.

I have been struck by how this sensibility has found expression in the Israeli education system. One of my sons was enrolled in an afterschool science club. At the end of the semester parents were invited to see the projects that the kids had been working on. It turned out the subject of the week was polymers and the kids had to figure out which ingredients would make the most effective polymers. But that was not the end of the exercise. After creating their gooey mixtures, the youngsters were told that they had to set up tables to market their polymers to the visiting parents, which they did with enthusiasm. It occurred to me that at the schools my kids had attended while on postings abroad, the exercise would almost certainly have ended with the creation of the goo. But for the Israeli science club this was unfinished business, until you could figure out how to take it to the next, practical phase.

The Talmud takes pains not only to tether its arguments to the real world, but also to real people. The cases discussed are almost never described in purely abstract terms, using dehumanising terms such as 'plaintiff' and 'defendant'. Rather, the individuals involved are given faces, or at least names, most commonly Reuven and Shimon. We never lose sight of the fact that the issues we are discussing have impact on the real world, and on real people.

Taking a moment to reality test our arguments, and to ensure that we are talking about real people and real situations, is a good way to make sure that we don't let ivory-tower considerations disconnect us from the realities of this world, and the real-world needs and experiences of the people who live in it.

Chapter 14

Black Fire on White Fire – Words and Silence

The tongue has the power of life and death.

Book of Proverbs 18:21

The rabbis describe the Torah as being 'black fire written on white fire'. The 'black fire' is the letters and words inscribed in ink; 'white fire' describes the spaces between and around them. Both are needed for the whole to make sense. And both need to be treated with profound respect and caution.

Black fire: the power of words

The Chilean novelist Isabel Allende opens her collection *The Stories of Eva Luna* with a short story about the power of words. The story, 'Two Words', tells of a young woman, born into a family 'so poor they did not even have names to give their children'. She cannot read; indeed she has never even seen the written word. One day the sports page of a newspaper blows across her feet and, although she cannot understand it, she becomes captivated by its writing and begins to learn. After assessing the options otherwise available to her, to become either a servant or a prostitute, she chooses to become a seller of words. She buys a dictionary, studies its contents, and then throws it into the sea: 'It was not her intention to defraud her customers with packaged words.' Years later she is captured by soldiers and taken to meet the Colonel, a military hero, who tells her he needs a speech that will enable him to become President. Partly out of fear, partly out of attraction towards the handsome soldier, she crafts a speech. Allende describes her at work:

She discarded harsh, cold words, words that were too flowery, words worn from abuse, words that offered improbable promises, untruthful and confusing words, until all she had left were words sure to touch the minds of men and women's intuition.[1]

She gives the Colonel the speech, along with two extra words which, she assures him, are for his eyes alone. We never learn what the two mysterious words are, but by the end of the story the colonel has won the presidency, and the young woman his love. When I've been asked to teach classes on speechwriting, I've often suggested to participants that they read this story, as a reminder of the awesome power of words to change minds and hearts. Because words are so readily available, it's a lesson we can easily lose sight of.

It's also a lesson that is apparent in the Jewish tradition. In the book of Genesis, the world is created with words, the repeated command: 'Let there be . . .' So too in our own lives, the tradition teaches, words have concrete effects. In Hebrew the word for a 'word', *davar*, also means a tangible object. The word *davar* also comes from the same root as *devora*, a bee. Words themselves, the tradition suggests, can be honey or can sting, the choice is in our hands.[2] This idea is reflected in a host of Jewish laws dealing with caution in speech, prohibiting slander or disparaging remarks about others. Turning on its head the English proverb that sticks and stones may break my bones, but words can never hurt me, the tradition is insistent that words can cause genuine harm, with the rabbis likening destroying another's reputation or embarrassing them in public to a kind of murder.

Words can change things on a spiritual level too. Blessings over food can change its status, verbal confession on Yom Kippur can bring atonement, marriage and divorce are effected by verbal declarations. A child growing up in this environment inhabits a kind of Hogwarts. Their incantations may not be able to make a feather fly or an ogre fall, but they too can have real effects.

On a more mystical level, the kabbalistic Jewish tradition

ascribes spiritual force to words and to the letters that comprise them. It is hard to make a pun in Hebrew, since if words appear or sound similar, that is understood as being a mark of deep connection rather than a cause for humour. The numerical values that are ascribed to each of the letters of the alphabet give rise to the kabbalistic practice of *gematria* – finding hidden connections and meanings. For example, the name of God, *Elo-him*, has the same numerical value (eighty-six) as the word for nature, *hateva*, suggesting that God can be seen through nature. Words are never just words.

The scroll and the scribe

One of my sons and I decided, as a joint project, to study the art of *sofrut*; that is, the craft of the scribe who writes holy texts on parchment. Jews are often called the People of the Book, but more rightly they should be called the People of the Scroll, since the holiest texts, including the five books of Moses, are read from a handwritten parchment. Learning the rules of the scribe includes attention to countless minutiae, from those governing the quill and the parchment, to the myriad traditions concerning the shape and form of the letters themselves. Any tiny addition or omission, a crack in a letter, or a point where two letters kiss each other, can render an entire scroll invalid. Attention must be given not only to the order in which letters are written, but also to the scribe's intention in writing them. To preserve authenticity, a scroll should not be written from memory, but copied from a prior scroll.

An intriguing story in the Jerusalem Talmud highlights, but also mischievously subverts, the tradition's insistence that texts be copied faithfully. It tells of a rabbi who arrived in a town on the Purim holiday and discovered that they did not have a scroll of the book of Esther, which is read on that day. He called for parchment and a quill and wrote the entire book, ten chapters in all, from memory. 'But, Rabbi,' objected one of the villagers, 'the law states that a scroll cannot be written from memory: it must be copied from another scroll.' 'Very well,' replied the rabbi, and called for more parchment. He then wrote a new scroll – copying it from the first one he had written.

The process of learning these traditions was painstaking, but also surprisingly moving. Dipping the quill in the ink and then forming shapes on parchment to create a new copy of a holy text felt humbling and uplifting. While I was studying the skill and writing out my first holy text, I felt that in some way my antennae were more sharply attuned to the power of letters and words. Some weeks after I had begun the course, I visited a synagogue that I occasionally attend and was given the honour of being called to make one of the blessings over the Torah scroll. As I looked into the Torah at the text that was about to be read, I happened to notice a slight error which could invalidate the scroll – something I would certainly not have noticed had I not been made more alert to such things as a result of my studies. I pointed it out to the rabbi of the synagogue. On checking, he determined that this indeed was an invalidating error, and had to call in a professional scribe to repair the scroll. He thanked me effusively for my sharp-eyed attention – though I should note that I have not been called up to bless the Torah again in his synagogue!

The same care that we are called on to exercise in writing a holy scroll is also called for in crafting the words of our conversations. Here too we are playing with fire. Not least of the difficulties that using words creates is that we cannot always be certain that what we mean to say is what is understood by our counterpart. Every language has its own historic echoes that give layers of nuance and association. The drive of international brands to standardise their advertising around the world has given rise to a host of cross-cultural misunderstandings. When Pepsi launched their brand in China in the 1960s, adapting their international slogan 'Pepsi Brings You Back to Life', the unfortunate Mandarin translation came out as: 'Pepsi brings your ancestors back from the grave'.

Even within the same language, differences of nuance can lead to misunderstanding. The British and Americans in conversation sometimes stumble over slight but usually unremarked differences in meaning. The word 'quite' in British usage generally signifies something a little *less* than, while in the US it indicates *more* than. So, an American is likely to take the British statement 'That was quite good' – indicating moderate approval – as a mark of great appreciation.

International diplomacy provides no shortage of examples in which a verbal misunderstanding can genuinely mean the difference between war and peace. In negotiations between Paris and Washington in 1830, a translator, confronted with the phrase *le gouvernement français demande*, rendered the French verb *demander*, meaning 'to ask', as 'the French government *demands*'. The US President was reportedly furious with their impertinence, until the mistranslation was spotted and corrected.

One of the primary United Nations solutions cited as a basis for resolving the Israeli–Palestinian conflict is Security Council resolution 242 of 1967. In a key paragraph it states that a just and lasting peace should include withdrawal of Israel armed forces 'from territories occupied in the recent conflict'. Reams of paper and hours of debate have revolved around the phrase 'from territories', with Arab interpreters insisting that this means withdrawal from *all* territories, while Israeli advocates argue that the definite article was deliberately not included to allow for a continued Israel presence in some areas.

If the definite article seems a small subject for differences of understanding, consider the Northern Ireland peace process, where debate has revolved around a single comma. In 1990 the UK Secretary of State for Northern Ireland, Peter Brooke, made a statement in which he said that Britain had 'no selfish strategic or economic interest in Northern Ireland'. Some listeners interpreted this to mean that Britain had no interests, whether selfish or strategic or economic, in Northern Ireland. Pointing out the absence of a comma between 'selfish' and 'strategic', however, Brooke was able to make his case that Britain did indeed have strategic and economic interests, but these were not motivated by self-interest.

If it is hard to communicate with words, however, we find it impossible to communicate without them. The best that we can do is to enter into our most difficult conversations with an awareness that we are playing with fire. And to remember that words used carelessly or harmfully are hard, even impossible, to undo.

A Hassidic story warns of the irreversibility of careless speech. A man goes to a rabbi and tells him that he has spread malicious rumours about his adversary. He would like to make amends. What should he do? The rabbi tells him he should take a feather pillow, tear it open, and scatter the feathers to the winds. The man does so and comes back to the rabbi. 'I did as you told me,' he reports. 'Am I now forgiven?' 'There is just one more thing you have to do,' advises the rabbi. 'You have to gather all the feathers and put them back into the pillow, for that is how far the rumours you have spread have reached.'

At the heart of each Jewish prayer service stands the most central prayer of the tradition, the *Amidah*. It begins with a verse from Psalms, a brief prayer to be able to pray properly: 'Oh Lord, open my mouth, so my lips can declare your praise.' Perhaps we should enter into our most sensitive conversations with a similar prayer, or at least an internal intent, that our lips may be guided to choose the words that will go from our heart to the heart of our listener.

White fire: the power of silence

Towards the end of my diplomatic posting in London, after several years of being invited to speak at rather grand fundraising dinners, I was again asked to speak at one such event. The red-jacketed master of ceremonies stepped forward to invite me to take the podium, for which there is a standard rather grandiose formulation: 'Pray silence for His Excellency the ambassador.' I like to think it was only through a slip of the tongue and not as an indication that I had outstayed my welcome that he instead bellowed: 'Pray for the silence of the ambassador!'

If, in the image of the rabbis, black fire is the words we choose, then white fire represents our silences. Silence is far more than the absence of words. The space around the letters not only gives them shape (a letter in the Torah scroll not entirely surrounded by blank parchment is invalid) but it has a voice of its own. It is, in the words of new age author Deepak Chopra, 'the space between thoughts, the place where insight can make itself known'.[3]

Silence, it is probably fair to say, is not a default Jewish condition. Our communal spaces and prayer houses tend to be loud, even boisterous. Indeed, the more traditional the synagogue, the less decorum you are likely to find there. Samuel Pepys records in his diary a visit to the leading synagogue of his day, in Creechurch Lane in the City of London, where he was astonished by the rowdy and chaotic proceedings: 'But Lord,' he wrote in dismay, 'to see the disorder, laughing, sporting and no attention, but confusion in all their service.' In the synagogue's defence we should note that the date of his visit, 14 October 1663, was actually the festival of Simchat Torah, which is characterised by lively and often disorderly dancing. But even in a regular service Pepys would have been unlikely to find the solemn quiet of his regular place of worship in the City of London, St Olave's Church.

Traditional Jewish study is also, as we have noted, collaborative and noisy. As Elie Wiesel once remarked: 'We have our silences in Judaism, we just don't like to talk about them.'[4] A Yeshiva quip has it that if the study hall is too quiet the students will lose their concentration. Israel's National Library has sought to balance the silent ethos of a Western library with the noisy debate of a Jewish study hall by surrounding the central reading room with smaller breakout 'loud rooms' for traditional study.

Silence can take many forms. Jewish life has its own taxonomy of silences, each with its different timbre and each serving a different purpose. While synagogues, as Pepys discovered, are rarely filled with reverent quiet, the central prayer of the service, the *Amidah* prayer, is recited by all while standing in contemplative silence. Similarly, when the *Yizkor* memorial prayer is said on major festivals, a sombre hush descends on the congregation as they recall departed relatives.

Twice a year the entire people of Israel come to a standstill, marking remembrance for the victims of the Holocaust, and for the fallen in the wars for Israel's survival. Even the cars stop on the highways, and drivers get out and stand in silence. Not exactly silence, mind you – the siren, reminiscent of the shofar, is the call to this moment, but then all are joined in wordless memory, in a unity beyond any words.

Silence also helps us to orient ourselves in environments of uncertainty. A thoughtful suggestion from the rabbis advises that a visitor to a house of mourning should remain silent until the mourner speaks. It's a simple and sensitive recognition that we don't know what mood the mourner is in. They may wish to talk about the person who died, or about something else entirely. Our silence gives them the opportunity to set the tone. At the very least it prevents us from putting our foot badly wrong. In the Bible, the long-suffering Job loses patience with his so-called friends and their endless attempts to comfort him. 'Be silent,' he tells them, 'and I will teach you wisdom.'

In negotiation theory 'The Negotiator's Dilemma' describes a fundamental challenge for any negotiator. The dilemma arises from the fact that we often do not know whether we are negotiating in a cooperative environment or a competitive one. The tactics that are likely to help us in one environment are actually likely to undermine our cause in the other. For example, if we are negotiating in a cooperative environment, it will make sense to share our genuine interests with our counterpart so we can explore how to craft a deal that maximises the value of the outcome for both of us ('I prefer the orange segments, you want the peel'). But if we are facing a counterpart with a competitive mindset, this strategy is likely to make us vulnerable and to be taken advantage of ('I know you prefer the orange segments. I actually prefer the orange peel but I'm not going to tell you that because I might be able to get all of the peel and some of the segments as well').

This dilemma lies at the heart of a classic negotiation training exercise. Usually conducted in silence, in groups of four, with a series of rounds, players have to work out in each successive round whether to cooperate or compete. A pay-off table setting out the points received for each outcome ensures that if the group manages to cooperate as a whole, they will be well rewarded, and if all are selfish they will pay a price. But if just one person defects and goes on their own, they will profit even more than if they had cooperated, while the others will suffer. In short, success depends on picking up cues from the other players regarding their willingness to collaborate. I have had the opportunity to teach this exercise in the course of negotiation training in a number of countries. I've regularly found that Israeli negotiators, particularly Israeli men, tend to score low. The primary reason, I have realised, is that, whatever their other strengths as negotiators, they are uncomfortable with silence, and as a result they miss out on cues that could provide valuable information about the context in which they are operating.

I tried to convey the dangers of prematurely breaking silence in *Winner's Curse*, a play I wrote about international negotiations, which ran at London's Park Theatre in 2023. One of the characters, an eager young negotiator, is bursting with ideas for resolving the conflict and cannot resist sharing them in the very first round of the negotiations. Later, he asks his mentor, an experienced negotiator, if there is anything he missed. The mentor replies:

Just one little thing. Silence. The most important thing at the negotiation table is not what you say. It's what you hear . . . if you are quiet for long enough. But what did we glean? Nothing. We were too busy batting our own balls.

It's a lesson that Seinfeld's friend Kramer clearly needs to learn in an episode of the long-running sitcom. Having been burned by a spilled cup of coffee from Java World, his lawyer encourages him to sue the coffee shop chain. The Java World executives are keen to settle quickly and come to the first meeting ready to commit a large sum, together with a promise of free coffee in their stores. At the settlement meeting, they start with the offer of free coffee, but before they can go on to talk about financial compensation, Kramer interrupts excitedly: 'I'll take it!'

Silence is a critical tool for the negotiator, but even patient listening may have its limits. In one set of international negotiations, I found myself with a counterpart who was loquacious, to say the least. With the slightest invitation or provocation, he would launch into a passionate and interminable monologue about the justice of his cause and the righteousness of his grievance. The speeches may have been therapeutic for him, but it was hard to see how they made reaching an agreement any easier. After being on the receiving end of these orations rather too many times I discovered a surprisingly effective way of short-circuiting them. Each time he launched into another set-piece monologue I would conspicuously stop writing notes, put the cap on my pen and place it on the table in front of me. Changing the tone of my silence to hint that his diatribes wouldn't make it into the record helped us get back to business.

Western societies tend to be unforgiving of silence. To those of us raised in such societies, silence, certainly beyond a few short moments, can feel very awkward.

If Westerners tend to one end of the spectrum, the Japanese tend to the other. Japanese business people, researchers have found, are more likely to wait until the end of others' comments and then pause, sometimes for as long as eight seconds, before responding, twice as long a silence as American business people conventionally tolerate.

Susan Scott, in her book *Fierce Conversations*, gives an example of Japanese sensitivity to the things that can only be heard in silence. She describes participating in a business meeting in Tokyo, in which she notices a young woman writing continuously. Following the meeting, she comments that it was good to have someone capturing everything that was said. 'She wasn't writing down what was said,' explained her host. 'She was writing down what was *not* said.' 'But she never stopped writing the entire time,' said Scott. Her host just smiled.[5]

We may not be able to change our cultural baggage, but we can try to adopt practices that may help us capture the things that are not said. Quaker Christians place a great emphasis on their communal life and thoughtful communication. Their services are based on the principle that one should only speak when directly inspired to do so and in their discussion groups participants are asked to wait at least a minute before speaking after someone else has finished, to quiet the noise of 'popcorn style' discussion, with comments popping off one after another. A powerful tool in conflict resolution discussion groups is to invite people to ask questions that are on their mind, but to leave them unanswered. The silence that follows a heartfelt question can allow for more and deeper insight than any single answer.

As well as adopting practices that encourage silence, we can also create contexts in which silence may feel less awkward. Particularly if we anticipate that a conversation may be sensitive, having it while walking in the hills or drinking a good whisky in front of a crackling fire are two classic contexts that allow for long pauses and remain as effective as ever.

Silence is not just an opportunity to hear others better. It has its own voice. Or it may enable us to hear the voices that are easily overlooked. The writer Catherine Blyth, in *The Art of Conversation*, suggests a series of practices to 'relish silence':

Inevitably time feels impoverished, experience intangible, if we don't notice spending it. Fast for a day: no TV, computer, music, PlayStation, film. Unplug the toys, plug in, be a tourist in your world, and you'll find there is no silence: too much is going on.

What will you see? Who will you meet? Perhaps you'll have a conversation.[6]

The practices Blyth recommends, the whole idea of unplugging from our devices for a day, sound remarkably like the traditional Jewish Sabbath. We can see islands of silence as the sabbaths of our conversations. Just as there is more to Shabbat than not working, so is there more to silence than not speaking.

The Bible describes the voice that can only be heard in silence in its dramatic description of the vision of the prophet Elijah, standing on the mountain waiting to see the Lord. As described in the book of 1 Kings:

> The LORD said, 'Go out and stand on the mountain in the presence of the LORD, for the LORD is about to pass by.' Then a great and powerful wind tore the mountains apart and shattered the rocks before the LORD, but the LORD was not in the wind. After the wind there was an earthquake, but the LORD was not in the earthquake. After the earthquake came a fire, but the LORD was not in the fire. And after the fire came a gentle whisper [*kol demama daka*]. When Elijah heard it, he pulled his cloak over his face and went out and stood at the mouth of the cave.[7]

Usually translated as 'the still small voice' or 'gentle whisper', the Hebrew phrase *kol demama daka* more accurately means 'the slender voice of silence'.

The famous passage suggests that a learning process is required. Before Elijah hears the voice, he needs to learn where God's voice cannot be heard – it is not in the wind, nor in the earthquake, nor in the fire. Only after learning to exclude the noise is he able to hear the slender voice in which God appears.

The twentieth-century rabbi Shlomo Wolbe noted that keeping silence is not a natural instinct but one which needs to be developed:

Silence is something one has to learn. Since a baby knows to talk, he babbles just as it pleases him, but silence needs to be learned because it is a great skill. The nature of a person is their solitude: only in that does the soul and spirit develop their strength.[8]

Over the centuries Jewish tradition has sought ways for us to learn the skill of silence. The Mishnah relates that the sages of the Great Assembly which led the Jewish community two millennia ago would sit for an hour in silence before they were ready for prayer. Some 1,500 years later, the medieval kabbalists took this practice much further, instituting speech fasts, extended periods of time when they would refrain from speaking, particularly ahead of the high holidays. The Mussar movement of the eighteenth century, which focused on personal and spiritual development, saw silence as a key soul trait that needed to be nurtured and developed. Curiously, it seems that the founders of the Mussar movement were influenced by the ethical monographs of Benjamin Franklin, which had been translated into Hebrew, and which listed silence as one of the thirteen key virtues. Franklin advised: 'Speak not but what may benefit others or yourself; avoid trifling conversation.'

We are accustomed to telling our children to 'be seen and not heard'. As adults we should remember to pay attention to this advice ourselves. Modern conversations tend to have all the wind and quake and fire that surrounded Elijah. The challenge is to find the slender quiet moments within. Silence is the most open of questions, the best of teachers. And while we may learn from noise, we change in silence.

Chapter 15

A Place for Jesters in Heaven

A rabbi who doesn't laugh isn't serious.

Rabbi Yehuda Leon Ashkenazi

The atmosphere in the Israeli–Palestinian negotiation room in our early negotiations in the 1990s was often tense, and there was no shortage of issues that were sensitive and hard to address. In the course of discussion about legal cooperation between the two sides, one of the unspoken issues was corruption within the Palestinian legal system. It was one of the Palestinian negotiators who helped diffuse the sensitive topic, and enabled us to broach the issue, by telling a traditional Palestinian joke:

A plaintiff in a court case was worried that he would lose his case, so he went secretly to the judge and offered him a bribe. The judge took the bribe and promised him he would decide in his favour. Unbeknown to the plaintiff, the judge had also taken a bribe from the other side in the case, and at the end of the case issued his judgment against the plaintiff. Furious, the plaintiff went to the judge's chambers. 'You took my money,' he exclaimed. 'How could you decide the case against me?' 'Don't you see?' the judge answered calmly. 'I wrote my judgment in such a way that you will be sure to win on appeal!'

Often, the greater the tension, the greater the laughter. In 1960, British Prime Minister Harold Macmillan was addressing the United Nations when the Soviet leader, Nikita Khrushchev, started shouting and hammering on his desk with his shoe. Macmillan paused and to great laughter said: 'I'd like that translated, if I may.'

In Israel's foreign relations, too, humour has been useful as a tension reliever. In the 1970s President Anwar Sadat of Egypt would often banter with Israeli Foreign Minister Golda Meir, calling her 'the old lady'. Meir returned the favour on the day after Sadat's first grandchild was born, telling him that she was speaking 'as a grandmother to a grandfather'. And in the 2000s Prime Minister Ehud Olmert, on receiving a visit from Palestinian President Mahmoud Abbas, after both had recently had prostate surgery, joked that the time had come for a 'two prostate solution'.

Still, for anyone planning to use humour in the sensitive area of foreign relations, caution is advised. Boris Johnson, usually a master of the mischievous gag, missed the mark when, as Foreign Secretary, he welcomed foreign ambassadors to a reception with the greeting: 'We have invaded, defeated or conquered most of your countries, but we are here as friends.' Many envoys were horrified at what the Foreign Secretary evidently considered a joke.

The Talmud clearly identifies the ability to use humour to diffuse tension as a gift, even a heavenly one. It tells a surprising story of a certain Rabbi Beroka who was standing with the prophet Elijah in the marketplace. He asked Elijah, 'Is there anyone here who merits a place in the world to come?' Elijah pointed out two brothers. Rabbi Beroka ran after the two brothers and asked them what their business was. They replied, 'We are jesters. We make sad people laugh. And when we see two people in a quarrel, we use humour to make peace between them.'[1]

Over the centuries of Jewish history, humour has served as more than a peace-making relationship builder. It's been a source of resilience, even a key to survival. When I visited refuseniks suffering persecution in the Soviet Union, I learned how important anti-establishment humour was in maintaining their spirits. One popular joke based on a true story described a KGB interview with a refusenik trying to leave and emigrate to Israel:

KGB: Comrade Lev, you understand that we cannot allow you to leave, because you are privy to state secrets. Why are you applying for an exit visa to leave?

Lev: But in my field of science, we are decades behind the West!

KGB: *That* is the state secret!

And a favourite from my friend and former refusenik, Rabbi Leonid Feldman:

Brezhnev is planning a state visit to Poland. He wants to present his hosts with a painting of 'Lenin in Poland'. However, the Russian school of painting is very realistic, and since Lenin never actually visited Poland, no artist willing to paint the picture can be found.

Finally a Jewish artist agrees to take the commission. A little while later, the artist is back at the Kremlin for the unveiling. Brezhnev pulls back the drapes only to see a picture of Lenin's wife, Nadya, in bed with Leon Trotsky.

'What's this?' asks Brezhnev. 'Where's Lenin?'

The artist replies, 'In Poland!'

The power of humour to preserve human dignity against persecution has never been more powerfully expressed than in Viktor Frankl's extraordinary psychological memoir of his experiences in a number of Nazi concentration camps, *Man's Search for Meaning*. He describes the role played by humour in enabling inmates to hold fast to a sense of their humanity:

Humour was another of the soul's weapons in the fight for self-preservation. It is well known that humour, more than anything else in the human make-up, can afford an aloofness and an ability to rise above any situation, even if only for a few seconds.[2]

Frankl describes how he suggested to a fellow inmate that every day they should invent at least one amusing story about an incident that might happen after liberation. On one occasion Frankl forced a smile from a fellow inmate by suggesting that their habit of asking the cooks to ladle the soup from the bottom of the pot so as to include a precious few bits of potato or the odd pea might now be ingrained. Frankl invited his friend to imagine attending an elegant dinner party in the future, where they would suddenly forget themselves and beg the hostess to serve the soup 'from the bottom'! Frankl would later develop the insights he drew from his experiences into a school of psychotherapy which he termed logotherapy.

If, in times of persecution and powerlessness, humour can help preserve our dignity, in times of comfort it can serve the opposite purpose, helping to puncture our delusions of grandeur. A host of Jewish jokes serve this moral function, calling out our reluctance to look ourselves, and our flaws, squarely in the mirror. Here are two of my favourites. The first takes a swipe at false piety:

Yom Kippur, the holiest day of the year, reaches its climactic moment. The rabbi, at the front of the congregation, over-whelmed by emotion, throws himself down on hands and knees and cries out to his Creator, 'Before You, I am nothing!'

The cantor, also overcome, prostrates himself: 'Before You, O Lord, I am nothing!'

The lowly beadle of the synagogue is so moved by this sight that he too falls to the floor, shouting: 'Before You, I am NOTHING!'

The rabbi looks condescendingly at the beadle and then turns to the cantor and sneers: 'Look who says he's a Nothing!'

And the second at ingratitude:

A Jewish grandmother takes her grandson to the beach. The boy is building sandcastles when suddenly a massive wave comes and sweeps him out to sea. Panic-stricken, the grandmother turns to heaven. 'Oh God, please bring him back! Please let him live!' Suddenly, an even bigger wave bursts out of the ocean, setting the little boy gently down at the grandmother's feet, still holding his bucket and spade. She scoops him up into a hug. Then she stares up at the sky and scowls: 'He had a cap.'

It's often suggested that this type of Jewish humour is European in origin, but in fact it goes back much further. The grandmother who takes her blessings for granted and only notices the missing cap has echoes as far back as the Bible itself. Following the miracles and wonders of the Exodus, the children of Israel turn to Moses, asking with sharp irony: 'Were there not enough graves in Egypt that you had to bring us out here to die in the desert?' (A funnier contemporary take on the Exodus story has Moses' wife turning to him in exasperation: 'Moses, we've been wandering for forty years in the wilderness. Ask directions already!')

Recognising there are truths that need the trappings of humour to come forth into the light of day suggests that we should make space for humour in our lives – and in our arguments. In the cycle of the Jewish year, the festival of Purim, marking the rescue of the Jews of Persia from the evil Haman by the heroic Queen Esther, has become a lively carnival-type occasion, characterised by partying and fancy dress. It's also an occasion when things that might not normally be said can find expression. The traditional concept of the Purim spiel, a show consisting of satirical skits, gives school and Yeshiva students licence to make fun of their teachers' idiosyncrasies more or less with impunity.

Within the Yeshiva world it's also a time when one can make fun of the very logic that lies at the heart of Talmud. Indeed, there is a longstanding tradition of writing satirical passages of quasi-Talmud, often called 'Purim tractate', which take Talmudic logic to comic extremes, debating (for example) the precise amount of alcohol that needs to be imbibed on the festival.

Across the Jewish world, Purim has become a kind of April Fool's Day, with a tradition of mischievous pranks and leg-pulling. Israeli and Jewish newspapers will have pages of parody news stories making fun of themselves or others. When I was a student in London, a group of friends and I were invited by a popular Jewish radio show, *You Don't Have to Be Jewish*, to take over their show on the Purim festival and replace the usual interviews with parodies. The veteran host Michael Freedland was a total sport, and interviewed us with studied seriousness about plans to send the President of the Jewish Board of Deputies on to a solidarity mission into space, an Arts Council grant to erect symbolic 150-foot-high Matzah in Hyde Park, and a new Chair for Better Sermon Jokes for Rabbis to be established at Jews' College. We thought the whole thing had been very funny, but when I spoke to my grandmother after one such broadcast, her only comment was that the news stories had been very strange indeed.

Heavenly laughter

If being a jester makes one deserving of a place in heaven, it comes as little surprise that Jewish tradition suggests that humour itself is a godly quality. The Talmudic story we mentioned in the Prologue, in which God's own opinion, proven by a series of miracles, is outvoted by the rabbis in the study hall, ends with a surprising postscript. Rabbi Nathan, one of the rabbis involved in the debate, meets Elijah the prophet who is visiting earth from heaven. Nathan asks Elijah: 'What was God doing at that time when His Heavenly voice was disregarded?' Elijah answered: 'He laughed and said: "My children have triumphed over Me; My children have triumphed over Me."'[3]

The Jewish conception of heaven is not one of humourless bliss. Heaven, we have seen, is described as a study hall, a place of arguments, but it's also a place of laughter. The Jewish vision of future redemption is itself one of joy and laughter. Psalm 126 describes the return of the exiles to Zion 'with mouths full of laughter and tongues full of joy'.

Far from being a cause of aggravation or frustration, constructive arguments are themselves seen as a source of joy. A surprising statement in the Talmud prohibits the study of Torah on the fast of Tisha B'av. This is the saddest day in the Jewish calendar, commemorating the destruction of both ancient temples as well as other tragedies in Jewish history. The reason for the prohibition? The study of Torah will create a sense of joy that is not fitting for the occasion. Thus study, except for certain designated sombre passages, is prohibited.

The argument that we aspire to is one which brings joy, even when, perhaps especially when, we are being argued against, challenged and even defeated. In the introduction to his great work, the *Noda B'Yehuda*, the eighteenth-century sage Yehezkel Landau addressed the critical comments he had received on an earlier edition of the work. Like Daniel Kahneman responding to Adam Grant's corrections to his research ('That was wonderful . . . now I'm less wrong than before'), Landau expressed his delight and appreciation: 'Even though his hand is outstretched and his sword sharp,' he noted in relation to one acerbic critic, 'his comments gave me great pleasure.'[4]

The joy of argument can be empowering too, giving us a confidence we might not otherwise have. During the Second World War, physicist Richard Feynman was one of the youngest scientists to be posted to the Los Alamos Laboratory in the US, working on the Manhattan Project. He was daunted by the world-famous experts working in the centre, whose reputation and brilliance were intimidating. In the end, it was the joy of argument that gave him the confidence to raise his voice. He describes one such conversation with the brilliant atomic physicist Hans Bethe:

All the big shots except for Hans Bethe happened to be away at the time, and what Bethe needed was someone to talk to, to push his ideas against. Well, he comes in to see this little squirt in an office and starts to argue, explaining his idea. I say 'No, no, you're crazy. It'll go like this.' And he says, 'Just a moment,' and explains how *he's* not crazy, *I'm* crazy. And we keep on going like this. You see, when I hear about physics, I just think about physics and I don't know who I'm talking to . . .[5]

The fact that our arguments are about serious subjects does not mean they should not be a source of joy. Indeed, if we can find joy at the heart of the dispute then the joy that we feel, and share with our counterparts, even as we disagree with them, will help the whole process be more effective. It also suggests a litmus test for the quality of our arguments. As we have seen, the rabbis asserted that a defining characteristic of an 'argument for the sake of heaven' is that it will endure. But if we do not have the patience to wait an eternity, we might propose an alternative rule of thumb: did the argument bring us joy?

Community: No Argument is an Island

Rabbi Elazar said, 'I shall go to Dyomset, a beautiful place with beautiful and delightful waters.' But the others said, 'We shall go to Yavneh, where there are scholars in abundance who love the Torah.'

According to the account the results were clear:

> Because Rabbi Elazar went to Dyomset – a beautiful place with lovely and delightful waters – his name was made least in the Torah. Because they went to Yavneh, where there are scholars in abundance who love the Torah, their names were magnified in the Torah.[1]

Good arguments don't happen in a vacuum. Our environment influences us for better or for worse. What might an environment geared to more constructive arguments look like? It might create social contexts that encourage deeper, learning conversations. It could recognise that constructive argument is not an instinct, but a skill that needs to be learned, and constantly honed. And it would nurture the critical social habit of living in difference.

Chapter 16

Creating the Right Environment

You can't fight in here. This is the War Room!
Peter Sellers as US President Merkin Muffley in *Dr Strangelove*

As a young child I once saw my mother carving two small doves out of clay, each with a small hole in its back. She and my father had just come back from the cinema where they had seen the film *Tom Thumb*. The film starts with an argument between a childless couple, a woodcutter and his wife. The woodcutter has been granted three wishes by a fairy. He wishes for a sausage. His wife, furious at the wasted wish, wishes for the sausage to be stuck on his nose. Sadly, the couple then waste their last wish to restore his nose. Devastated at the lost chance to have a child, the two cannot speak to each other. On the mantelpiece of their cottage are two porcelain doves, each holding a candle. The husband and wife light the candles and turn to face each other. An inscription on the base of the doves instructs them: 'Let not the sun go down on your wrath.' And indeed, before the candles have burned out, the two have overcome their sparks of anger.

I think that moment in the film resonated with my mother because she intuited that our arguments need to be placed in a context that reminds us of the ties that bind us, especially when we are addressing the most painful and intimate of conversations.

The Bible gives us two accounts of difficult conversations between childless couples, one showing how badly such conversations can go, and another how they might go better.

The first, one of the most painful conversations in the Bible, is between Jacob and his wife Rachel. It is all the more tragic since their relationship begins as one of the great love stories in the

Bible. Jacob falls in love with Rachel and then promises her wily father Laban that he will work for seven years to marry her. When Laban tricks him into marrying his older daughter Leah instead, Jacob agrees to work a further seven years for Rachel. Genesis 29:20 tells us these years of hard toil 'seemed like only a few days to him because of his love for her'. Their love, however, is not enough. Rachel is barren and becomes fiercely jealous of her sister Leah, who has child after child. In her anguish, she turns to Jacob and implores, 'Give me children, or I'll die!'

Instead of compassion, Jacob is consumed with anger. Perhaps he too is frustrated that he cannot have children with his beloved wife. Perhaps he is hurt by her implication that she, for whom he worked fourteen years, sees no value in her life with him if there are no children. Whatever the reason, Jacob blurts out a hurtful reply: 'Am I in the place of God, who has kept you from having children?' The emphasis in the sentence, it should be clear, is on the word 'you'. The fertility problem, he emphasises, is Rachel's – he himself has proved his virility by siring children with Leah.

Rachel's response is to offer Jacob her maidservant Bilhah as a surrogate to have children that she will raise. Why has she not made this offer before? Perhaps, before, she loved Jacob too much to share him. But Jacob's harsh words have had their effect. Now she feels the distance between them sufficiently to allow another woman to come between them. Sadly, the rivalry is destined to continue to the next generation, between Bilhah's children and her own.

A similar situation, but a very different response, is described in the book of 1 Samuel. The book begins by describing the events that led to the birth of the prophet Samuel. His father, Elkannah, has two wives, Peninah and Hannah. Hannah is deeply loved by Elkannah, but, unable to have children, she is teased and tormented by Elkannah's other wife Peninah, who by now has several children. Elkannah's response in 1 Samuel 1:8 is very different from Jacob's: 'Hannah, why are you weeping? Why don't you eat? Why are you down-hearted? Don't I mean more to you than ten sons?' He addresses her tenderly by her name (incidentally, individuals are addressed by name only rarely in the Bible, and almost always by God when they are). He sees her pain and her tears. He has noticed that she has lost her appetite. And then, gently, perhaps with a hint of humour, he reminds her that he too is in pain. He loves her and hopes for her to love him back.

Eventually both Rachel and Hannah do have children, their respective firstborns being Joseph and Samuel. Joseph grows up to be the viceroy of Egypt, and saves his family from famine. Samuel becomes one of Israel's greatest prophets, and shepherds the Jewish tradition through the critical transition from the period of leadership by the judges to the establishment of the monarchy. Joseph's life, though, will remain overshadowed by sibling rivalry and jealousy, suggesting that the sins, or at least the arguments, of the parents may indeed be visited on the children.

How might we create relationships which are resilient enough to survive our arguments? What might they look like? Milton's *Paradise Lost* ends with a moving description of the moment when Adam and Eve, having eaten the forbidden fruit, are exiled from Eden:

> The World was all before them, where to choose
> Their place of rest, and Providence their guide:
> They hand in hand with wandring steps and slow,
> Through Eden took their solitarie way.[1]

It is hard to imagine a greater loss than the loss of paradise, and Adam and Eve would certainly have had cause for harsh words. But touchingly, even at this moment of tragedy, Milton describes them making their way 'hand in hand', their relationship intact.

The truth is that our arguments are embedded in our relationships. We will often spend hours honing the points that we plan to make in support of our case. But alongside the question of whether our points, our claims and counterclaims, are ready, we would be wise to ask whether our relationship is ready for the argument we are about to have.

That is not to say that every area of disagreement has to be aired. Some things may be better not dragged to the surface. A story is told about an elderly couple who are asked to explain the secret of their long and happy marriage. 'Well,' says the husband, 'for my part I believe in always being caring and considerate. After all, the letter "i" doesn't appear in the word "marriage".' 'And for my part,' adds the wife, 'I never correct my husband's spelling!'

But more often, and more productively, having a strong relationship means that we feel ready to say the things that need to be said.

The values that bind

If you want to feel a sense of hope for the possibility of peace in the Middle East, go to an Israeli hospital. You will witness a level of cooperation that transcends religious and ethnic boundaries. In an operating theatre it is by no means unusual to see a Russian surgeon, an Arab anaesthetist, and a team of religious and secular nurses of every political persuasion, all working together to save the life of a patient who could be of any faith or background.

During my army service I spent three months training as a combat medic. At the ceremony marking the end of the course, we took the combat medic's oath, some version of which is sworn by medics in militaries around the world. It swears to offer medical assistance to the needy 'without regard to whether they are friend or foe'.

I remember that, even as I was making this oath as a young soldier, I wondered dubiously whether such a high aspiration could ever really be implemented in practice. But some days later I was stationed in an emergency room and a would-be terrorist in his early twenties was brought in on a stretcher. He was seriously injured. His injuries, it turned out, were self-inflicted – an explosive device he had been preparing for use had blown up in his hands. I was surprised and moved to see that the medical protocols and treatments he received were identical to those that any Israeli patient – including his victims, had he succeeded in carrying out the planned attack – would have received.

Not only in Israel, but around the world, healthcare seems to be a unique arena in which we find ourselves able to rise above difference and work together in pursuit of a common purpose. Is there a way that we can bring this spirit into our debates?

Mediator and conflict resolution expert Adar Cohen suggests crafting what he calls a 'gem statement' to serve as a reminder of the core value or emotion that holds the relationship together.[2] Particularly at moments of high emotion, it can be hard to take time to distil such a gem statement. Cohen suggests a thought experiment that can help. Think about the person with whom you need to talk, he suggests, and allow yourself to imagine that you have just finished having the best possible conversation with them. You were heard fully. If an apology was appropriate, you received an excellent one. You've reached an understanding that gives you confidence in the future of the relationship. Now, in this imaginary scenario, ask yourself what you would say to them in *that* moment. What would come to the forefront as being true in the relationship, once you're not consumed with negative feelings? Write down the first thing you think of. Cohen says you can follow up with other things too, but usually the first one is the real deal. He gives a few examples: 'We've kept on fighting in part because neither of us is willing to walk away from this friendship. That's something.' Or: 'Even when we can't agree on Dad's medical care, I've never doubted your good intentions. I know you want the best for him.' Once you've identified the gem statement, there's one small step left to take – actually saying it to your counterpart. If you are willing to repeat the statement to them, that may be a sign that your relationship is ready.

A gem statement may enable us to address a particular relational challenge, but we often don't need to go through the process of crafting one to give expression to our shared values or feelings. We can convey our common bonds in many ways. Within the Jewish and Israeli world, many conversations over the most provocative political and personal issues take place over the Friday night dinner table. With a candle lit for each member of the family, parents laying their hands on the heads of their children – even adult children – to whisper an ancient blessing, and a meal spiced with recipes and songs handed down from grandparents to grandchildren, there is no need to verbalise the implied gem statements that remind us of the truth that we are family together.

Can we bring a Friday night spirit into our other conversations, even our most difficult ones? During the 2012 violence in Israel and Gaza, when I was serving as Israeli ambassador in London, I received an invitation from Vincent Nichols, the Archbishop of Westminster, to join him, together with the Palestinian ambassador, for a meeting to talk about the Middle East and pray for the people of Israel and Gaza. When I arrived at his residence I was surprised to find that the only participants in the meeting were the Archbishop, the Palestinian ambassador and myself. Then the door opened and one more person entered – a young choirboy from Westminster Cathedral. For a few extraordinary minutes we sat in reverent awe as the angelic voice of the choirboy sang out a Christian psalm for peace between Jews and Muslims in the Middle East. As you might guess, we didn't then go on to solve the Middle East conflict, but something in our conversation was made different by the pure choral notes that rose above the differences that divided us.

The location and circumstances in which we conduct our conversation can create a powerful context to change attitudes. In the world of conflict resolution, it is common for warring parties to visit post-conflict situations. Doing so conveys a powerful message that even in conflicts that seem insoluble we can in time find a resolution. I had such an experience when I visited Northern Ireland together with my Palestinian counterpart in the Israeli–Palestinian Culture of Peace negotiations. There was much for us to learn from the experiences of the two sides in the years after the Good Friday peace agreement, but I think that for both of us the most inspiring aspect was to see how hard it was, not only to reach a peace agreement, but to keep it alive after the initial celebrations. Every official we met with described the extraordinary efforts required to maintain the peace, and indeed when we visited, not a single one of the 'peace walls' separating rival Protestant and Catholic groups in Belfast had yet been taken down. None the less, hearing about these challenges was indeed inspiring. It made peace seem real to us, not just a distant utopia. Peace, the context seemed to suggest, is not about finding a solution to all of your problems. Rather, it means changing one set of problems for another – but they happen to be a much better set of problems to have.

With the significance of physical locations in mind, while in Northern Ireland we were interested to learn what had happened with the Maze prison. Memorialising sites which are seen very differently by two sides to a conflict is a complex issue, and the Maze prison is a prime example. Used to detain paramilitary prisoners during the years of the Troubles, it was the site of many hunger-strikes and vigorous protests. Seen by republicans as an icon of resistance and by unionists as a reminder of acts of terror, the question of what to do with it presented a serious challenge once peace was achieved. The idea under discussion at the time of our visit was that the site would be repurposed as a 'conflict transformation centre'. For us, as visitors from the Middle East, aware of how powerful the experience of being in a post-conflict environment could be, this seemed like a powerful and positive idea. At the time of writing, though, the project has not progressed, suggesting that the shadows of conflict are long indeed.

Sometimes the context that shapes our conversation can be as basic as the seating arrangements. In international diplomacy these are notoriously complex. Within the United Nations, where nations are seated alphabetically, Israel should, strictly speaking, be seated next to the Islamic Republic of Iran. The UN's canny bureaucrats, recognising that this could be problematic, decided that within the UN system Iran should be referred to as 'Iran (Islamic Republic of . . .)' – a small tweak which ensures that the representative of Ireland takes their seat as a buffer between the two potential combatants of Israel and Iran.

But a helpful seating arrangement can achieve more than simply conflict avoidance. It can signal a commitment to cooperation and common goals, thus opening the path to resolution. As a student at Harvard, I had the privilege of getting to know Jamil Mahuad, former President of Ecuador. He had been a Nobel Peace Prize nominee for his role in ending the long-lasting conflict between Ecuador and Peru. Jamil told me that before meeting with his Peruvian counterpart, Alberto Fujimori, he consulted with Harvard negotiation professor Roger Fisher. Fisher advised him that in their first meeting Jamil should seek to achieve only one thing: a photograph in which he and Fujimori were seated, not across the table from each other, but on the same side, looking at a map together. The goal was to send a message that, although the two sides might have serious differences, here was a collaborative effort to reach a resolution. Jamil succeeded in securing the photograph, which was duly published in the newspapers of both countries. The peace agreement that eventually resulted from those negotiations ended the longest-running war in the Western hemisphere.

The realisation that working side by side can be more effective in addressing our differences than sitting face to face was creatively demonstrated by the British politician Lord Victor Mishcon. He cared deeply about the prospects for peace in the Middle East and in the early 1980s he invited King Hussein of Jordan and Foreign Minister of Israel Shimon Peres to his home for dinner. At the end of the evening, the two guests got up to leave. 'You can't leave yet,' said Mishcon. 'What about the washing up?' When the two men realised that Mishcon wasn't joking, they took off their jackets, rolled up their sleeves, and continued their conversation as they cleaned the dishes at the sink.[3]

Conducting our conversations side by side, whether at the negotiating table or the kitchen sink, is one way to nurture a more constructive mind-frame. Another is to engage through shared passions and texts. We can meet, as it were, on the page. On one occasion my embassy staff felt it was important for me to meet with senior church leaders at the General Synod of the Church of England, but they had not been able to arrange this, since 'political' speakers were not allowed. I suggested to them that instead of my speaking to them about political issues, we would instead have a joint Bible study session in which I would try to show how the Hebrew text of the Bible incorporates insights that are impossible to capture in translation. The organisers were happy with this, and in fact the initial Synod session led to a series of joint Bible study sessions and an opportunity to build valuable relationships. The common ground we found to meet on was provided by our shared text.

Restructuring the framework

Often the very structure in which we are having our discussion corrals us into positions with little room for nuance or empathy. Yale law professor Stephen Carter shares his frustration about trying to discuss complex issues on television talk shows: 'What immediately strikes me, whether as viewer or participant, is how difficult it is to construct an argument within the time-conscious frame of the medium.' But the challenge runs deeper than the lack of time available. Carter suggests that there is a fundamental misalignment between the goals of the media and the idea of a genuine conversation: 'The media fundamentally disbelieve in – or rather, are unable to squeeze profit from – the possibility of humans reasoning together to find truth.'[4]

A funny sketch in 1980s comedy show *Not the Nine O'Clock News* parodied the dependence of talk show discussions on rival viewpoints. An interviewer introduces his two guests to discuss youth vandalism. The first, a stuffy old-school conservative, insists that the only way to deal with the troublemakers is to 'cut their goolies off'. The interviewer then turns to a trendy female social worker for another opinion. She expresses understanding and empathy for these young people. She knows them and the challenges they face, she says, and then adds that the best way to address the problem is to 'cut their goolies off'! The hapless interviewer finds himself hopelessly arguing against two guests in total agreement – something which of course would never happen in practice!

CNN analyst and author Van Jones has written about the unspoken rules that dominate any discussion in the media, including: 'Always attack your opponent's views, even if she has made a good point', 'Defend your own side at all costs' and 'Expose your opponent's weaknesses; conceal your own'. He warns that the 'nightly "death match" between talking heads is in danger of reducing our national discourse to a farce'.[5]

Stephen Carter may be right in suggesting that the gap between the desire for genuine truth-seeking discussion and the desire for ratings in television formats is unbridgeable. But in our own contexts we can think about shaping frameworks for discussion that welcome rather than penalise nuance and understanding.

I recently attended a conference on divisions in Israeli society held at the Van Leer Institute in Jerusalem. The organisers had given thought to precisely this question. How could they encourage panel participants to break out from behind the labels that defined and constrained them? They decided that instead of the usual panels about Israeli society, in which each sector (secular, ultraorthodox, Arab and so on) had its own representative to defend them on each topic, each panel would relate to only one sector and present a range of voices within that group. The result was a far richer and franker conversation, and one which served to break down the sense outsiders often have that each such group is monolithic.

Another way to ease the pressure created by having sensitive conversations in front of the world at large is to take them off-line, and address the most difficult issues away from the public eye.

In 1994, in a brutal shooting attack at an abortion clinic in Boston, two people were killed and five injured. Following the attack, Laura Chasin, a family therapist and philanthropist from the Rockefeller family, was watching a televised debate on abortion. In the high decibel exchange, the respective pro-choice and pro-life advocates were totally unable to communicate with each other. Barely able to quieten the verbal attacks and counter-attacks of the participants, the moderator lamented, 'There's nothing going on here but a lot of noise.'

Chasin wondered whether there might be a better way of conducting the dialogue and, together with colleagues at the Family Institute of Cambridge, Massachusetts, convened a series of small dialogue groups to talk about abortion. All groups were evenly balanced between people who described themselves as 'pro-choice' and 'pro-life' and, most importantly, the groups met away from the public eye. At the start of the process, which took place over several years, many of the participants found their positions hardening, but over time, as the relationships deepened, they found they were able to think about the issue in more nuanced, less simplistic ways. Taking the conversation off-line succeeded in lowering the identity stakes and opening up ways of communication that had seemed unimaginable before.

I certainly noticed this in my own negotiation experience. Often international negotiators are charged with two separate functions: first, trying to reach agreement with the other side, and second, defending their side's position to the international community. The members of the Palestinian Negotiation Support Unit, for example, would serve both as negotiators at the table and as spokespeople in the media. These are two very different tasks, and ones which require very different attitudes. Success in the negotiation room calls for creative thinking and empathy, while most media formats tend to reward forceful and even intransigent positions. I suggested to my counterparts that it might be helpful to divide their team into two, so that at least the people sitting at the table would not be the same ones who had only moments earlier been broadcasting more extreme and inflexible positions. For my part, during the period I was involved in the peace talks, I asked to be excused from any spokesperson assignments so that I would feel freer to think more flexibly and openly in the negotiation room.

Another way of lowering the temperature around hot-button issues is to create environments in which the issues themselves do not take centre stage, but are addressed in a broader and less divisive context. Media entrepreneur Eli Pariser has noted that some of the best American political discussions online take place in sports team forums and bulletin boards.[6] The fact that the participants start from the knowledge that they have common ground, a shared love of their team, means that they are less likely to feel their identities are invested in their political positions and so are more at liberty to be open to alternative viewpoints – both across the table and within themselves. (One cannot help wondering whether we might also find less emotive and more substantive discussion of sports competitions if they were to be conducted in political forums and bulletin boards.)

I have also had the opportunity to participate in a number of 'Track 2' processes, discreet dialogues aimed at advancing relations between Israelis and Palestinians. One of the most effective, in terms of building relationships and nurturing deep and frank discussion, involved representatives from the two sides who had previously been members of their respective negotiating teams. The originality of its approach was that a key ground rule was set for the group: these discussions would not directly address any of the substantive issues at the heart of the conflict. Instead, they would revolve around process issues, encouraging the Israeli and Palestinian participants jointly to explore different approaches to the conduct of negotiations and to consider whether any of these tools and techniques might help improve the ongoing process of negotiation. The fact that we were engaged, ostensibly at least, in a joint exploration, rather than the more traditional arm-wrestle over the same old issues, created a space for building a collaborative dynamic. The real issues in the conflict, of course, were not forgotten, but we found that in coffee breaks and after-hours discussions, these were talked about with an openness that might not have been possible otherwise.

Our arguments do not take place against a blank canvas. The context in which they occur can serve to highlight our differences or remind us of the ties that bind us. We can help shape this context by looking for ways to remind ourselves of these ties and shared values. This can be explicit, as Adar Cohen suggests, through the declaration of a gem statement, or implied by our environment, whether the angelic notes of a choirboy or the lively family debates at a Friday night dinner.

Chapter 17
Sharpening the Skills – In Others and Ourselves

'What I believe' is a process rather than a finality.

Emma Goldman

When teaching workshops on negotiation, I'll often ask participants to raise their hands to the height that indicates how much of their time at work is spent negotiating; that is, using communication to try to advance their interests. Most of the hands indicate well above fifty per cent. When I go on to ask how much time at home, with family and with kids, is spent in negotiation, almost all the hands shoot high up in the air. But the kicker comes next. Seeing how much time is spent on this exercise, I'll ask the group to raise their hands again, this time to indicate how much time and thought people have put in to learning how to negotiate better and more effectively. This time the hands invariably remain low, indicating a number close to zero.

In the first class I took at Harvard Business School, I was surprised to see a number of second-year students sitting at the back of the hall. I was puzzled. Had they not taken this course before? Had they failed and now needed to retake it? No, I was told, these were the 'Skydeck'. Their job was to follow the class discussion and afterwards point out to students how their contributions could have been more useful or effective.

Most of us, however, so rarely stop to think about how effective we have actually been in our conversations, and how we might be better in the future. But none of the practices we have looked at are instinctive. Many are hard. They rub up against our own prejudices. And it is more tempting to surround ourselves with a cocoon of comforting and confirming opinions, reassuring ourselves that our opinions are uniquely balanced and objective.

Now that we've looked at a range of practices that are designed to improve the quality of our arguments, we should perhaps ask more broadly how we might begin to educate ourselves to be better, more effective arguers. We've seen that educators in South Korea have adopted Talmud study, and in particular the *havruta* methodology, as one way to do this. But outside a wholesale commitment to teaching Talmud, what particular practices should we seek to teach and nurture?

We could begin with the *shakla ve'tarya* exercise that lies at the heart of Talmud study. As we have mentioned, students of Talmud rarely focus on the final legal rulings themselves. Indeed, the practical conclusions of the rabbinic arguments are for the most part not even stated in the Talmud. What students study is the argument itself. They will often test their knowledge of a tractate by trying to reconstruct its *shakla ve'tarya*. As we have seen, this phrase, literally meaning 'give and take', and also used to describe bargaining in a market, refers to the chain of arguments and counterarguments, proofs and counterproofs, that make up the backbone of the tractate. From a young age, children will be asked to recite the to and fro of the discussion, making sure that no key argument, logical step or piece of evidence has been omitted.

It is striking that in modern life we so rarely do this simple exercise. Considering how much time we spend debating our differences, and how significant are some of the decisions that we reach, we rarely step back to think about the process of debate and dialogue that leads to the final conclusion. As we have noted previously, Daniel Kahneman advises major organisations making important decisions to adopt a very similar practice, keeping a 'decision journal' to record the to and fro of the arguments for and against, along with whatever alternatives were considered.

It sounds like a simple exercise, but it doesn't come easily to us. That's a point that Malcolm Gladwell had to learn the hard way. Gladwell has a brilliant mind and is a gifted speaker. So he was shaken when, in a public debate on media bias, he was roundly defeated by the talented British writer and speaker Douglas

Murray. But rather than try to bury his embarrassment, he decided to make it a learning experience by going to debate school. He charted the process on his podcast, *Revisionist History*.[1]

One of the key points that his new coaches from the Brooklyn Debate League stressed, after hearing a recording of his disastrous performance, was that he had been hopelessly sidetracked, and had lost track of the lines of argument in the debate. To show him what that meant, they played a game that is used to coach high school debaters. The idea is to train them to follow the to and fro of the debate, but with imaginary playing cards rather than with arguments. Here's what it sounded like:

Hello, my name is Sasan and I'll be speaking on the affirmative today. My first argument is the three of hearts, and we know that's true because of the four of diamonds. You can't forget about the jack of spades. You know, a lot of people tell me ten of diamonds. But what those people don't realise is, first off, ace of hearts. Secondly, the six of clubs and finally the nine of spades.

That was the speech for the proposition. Now Gladwell was invited to hear the speech for the opposition:

I disagree with everything that guy said. He says three of hearts but it's more like the seven of diamonds. People like to talk about jack of spades, but what they don't realise is king of hearts. Ten of diamonds is okay, if you don't remember that the ace of spades is there. And as far as the ace of hearts goes, more like the two of hearts. Finally, they brought up the nine of spades, nine of spades, nine of seriously, because have you never heard of the queen of clubs?

For Gladwell this was a sobering experience. 'How did I do?' he asked, then reported: 'I was terrible. I could keep up for the first minute or so. Then I fell behind. I missed things. Sasan gets up and talks about playing cards and I can't keep up.'

It's not surprising though. Not just in the world of debating, but in meetings and discussions of every type, we have been trained to think in binary terms: which argument wins out? How do we advance our own case? This doesn't just make us worse as debaters. It also means that when we leave a discussion or meeting, we are leaving a great deal of its value behind us. If the opinions and possibilities that didn't win out are forgotten, the insight that they hold – which may include arguments that in other contexts could win out – will be lost.

As Gladwell discovered, capturing all sides of an argument is something that doesn't come naturally to us. It requires effort. In the world of the Yeshiva, students have study partners to act as a sounding board and help them check the accuracy of their recollection. Awkward as it may feel at first, this may be a good way to start, finding an 'argument buddy' with whom we can debrief after serious debates, and whom we can ask for help in this task: 'I'm trying to reconstruct the flow of that discussion, can you help by pointing out what I've missed?'

Embracing complexity

Another practice we could do well to adopt and nurture is to embrace complexity. Talmudic thinking, as we have seen, is not binary in its conclusions. Different views, often contradictory, are seen as capable of coexisting. Maybe one is more relevant for a particular situation, and another for a different one, or maybe there are unseen perspectives from which the apparent contradictions melt away.

This approach is reflected in the very text of the Hebrew Bible. The standard version is not a monolithic text. Rather, around the text of the Bible, circling it like the rings of an ancient tree, are commentaries from different generations, many of which do not hesitate to take issue with each other, arguing not only across the page but down the ages.

For David Bonett, it was seeing such a Bible that began his journey to Judaism. Bonett was serving a thirty-month sentence in a

US prison for selling drugs when he saw a fellow inmate studying the weekly Torah portion. He was intrigued by the competing commentaries on the page, which was so different from the approach in the church he had grown up in: 'The way I grew up with religion, it was, "This is what it means." There was no debate. And if you disagreed, that was wrong and you're on your way to hell.' Fascinated by the idea of a religious life that left room for different interpretations, he began studying Judaism, and today, as David Ben Moshe, lives in Jerusalem.

The sensibility that differences are not to be avoided or resolved but embraced is one that can be inculcated in youngsters, even from an early age. Regarding the verse that states Noah was 'a righteous man *in his generation*', for example, a child in Hebrew school will be taught the opinion that this description emphasises that Noah was righteous *despite* his evil generation and so was especially righteous, and at the same time the entirely contrary view that *only in comparison to* the evil generation in which he lived was he to be considered righteous. The young student will be encouraged to hold both of these contrary views as part of a cherished holy tradition.

A similar approach applies with regard to Jewish customs. For example, the end of the Sabbath day is marked with the Havdalah ceremony. At one point in the ceremony it is customary to raise one's hands towards a candle flame. Ask children why we do this and you will get a host of responses, from the legalistic (we are not supposed to make a blessing on the flame unless we use it, so we 'use' the flame to look at our fingers), to the symbolic (we see our fingernails are clean because we have not worked through the Sabbath) to the metaphorical (we note the difference between dark and light, reflecting the blessing that distinguishes between light and darkness). There is no sense of any particular answer being right or wrong. We may have a preference for a particular explanation, but all are celebrated as facets adding sparkle to the tradition. And the child grows up with a notion that varieties of viewpoints can coexist, and choices are not always one or the other.

We often think that children need to be taught in simple, clear categories, and that nuance is something that should be introduced later in their education. But the Jewish tradition encourages the introduction of complexity at an early age. I once saw master educator Avraham Infeld demonstrate a particularly creative and vivid way of doing this to a class of young people in Jerusalem. He was teaching the Purim story of Esther, and explaining the three choices that confronted the Jews of Persia in the face of the edict to destroy them: to turn to God through prayer; to turn to the king through diplomacy; or to take up arms and fight (in fact, in the story, they do all three). To convey the dilemma, he posted three labels on walls of the classroom: 'Prayer', 'Diplomacy' and 'Battle'. He then asked the youngsters to move their chairs and sit at the place in the room that reflected the balance of these three approaches that they identified. As the class discussion continued, he urged the students to move their chairs to reflect how their position was changing. Not only was it an effective way of conveying the need to balance competing values, the shuffling of the chairs to new places was a beautiful physical expression of minds thinking and changing throughout the debate.

A *scientific addendum*

It has sometimes been suggested that the Jewish tradition's openness to embracing apparently contradictory positions may in part explain the disproportionate contribution of Jewish thinkers to modern science, particularly in areas like modern physics, which requires an openness to theories that seem to contradict established principles. There is no real way to gauge whether this is true, but one can readily wonder whether being raised from an early age with a sensibility that is open to apparently irreconcilable positions (Noah was both better and worse than the righteous of other generations) may help nurture a frame of mind in which it is easier to think of light as both a wave and a particle, and of Schrödinger's cat as both dead and alive.

Whether or not Jewish scientists themselves have attributed their insights to a sensibility nurtured by the Jewish tradition, this is a conclusion that has often been held by antisemites. The extraordinary advances in physics in the early twentieth century, made in large part by Jewish scientists, were roundly rejected by Nazis and their supporters. In the 1930s a fierce campaign was waged by two German Nobel laureates, Philipp Lenard and Johannes Stark, against what they termed 'Jewish physics'. Unlike the purity of Aryan 'Deutsche Physik', they insisted, Jewish physics was a degenerate fraud which relied on spinning webs of abstract theory. 'The Jew is innately driven,' they alleged 'to mix facts and imputations topsy-turvy in the endeavour to secure the court decision he desires.' The fact that these topsy-turvy theories turned out to be empirically correct did nothing to alter their prejudice, and there is a historic irony in the fact that the Nazis deprived themselves of access to critical scientific advances being made under their noses, because they were convinced that these were a result of uniquely Jewish ways of thinking.

This tendency to see something objectionable and characteristically Jewish in the embrace of complexity still surfaces in antisemitic discourse. Writer and comedian Stephen Fry, whose mother is Jewish, wryly captures this suspicious voice of the antisemite in his memoir *Moab Is My Washpot*:

[Jews] are part of that parade of pale, clever men, who, at the turn of the century, confused the healthy world with all that talk of relativism and doubt and those weird ideas about determinant history and the divided self . . . reading things into things. It's their bloody *torah* and their damnable *talmud*, simply encourages too much of reading things into things and too much smug rabbinical clever-clever cleverness.[2]

The scientific apologists for the Nazis prided themselves on their excellence in empirical physics, arguing that their Jewish counterparts were ignoring the practice of experimental physics and engaging in disconnected flights of abstract fancy. Ultimately, though, it was the so-called 'Jewish physics' – developed, we should note, with the involvement of many non-Jewish scientists – that proved to match the reality.

Never too young

Acquiring and honing these and other skills and habits we have discussed is a lifelong endeavour, and one which it is never too young to begin. At what age should young people be encouraged to take part in constructive debate? In 'The Ethics of the Fathers' the rabbis suggest the age of ten, though the Talmud itself seems to argue for younger still. In a striking Talmudic passage, the sage Yehoshua ben Hananiah says that while he was rarely bested in an argument, he was once defeated by a young girl, and once by a young boy (the Talmudic language suggests the children were very young indeed – even toddlers). He describes the incident with the young girl as follows:

> One time I was walking along the path, and the path passed through a field, and I was walking on it. A young girl said to me: 'My Rabbi, isn't this a field? One should not walk through a field, so as not to damage the crops growing there.' I said to her: 'Isn't it a well-trodden path in the field, across which one is permitted to walk?' She said to me: 'The path has been trodden by dishonest people like you.'[3]

If the young girl gives the eminent rabbi a lesson in moral responsibility, the young boy gives him one in logical thinking:

> One time I was walking along the path, and I saw a young boy sitting at the crossroads. And I said to him: 'On which path shall we walk in order to get to the city?' He said to me: 'This path is short and long, and that path is long and short.' I walked on the path that was short and long. When I approached the city I found

that gardens and orchards surrounded it, and I did not know the trails leading through them to the city. I went back and met the young boy again and said to him: 'My son, didn't you tell me that this way is short?' He said to me: 'And didn't I tell you that it is also long?' I kissed him on his head and said to him: 'Happy are you, O Israel, for you are all exceedingly wise, from your old to your young.'[4]

For young children who have studied these and other such passages over the generations, the message is an empowering one. Far from being told to be 'seen and not heard' the message is that they too have a voice, and something to contribute to the argument. They may even have a point of view that can defeat the greatest sages.

This message is more than simply recognising the intellectual capacity of young people to absorb and comprehend. It puts a high value not just on their ability to learn, but also on their ability to innovate and contribute fresh thinking. The Talmud describes a conversation between Rabbi Yehoshua and two of his students walking home from their studies. 'What did you innovate in the study hall today?' he asked them. Intimidated by the great sage, they responded meekly: 'We are your students, we drink from your waters.' 'Even so,' responded the sage, 'there can be no true study without fresh ideas and innovation.'[5]

To this day, in traditional Jewish bar mitzvah ceremonies, young men, and now more frequently young women too, are expected not only to show that they can chant from the Torah – no small challenge, considering the written text in the scroll has neither vowels nor musical notation – but also to give a 'drash', a speech developing an idea in Jewish law. In addition to drawing from a range of sources, they are expected to add new insights of their own. In short, a young member of the community is invited to join the conversation of generations, and add their own fresh voice to the dialogue.

The skills needed to ensure genuine learning in our conversations may not come naturally. This can be especially true in the social media environment where so much of the 'noise' seems to encourage precisely the opposite, creating echo chambers, rewarding more extreme positions in any discussion, and encouraging a tribalism that makes it hard to give due weight to the opinions of others. All the more reason for us to hone these skills in ourselves and commit to teaching them to the next generation, recognising that having better arguments will always be a work in progress.

Chapter 18
Living with Difference

A work of art does not answer questions, it provokes them; and its essential meaning is in the tension between the contradictory answers.

Leonard Bernstein

A favourite Jewish joke tells of a new rabbi who comes to a well-established congregation. During the Sabbath service he is shocked to see a fight erupt. When the time comes to recite the Ten Commandments, half of the congregation stand and the other half sit. The half who stand say, 'We have always stood for the holy Ten Commandments', while the half who remain seated say, 'No part of the Torah is more holy than any other, we have always remained seated.' And both sides start yelling at each other.

Appalled by this disrespectful spectacle, the rabbi insists that they must clarify the original tradition of the congregation. In accordance with Talmudic tradition, he selects a delegation of three – one who stands, one who sits, and the rabbi himself – to visit Mr Levy, the last surviving founder of the congregation, now resident in an old people's home nearby.

They travel to the home and enter the room of the founding member. The man who stands in the service rushes over to the old man and says, 'Isn't it the tradition in our synagogue to stand for the reading of the Ten Commandments?' 'No,' the old man answers in a weak voice. 'That isn't the tradition.' The other man jumps in excitedly, 'So it's our tradition to sit?' 'No,' the old man says. 'That isn't the tradition.'

At this point, the rabbi cannot control himself. He cuts in in desperation. 'But Mr Levy, you have to help us. You can't imagine what is going on in the service – the people who are standing yell at the people who are sitting, the people who are sitting yell at the people who are standing . . .'

'*That's* the tradition!' says Mr Levy.

Some arguments need to be resolved. But not every difference needs a resolution. Or perhaps not now. In the Talmud, many arguments remain unresolved and yet it turns out we can live with difference. The Schools of the sages Hillel and Shammai, for example, had different traditions regarding who was allowed to marry whom. But notwithstanding their differences of opinion, the Talmud notes, they still made sure that children of the two schools were able to marry each other.[1]

When a debate cannot be resolved the Talmud will often declare *Teyku!* or 'Let it stand!' In modern Hebrew the term has come to mean a 'draw' or 'tie' – it is the word used for a draw in a football match. A rabbinic tradition teaches that irresolvable difference will have to wait for the return of Elijah the prophet when he comes to herald the Messiah. According to this tradition the term *Teyku* is an acronym for the phrase: 'The Tishbite (a name for the prophet Elijah) will have to be the one to resolve such questions and difficulties.'

Why should Elijah, rather than Moses, be the one to whom unanswerable difficulties are addressed? The rabbis find the explanation in the Bible's description of Elijah departing this world by ascending to heaven in a chariot. Since he never truly died, Elijah remains above time and will be able to resolve differences having regard to the needs and spirit of the age. The implication is that different positions may be equally correct, but for different times. Pending the arrival of Elijah, whom tradition describes as heralding the future arrival of the messianic age, we agree to live in uncertainty, open to a variety of possibilities.

While the term *Teyku* may be used in relation to specific issues that cannot be resolved, the spirit of living comfortably with contradiction is part of a broader sensibility. We've noted that Jewish children are inculcated towards an openminded perspective that embraces alternative viewpoints. The questions of Noah's righteousness, and why we hold our fingers to the light after Shabbat, all invite the answer *Teyku*. All of the above. *Teyku*, with its validation that certain issues can remain without final resolution, can help enable us to live with conflicts, even if we cannot fully resolve them. The book of Genesis provides an example of such a constructive non-resolution.

Jacob has been working for his uncle Laban for twenty years when he senses that his uncle's attitude to him has changed, and his life may be in danger. Gathering his wives and children, he leaves his uncle's house secretly at night. Laban chases after him and catches up with him. The two have a stormy argument, in which all the levels of difficult conversation – facts, feelings, their identities – are bared with raw emotion. Finally, the two reach a reconciliation and agree to make a pact. To mark it they gather stones and build a mound together. As the Bible recounts:

> So Jacob took a stone and set it up as a pillar. He said to his relatives, 'Gather some stones.' So they took stones and piled them in a heap, and they ate there by the heap. Laban called it *Jegar Sahadutha* ['mound of witness' in Aramaic], and Jacob called it *Galeed* ['mound of witness' in Hebrew].[2]

The two sides reach agreement, but not quite on everything. They agree to build a pile of stones, but each insists on calling it by a different name, in their preferred language. It is this latitude that leaves room for their fragile agreement to hold.

Negotiation expert William Ury advises parties at sensitive talks to 'leave room for the victory speech of the other side'. You don't have to think that their victory speech is as good as yours, but you have to let them go home with something, a story that they can tell themselves and those who sent them.

I've mentioned the unusual post box/ballot box constructed as part of the negotiations between Israel and the Palestinians in the

1990s. The forty-five-degree angle of the slit enabled one side to declare it was in the side of the box, like a post box, and the other to say that it was in the top, like a ballot box. *Teyku*, we might say.

On another occasion in these negotiations, the decision to live in difference was not a conscious one. The way in which we negotiated was using what is sometimes called the 'single text' negotiation method. After several rounds of exchanging draft proposals, and inching closer together in our positions, we would prepare a 'merged version'. This was a single text in which the different wordings preferred by the respective sides would each be included alongside each other, with the initials 'P' or 'I' to indicate each side's preference. Over subsequent rounds of talks we would work to bridge the gaps, slowly removing all the initialled sections until we could reach a fully agreed version.

One of the major agreements reached between us was hefty indeed. It ran to several hundred pages and included a host of annexes on security, civil and legal matters. With political pressure from the leadership of both sides, we worked round the clock to finish the agreement before the signing ceremony. Only after the ceremony, when all was signed and sealed, did we suddenly realise that in fact one of the annexes to the agreement had not been fully confirmed, and still included differing language with our separate initials indicating the Palestinian and Israeli preferred options. At least as far as that annex was concerned, we had effectively signed different agreements! Somehow or other, in the years that followed, the relevant officials charged with implementing those provisions managed to make it work. I won't specify what the annex was, but diligent researchers are welcome to hunt it down.

Whether entered into deliberately or not, living with difference is no easy option, but an uneasy peace may be better than none at all. Another passage in the book of Genesis, also about Jacob and stones that he uses to construct an altar, embodies this message.

Years before the argument with Laban, on his original flight from his brother Esau, Jacob settles down for the night. The Bible describes how he gathers stones to place under his head, then falls asleep, and dreams the famous vision of a ladder rising to heaven with angels ascending and descending. When Jacob wakes in the morning, realising that the place he has slept in must be holy, he seeks to build an altar. To do this, he takes the stone on which he has rested his head during the night and anoints it as an altar. The Midrashic commentary notes that the text describes Jacob as collecting 'stones', in the plural, on the night before, but in the morning the 'stone' he uses is described in the singular. Seeking to answer the question of whether there were many stones or a single one, the Talmud quotes Midrashic legend:

> Jacob indeed took several stones. The stones began quarrelling, each one saying, 'Upon me shall this righteous person rest his head.' So God combined them all into one stone, and the quarrelling ceased. Hence, when Jacob awoke, we read, he 'took the stone' in the singular, since all the stones became one.[3]

Many years ago, I heard a rabbi (whose name I have sadly forgotten) ask a question on this Midrash, as follows. 'Why, if God was going to do a miracle, did he turn the small stones into one stone? Why didn't he, for example, turn them into a feather pillow, so that the righteous Jacob would have a soft place to rest his head?' The teacher's answer, simple but powerful, was that peace is hard. It's not soft like a feather pillow. It's as tough as a stone, but better than conflict.

As I learned from visiting Northern Ireland with my Palestinian negotiating partner and seeing the challenges of keeping a fragile peace alive, peace does not mean finding a solution to all our problems. Instead, it means replacing them with a better set of problems. So too with our hardest conversations. Living in difference is not easy, but it beats the alternatives.

Conclusion

Chapter 19

Beyond Dispute

Don't just argue with reason, argue with love.

Dalai Lama

The Mishnah teaches: 'When two sit together and words of Torah are spoken between them, then the Divine Presence rests with them.'[1] The study hall where learning and arguments take place in a traditional Yeshiva also serves as the synagogue, with students breaking from their studies for morning, afternoon and evening prayers. Although the practical reason for this is one of space, it also reflects the understanding in Jewish thought that the worlds of prayer and of holy argument are not far apart. Not only through prayer, but also through argument, we can encounter the divine. So one might make a case that as we enter an argument, we should prepare ourselves as we do for prayer.

If we engage in a moment of self-reflection before we enter an argument, we may realise that we are not yet ready to have this debate. Perhaps we will realise that we have more work to do on ourselves before we can engage with others on this issue.

The eighteenth-century rabbi Moshe Sofer described the attitude that we need to cultivate for a truly learning conversation:

> Our motivation should not be to take sides between one position and another, or to try to bend the other side to my own view, but rather to be ready, if my counterpart's arguments are persuasive, to retract, and if they are not, to hold firm to my view.[2]

The mark of readiness to enter the conversation, he suggests, is whether we are prepared to change our view. It is reported that Robert Redford begins meetings at his Sundance Film Festival by

233

telling participants: 'I am inviting you to influence me. I want to be different when this meeting is over.' If our goal is simply to bend the other to our viewpoint, we are not ready. If, on the other hand, we are there not to defeat the other side, but to test our own thinking, willing to reconsider our arguments and change our position if necessary, then we are more likely to have a successful conversation.

The mark of success

So what does a successful argument look like? The popular 'flight' and 'fight' schools of argument have one distinct advantage: their criteria for success are abundantly clear.

For the 'flight' school, success means that the threat posed by Pandora's box has been kept at bay. Those difficult subjects that we fear to address can be safely tucked away and life goes on regardless, even though we are left with the nagging fear that at some point the box may spring open and threaten to destroy our relationship with the force of long-suppressed conflict.

For the 'fight' school, success lies in victory. Ideally our opponent will be left in a quivering heap on the floor, having been pummelled into submission by our inexorable logic. Ideally, this will have happened in front of an impressed crowd who are not only struck by our strength in argument, but will also be daunted, put off from challenging us themselves. So great is the glory that we give little thought to the fact that our position remains unchanged, we have learned nothing new, and the intimidated onlookers will be unlikely to challenge and deepen our understandings in the future.

But for a genuinely good argument, one that finds true resolution and helpful ways forward for all parties, the criteria for success are more elusive. Most difficult of all, the success of an argument can't be determined straight away. In the dictum of the rabbis: 'Every argument that is for the sake of heaven, it is destined to endure. But if it is not for the sake of heaven, it is not destined to endure.'[3] The rabbis do not exactly specify what the 'it' is that will endure, but what is clear is that we will have to wait to find out.

There are three possible interpretations of what is the enduring aspect of a good argument. Each of these suggests a different metric of success to which we should be aspiring.

The argument will endure

Unlike both the fight and flight schools, we are not aiming to win the argument decisively or to avoid it. Rather, we are aiming for the argument to be presented in its best possible form, with each side having distilled the truest, most convincing presentation of its case. To this end, we should ask ourselves a series of questions. Have we given voice to the truths on all sides, and preserved them so that we will not have to start from scratch when we revisit the debate in the future? Have we captured the knowledge that we have created, and the dissenting opinions along with them, so that, even if they didn't win the day today, they will have the opportunity, as Ruth Bader Ginsberg suggested, to speak to a future age? In short, have we treated the arguers as custodians of a treasure? Have we nurtured the argument with care and with passion, and have we handed it on, honestly and carefully, to provide insights to a new generation?

The resolution will endure

Many arguments do require practical resolution. Even if we feel there is value on both sides – even if 'both are the words of the living God' – in practice a single course of action needs to be followed. Is the course of action that we have arrived at resilient and sustainable? Do all sides feel that, even if their position has not been adopted, they have been fully heard? Some schools of mediation advise that mediators should facilitate discussion between parties to a conflict, but should not themselves make suggestions as to how the conflict might be resolved. The reason is because research suggests that while mediator-proposed solutions may help the sides reach agreement, in practice implementation of such agreements is more likely to fail. While the parties may have gone along with the mediator's suggestion, they did not themselves feel a sense of ownership and commitment to the resolution. Similarly in our own discussions we should ask: has the process been authentic and receptive enough that all feel invested in its outcome? Have we assured them that though the process has steered away from them today, it might yet allow them to win tomorrow?

The relationship will endure

The rabbinic dictum that an argument for the sake of heaven is 'destined to endure' is open to another interpretation: that when two people are engaged in a genuine process of truth-seeking, not merely the argument but also the relationship between them will last.

A truly good argument is not a sign of a poor relationship but of a strong and vibrant one. Rabbi Elazar Shach, as the leader of the ultraorthodox community in Israel, and Rabbi Yehuda Amital, a leading figure in the more liberal national religious movement, could hardly have been further apart on the religious spectrum in terms of their ideology. But they were, in fact, distant relatives and on one occasion the two met at a wedding. One turned to the other and said, 'We have become so estranged, we don't even argue any more!'

The better the relationship, the better the argument we should be able to have. But so too in reverse. The better the argument, the more it strengthens and deepens our relationship. As we have seen, the Talmud likens argument to iron striking iron, creating sparks of insight. But the process also tempers the iron itself, making it stronger and more resilient. A good litmus test for the quality of our debates is whether we emerge from them with our relationship damaged or improved.

From listening to love

Each of these measures of success has something in common with the others; none of them is predicated on the idea that an argument is a zero-sum game. To the contrary, they suggest that a successful argument is one in which both sides stand to benefit.

Is there any other human activity where neither side can claim victory, and where in effect there is no difference between giving and taking? There is. It is called love.

In advising managers, business consultant Quentin de la Bedoyere describes the process of active listening, and the need for managers to put aside their own interests and considerations to place themselves truly in the shoes of the speaker. 'I don't have a precise term to describe this kind of listening,' he writes. 'So in the absence of a better term, I call it . . . love.'⁴

It's surprising, to say the least, to meet the word 'love' in a hard-nosed book on business management, but it is, I think, wholly appropriate. Listening, true listening, is not a technique or series of calculated practices so much as a deep recognition of the humanity of the other and an attempt to reach out to a point of shared understanding.

What is true for listening is true too for arguing. In a true argument there is no winner and loser, and indeed a situation where you cannot distinguish between winning and losing, or between giving and taking, can truly be described as a relationship of love. In the Garden of Eden, when God creates Eve as a partner for Adam, he describes her as *ezer-knegdo*, traditionally translated as his 'helpmeet', but, as we have seen, better translated as his helper–opposer. Between parents and children too, the Talmud suggests that sparks of argument can fly in a way that only reflects a relationship of love. 'A father and son become enemies when they study, but they do not leave the study hall until they come to love each other.'⁵

Both our closest relationships and society at large can be enriched and strengthened by this sensibility. To be sure, in times when our debates seem irredeemably hostile and divisive this is a hard vision to hold fast to. But the resilience of the tradition of argument developed by a group of rabbis facing crisis and social breakdown two millennia ago should give us cause for hope. Today as then it remains true. Community born of agreement is fragile. Community united in the same raucous conversation is real and lasting. Our highest aspiration is not to resolve our arguments but to have meaningful ones, which bring us closer not only to the truth but to each other.

Acknowledgements

If I've suggested on occasion that the practices I have described in this book are rare, then the process of writing and editing this book has proven they are not always so. I have found myself surrounded by dear friends, teachers and colleagues for whom they are second nature. They have listened, questioned, collaborated adversarially, and shared stories and insights – all for the sake of heaven. So it is a deep pleasure for me to engage in the practice of owning up to my influences.

While my journey in Jewish learning has been rather haphazard, along the way I have been blessed with many wonderful teachers. Two in particular have left their imprint on my Jewish thinking and thus on almost every page of this book. I had the opportunity to study regularly with Rabbi Jonathan Sacks (of blessed memory) while I was posted in the United Kingdom. It is the custom for the Israeli ambassador to the UK to have monthly work meetings with the Chief Rabbi of the time, and in my posting I was wise enough to realise that the chance to have a *havruta* study partnership with Chief Rabbi Sacks was too good to pass up. I prepared the work items we needed to cover in advance so as to get our business out of the way quickly, giving us time to study together, a rare privilege which I treasured greatly. Going back further, Rabbi Joseph Telushkin has been an extraordinary teacher and friend for over forty years. He is not only the most wise and compelling writer I know about Jewish ethics, but he truly lives his teachings, with humanity and humour, in the most beautiful and inspiring way.

The Jewish version of 'It takes a village . . .' is that it takes a Jewish community, with a synagogue at its centre. In Jerusalem our family are blessed to be members of two wonderful and warm communities, headed by Rabbi Shlomo Wilk and Rabbi Shai Finkelstein respectively – two unique and original thinkers who have become cherished friends.

Many good friends read the manuscript in whole or in part and made many important and valuable comments. Very grateful thanks to Dr Tal Becker, Sally Berkovic, Neil Cohen, Rabbi Dr Daniel Gordis, Professor Daniel Jackson, Rabbi Dr Michael Marmur, Carly Maisel, Professor Ben Reis, Yifat Ovadia, Rabbi Dr Daniel Roth, Dan Sacker, Nigel Savage, Rabbi Yedidia Sinclair, Alex Stein and Ariella Taub. Heartfelt thanks also to my brothers Rabbi Jonathan Taub and Adam Taub, who offered learned and thoughtful feedback.

In the field of negotiation theory, I benefited greatly from time spent in Harvard as a Wexner Foundation fellow, and particularly from the teaching of Professors Roger Fisher of the Harvard Program on Negotiation, Michael Wheeler of Harvard Business School, and Brian Mandell of the Harvard Kennedy School of Government. On the practical level, I have learned much, especially about the role different faith traditions can play in conflict resolution, from my colleagues in the Mosaica Community Mediation Practicum: Sheikh Dr Eyad Amer, Sheikh Taiseer Mahamed and Rabbi Matanya Yadid.

With regard to researching Jewish sources, I owe a debt of gratitude to the curators at the National Library of Israel who guided me through its extraordinary collections, and also to the visionary geniuses behind the Sefaria library of online Jewish texts, perhaps the most exciting development in Jewish scholarship in our generation.

I have had the chance to road-test many of the ideas in this book with students in various classes and Difficult Conversation laboratories. I am extremely grateful to the Hartman Institute, the Pardes Institute of Jewish Studies, Shalem College and the Israeli Foreign Ministry diplomatic cadet training programme for giving me this opportunity. I would also like to pay tribute to two important Track 2 initiatives that I have had the opportunity to take part in: Israel–Palestinian Negotiation Partners and Tema/ Bridging Insights.

For helping me navigate the world of publishing, I am very grateful to my agent, Rory Scarfe of the Neil Blair partnership, and wish to express very special thanks to Ian Metcalfe at Hodder & Stoughton for his encouragement and meticulous and kind guidance.

My parents Brian and Esther (of blessed memory) set me on a path of Jewish study and involvement, and their relationship remains for me a shining example of a living gem statement. My parents-in-law Dr Henry and Paula Goldblum (of blessed memory) modelled a life of scholarship and joyful Jewish living which we have always tried to emulate.

My children, true thought partners as well as models of joyful and purposeful living, gave thoughtful and detailed comments. Deepest thanks to Judah and Leah, Sophie and Chanan, Aaron and Adiella, Reuven and Ayelet, Asher (whose suggested title for the book How to be an Argumensch was a strong finalist), and Amichai.

Above all, and beyond any argument, is my inexpressible debt to my wife and partner Zehava, an ezer-knegdo if ever there was one, a helper–challenger in all our shared enterprises, most especially our growing family. May the arguments of our children and grandchildren truly be for the sake of heaven.

Notes

Introduction: Can We Talk?

1. Years later I was delighted to reconnect with several of the study group participants in Israel, which they had finally been able to make their home.
2. Salman Rushdie, Speech on receiving the Chicago Tribune Lifetime Achievement Award 2015, reported at https://www.thefire.org/news/salman-rushdie-champions-free-speech-chides-coddled-students-chicago-tribune-award-ceremony.
3. Pew Research Center, *Beyond Red vs Blue: The Political Typology* (November 2021).
4. Cato Institute, *Summer 2020* National Survey.
5. Dale Carnegie, *How to Win Friends and Influence People* (Simon and Schuster 1936) 2024 edition, p. 140 .
6. Mehdi Hasan, *Win Every Argument, The Art of Debating, Persuading and Public Speaking* (Holt 2023) p. 246.

Prologue: From Crisis to Conversation

1. Jonathan Sacks, *Radical Then, Radical Now: The Legacy of the World's Oldest Religion* (HarperCollins 2001), p. 162.
2. Babylonian Talmud, Tractate Bava Metzia 59a–b.
3. Ilana Kurshan, *If All the Seas Were Ink* (St Martin's Press 2017), p. 10.
4. Edelman Trust Barometer 2022.
5. Robert D. Putnam, *Bowling Alone: The Collapse and Revival of American Community* (Simon & Schuster 2000).
6. Micah Goodman, 'The Talmudic Cure for Our Technology Sickness', *Sapir* 11, Autumn 2023.

Chapter 1: Rethinking Truth

1. Jacob Bronowski, *The Ascent of Man* (BBC 1973), 2011 edition, p. 285.
2. David Wolpe, 'To Err is Human: to Disagree, Jewish', *Sapir* Volume VII, p. 27.
3. Available at the Oxford Farming Conference website: https://www.ofc.org.uk/conference/2013/videos/frank_parkinson_lecture/mark_lynas_-_a_changing_perspective.
4. Interestingly, the Hebrew phrase 'Truth will grow up from the ground' (*Emet Me'eretz Titzmach*) is an acronym of its opening word EMeT, truth. We have not given up on truth, it suggests, but truth has taken on a very different form.
5. Jonathan Sacks, *The Dignity of Difference: How to Avoid the Clash of Civilisations* (Continuum 2002), p. 64.
6. *Midrash Vayikra Rabbah* I:14.
7. Dvorah Telushkin (ed.), *'Dear Ben': Writings of Benjamin Telushkin* (private publication 2022).
8. In fact, the Talmud relates, his scholarship was not lost. The sage Rabbi Akiva himself later came and elucidated the rogue *et*, explaining that it came to teach that alongside respect for the Almighty, one was obliged to hold in awe the sages who taught the Torah. In a beautiful irony, Shimon HaAssamoni, whose study was so purely motivated, is included among these sages, and so included within the *et* that he was unable to interpret.
9. Adam Grant, *Think Again: The Power of Knowing What You Don't Know* (Penguin Random House 2021), p. 46.
10. James O'Brien, *How Not to be Wrong, The Art of Changing Your Mind* (Penguin 2020), p. 9.
11. Ibid, p. 11.
12. Ibid, p. 205.
13. Yehuda Amichai, 'The Place Where We are Right' in *Poems 1948–1962* (Shocken 1962), my translation.

Chapter 2: Rethinking Difference

1. Mishnah, Tractate Eruvin 13b:10–14.
2. Babylonian Talmud, Tractate Gittin 5b.
3. A comment on Bertolt Brecht's poem 'Lao Tzu', quoted in Walter Benjamin, *Understanding Brecht*, trans. Anna Bostock, intro. Stanley Mitchell (Verso 1983), pp. 72–73.
4. Jonathan Haidt, *The Righteous Mind* (Vintage 2012), p. 343.

5. Babylonian Talmud, Tractate Berakhot 63b.
6. Joshua Wolf Shenk, *Powers of Two: Finding the Essence of Innovation in Creative Pairs* (Houghton Mifflin Harcourt 2014), p. xv.
7. Ibid, p. xvi.

Chapter 3: Rethinking Argument

1. Heard from my dear friend and teacher Maureen Kendler of blessed memory.
2. Mark Twain, *The Tragedy of Pudd'nhead Wilson's Calendar* 1893.
3. Mary Parker Follett, 'Constructive Conflict', lecture delivered to the Bureau of Personnel Administration Conference 1925.
4. Howard Kaminsky, *Fundamentals of Jewish Conflict Resolution* (Academic Studies Press 2017), p. 105.
5. Numbers 7:89.
6. Mishnah, Tractate Avot 5:17.
7. *Likutey Moharan* I, 122.
8. Jonathan Sacks, *Covenant and Conversation, Korach 5775*, https://rabbisacks.org/covenant-conversation/korach/when-truth-is-sacrificed-to-power/.
9. See Loretta J. Ross, TED Talk: 'Don't call people out – call them in' at https://www.youtube.com/watch?v=xw_720iQDss.
10. Babylonian Talmud, Tractate Menachot 37a.
11. Babylonian Talmud, Tractate Baba Batra 23b.
12. Ian Leslie, *Conflicted: Why Arguments Are Tearing Us Apart and How They Can Bring Us Together* (Faber 2021), pp. 231–32.
13. Archbishop Justin Welby, Presidential address to the General Synod, November 2015 at https://www.archbishopofcanterbury.org/archbishop-delivers-presidential-address-general-synod.
14. Babylonian Talmud, Tractate Baba Batra 165b.

Chapter 4: Developing a Robust Identity

1. Douglas Stone, Bruce Patton and Sheila Heen, *Difficult Conversations: How to Discuss What Matters Most* (Portfolio/Penguin 1999).
2. Monica Guzman, *I Never Thought of it That Way* (BenBella 2022).
3. Genesis 25:26–28.
4. The Hebrew name 'Israel' means: 'He who struggles with God'.

Chapter 5: Owning Up to Our Influences

1. Jonathan Freedland, 'Personality Politics', *Guardian*, 2 March 2007, https://www.theguardian.com/commentisfree/2007/mar/02/ishare someofjackie.
2. Babylonian Talmud, Tractate Sota 40b.
3. Jerusalem Talmud, Tractate Kiddushin 1:7.

Chapter 6: Separating the Argument from the Arguer

1. T Adam Grant, *Think Again* (WH Allen 2021), p. 64.
2. Joseph Telushkin, *Rebbe* (Harper Wave 2014), p. 140.
3. Among other places this is found in John Blundell, *Female Force: Margaret Thatcher* (Bluewater Productions 2011), p. 18.
4. Bertrand Russell, The Will to Doubt 1958.

Chapter 7: Adversarial Collaboration

1. Tokayer's English-Korean edition of the Talmud is also available on Amazon.
2. Ross Arbes, 'How the Talmud Became a Best-Seller in South Korea', *The New Yorker*, June 2015.
3. EunJung Chung, Byoung-Hee Lee, 'The Effects of a *havruta* Method on the Self-directed Learning and Learning Motivation', *Journal of Problem-Based Learning* 6(1) 2019, pp. 3–9; published online: 30 April 2019.
4. David W. Johnson, *Constructive Controversy, Theory, Research, Practice* (Cambridge University Press 2015), pp. 87–9.
5. Daniel Kahneman, *Thinking Fast and Slow* (Farar, Straus and Giroux 2011), p. 235.
6. Babylonian Talmud, Tractate Bava Metzia 84a.
7. Chaim Navon, *Teyku – 101 Great Jewish Arguments* (Yedioth Books 2014), Introduction (Hebrew).
8. Conor Frierdersdorf, 'The Highest Form of Disagreement', *The Atlantic*, June 2017.
9. Bo Seo, *Good Arguments: How Debate Teaches Us to Listen and Be Heard* (Penguin 2022), p. 96.
10. Margaret Heffernan, TED Talk: 'Dare to Disagree' at https://www.ted.com/talks/margaret_heffernan_dare_to_disagree?subtitle=en.

Chapter 8: Nurturing Dissent

1. Peter F. Drucker, *Management: Tasks, Responsibilities, Practices* (Harper Business 1993), p. 472.
2. Babylonian Talmud, Tractate Berakhot 58a.
3. Midrash Bereshit Rabba 42.
4. Abraham Joshua Heschel, 'Dissent' in Susannah Heschel (ed.), *Abraham Joshua Heschel: Essential Writing* (Orbis Books 2011), p. 106.
5. Jonathan Sacks, *Faith Lectures: Judaism, Justice, and Tragedy (2) Confronting the Problem of Evil*, November 2000, https://rabbisacks.org /archive/faith-lectures-judaism-justice-and-tragedy-confronting-the-problem-of-evil/.
6. Shmuel Faust, *Tihyu Hachamim, Timeless Wisdom – Practical Talmudic Thinking for the 21st Century* Hebrew (Kinneret Zmora Dvir 2023), p. 138.
7. Malcolm Gladwell, *Outliers: The Story of Success* (Back Bay Books 2011).
8. Cass Sunstein, *The Power of Dissent* (Harvard University Press 2002).
9. Cass Sunstein, *Why Societies Need Dissent* (Harvard University Press 2005), p. 27.
10. Mishnah, Eduyot 1:1.
11. Bari Weiss, Remarks at LA Press Club on receiving the Daniel Pearl Award for Courage and Integrity in Journalism, October 2021, available at https://www.thefp.com/p/the-daniel-pearl-award-for-courage.
12. Ruth Bader Ginsburg, interview with Nina Totenberg, NPR, in 2002.
13. Daniel Kahneman, *Thinking Fast and Slow* (Farar, Straus and Giroux 2011).
14. Rory Stewart, 'How to have a really good argument', https://www.bbc.co.uk/ideas/videos/how-to-have-a-really-good-argument/pocmk9tp.
15. David Brooks, *Nine Nonobvious Ways to Have Deeper Conversations* (New York Times 19 November 2020).

Chapter 9: Alternative Thinking

1. Warren Buffett, Annual Letter to Berkshire Hathaway Inc. shareholders 2009, https://www.berkshirehathaway.com/2009ar/2009ar.pdf.
2. Gary Klein, 'Performing a Project Premortem', *Harvard Business, September 2007*.

Communication: Words are All I Have

1. George Orwell, essay 'Politics and the English Language', 1946.

Chapter 10: The Seeing Ear

1. The word *shema* is almost impossible to translate, meaning variously: to hear, to listen, to pay attention, to hearken, to understand, to respond, to obey.
2. Mishnah, Eruvin 13:2.
3. Babylonian Talmud, Tractate Shabbat 31a.
4. Joseph Telushkin, *The Book of Jewish Values: A Day-by-Day Guide to Ethical Living* (Harmony/Rodale 2011), p. 187.
5. Quoted in Adam Grant, *Think Again* (WH Allen 2021), p. 59.
6. Mishnah, Tractate Avot 4:1.
7. David Brooks, 'Nine Non-obvious Ways to Have Deeper Conversations', *New York Times*, 19 November 2020.
8. Stephen Covey, *The 7 Habits of Highly Effective People* (Simon & Schuster 2013).
9. Jack Zenger and Joseph Folkman, 'What Great Listeners Actually Do', *Harvard Business Review*, June 2018.
10. 1 Kings 3:16–24.
11. 1 Kings 3:23.

Chapter 11: Better than an Answer

1. David Brooks, 'Nine Non - obvious Ways to Have Deeper Conversations', *New York Times*, 19 November 2020.
2. Jack Zenger and Joseph Folkman, 'What Great Listeners Actually Do', *Harvard Business Review*, June 2018.
3. Joseph Telushkin, *Rebbe* (Harper Wave 2014), p. 134.
4. Van Jones, *Beyond the Messy Truth* (Ballantine 2017), p. 128.
5. Report of the Secretary-General's Panel of Inquiry on 31 May 2010 Flotilla Incident, https://www.un.org/unispal/document/auto-insert-205969/.

Chapter 12: The Power of Storytelling

1. The Talmudic passage is from Tractate Ketubot 62b. Ruth Calderon's speech, with English subtitles, can be seen at https://www.worldjewish-congress.org/en/videos/israel/Flashback-MK-Ruth-Calderon-delivers-maiden-speech-11-1-2020.
2. Jonathan Rosen, *The Talmud and the Internet: A Journey Between Worlds* (Farrar, Straus and Giroux 2000), p. 7.
3. Babylonian Talmud, Tractate Baba Kamma 60b.
4. Jonathan Sacks, 'Law and Narrative', *Covenant and Conversation, Chukat* 2007–8.
5. Abraham Joshua Heschel, 'Halakhah and Aggadah', *Between God and Man* (The Free Press 1965).
6. Haim Nahman Bialik, 'Halakhah and Aggadah' in *Revealment and Concealment*, trans. Zali Gurevitch (Ibis Editions 2000).
7. Chip Heath and Dan Heath, *Made to Stick: Why Some Ideas Survive and Others Die* (Random House 2007), pp. 99–100.
8. James O'Brien, How Not to be Wrong: *The Art of Changing Your Mind* (Penguin 2020), p. 218.
9. Heath and Heath, Made to Stick, p. 165.
10. Uri Hasson, TED Talk: 'This is your Brain on Communication', February 2016, https://www.youtube.com/watch?v=FDhlOovaGrI.
11. Heath and Heath, *Made to Stick*, pp. 98–9.
12. Will Storr, The Science of Storytelling (William Collins 2012), pp. 153–4.
13. Amos Oz, *A Tale of Love and Darkness* (Mariner 2005).
14. John Steinbeck, interviewed by George Plimpton and Frank Crowther, *The Paris Review*, 1975.

Chapter 13: Connecting Ideas to Reality

1. Richard Feynman, *Surely You're Joking, Mr Feynman! Adventures of a Curious Character* (Ralph Leighton 2010), p. 85.
2. Babylonian Talmud, Tractate Yevamot 82b.

Chapter 14: Black Fire on White Fire

1. Isabel Allende, *The Stories of Eva Luna* (Scribner UK 2017), p. 9.
2. Midrash Devarim Rabbah 1:7.

3. Quoted in Susan Scott, *Fierce Conversations* (New American Library 2017), p. 284
4. Quoted in https://rabbisacks.org/covenant-conversation/bamidbar/the-sound-of-silence/.
5. Susan Scott, *Fierce Conversations*.
6. Catherine Blyth, *The Art of Conversation* (John Murray 2009), p. 286.
7. Shlomo Wolbe, *Alei Shor* (1966).
8. I Kings 19:11–13.

Chapter 15: A Place for Jesters in Heaven

1. Babylonian Talmud, Tractate Taanit 22a.
2. Viktor Frankl, *Man's Search for Meaning* (Better Yourself Books 2003, first published 1946), p. 46.
3. Babllonian Talmud, Tractate Baba Metzia 59b.
4. Yuval Cherlow, *Leshem Shamayim, The ethics of Machloket* (Maggid 2018), p. 97 (Hebrew).
5. Richard Feynman, *Surely You're Joking, Mr Feynman! Adventures of a Curious Character* (Ralph Leighton 2010).

Community: No Argument is an Island

1. Avot de-Rabbi Natan, Version A 14:6.

Chapter 16: Creating the Right Environment

1. John Milton, *Paradise Lost*, Book XII.
2. Adar Cohen, TEDx Talk, 'How to Lead Tough Conversations', https://www.youtube.com/watch?v=LZu16ZaLgJM.
3. Jonathan Sacks, *The Home We Build Together* (Continuum 2007), p. 173.
4. Stephen L. Carter, *Civility: Manners, Morals, and the Etiquette of Democracy* (Harper Perennial 1998), pp. 120–30.
5. Van Jones, *Beyond the Messy Truth* (Ballantine 2017), p. xiv.
6. 'Eli Pariser Predicted the Future. Now He Can't Escape It', interview in *Wired*, 24 May 2017, at https://www.wired.com/2017/05/eli-pariser-predicted-the-future-now-he-cant-escape-it/.

Chapter 17: Sharpening the Skills
– In Others and Ourselves

1. Malcolm Gladwell, 'Malcolm Goes to Debate School', *Revisionist History* podcast, https://www.youtube.com/watch?v=cGGCe2DlV88.
2. Stephen Fry, *Moab Is My Washpot: A Memoir* (Soho Press 2011).
3. Babylonian Talmud, Tractate Eruvin 53b.
4. Ibid.
5. Babylonian Talmud, Tractate Hagiga 3a.

Chapter 18: Living with Difference

1. Babylonian Talmud, Tractate Yevamot 14a.
2. Genesis 31: 45–6.
3. Babylonian Talmud, Tractate Chullin 91b.

Chapter 19: Beyond Dispute

1. Mishnah, Tractate Avot 3:2.
2. Hatam Sofer, Responsa Part 1, Orach Chayim 208.
3. Mishnah, Tractate Avot 5:17.
4. Quentin de la Bedoyere, *Managing People and Problems* (Gower 1988), p. 31.
5. Babylonian Talmud, Kiddushin 30b.

Select Bibliography

Bavel, Jay Van and Packer, Dominic J. *The Power of Us* (Little, Brown 2021)

Bedoyere, Quentin de la. *Managing People and Problems* (Gower 1988)

Blyth, Catherine. *The Art of Conversation* (John Murray 2009)

Brooks, Arthur C. *Love your Enemies* (Broadside Books 2019)

Cherlow, Yuval. *Leshem Shamayim, The Ethics of Makhloket* (Hebrew)

Colombus, Katie. *How to Listen: Tools for Opening Up Conversations When it Matters Most* (Kyle 2021)

Faust, Shmuel. *Tihyu Hachamim, Timeless Wisdom – Practical Talmudic Thinking for the 21st Century* (Hebrew)

Feynman, Richard. *Surely You're Joking, Mr Feynman! Adventures of a Curious Character* (Ralph Leighton 2010)

Fine, Gila. *The Madwoman in the Rabbi's Attic: Rereading the Women of the Talmud* (Toby Press 2024)

Goodman, Micah. *Mahapechat Hakeshev, The Attention Revolution* (Hebrew)

Grant, Adam. *Think Again:The Power of Knowing What You Don't Know* (Penguin Random House 2021)

Gringras, Robbie and Dauber Sterne, Abi. *Stories for the Sake of Argument* (FSA Publications 2022)

Grinstein, Gidi. *Flexigidity: The Secret of Jewish Adaptability* (Grinstein 2013)

Guzman, Monica. *I Never Thought of it That Way* (Random House 2022)

Haidt, Jonathan. *The Righteous Mind. Why Good People Are Divided by Politics and Religion* (Random House 2012)

Hall, Trish. *Writing to Persuade* (Liveright 2019)

Halbertal, Moshe. *Holadat Hasafek, The Birth of Doubt: Confronting Uncertainty in Early Rabbinic Literature* (Hebrew)

Hari, Johann. *Stolen Focus: Why You Can't Pay Attention* (Crown 2022)

Heath, Chip and Heath, Dan. *Made to Stick: Why Some Ideas Survive and Others Die* (Random House 2007)

Hidary, Richard. *Dispute for the Sake of Heaven: Legal Pluralism in the Talmud* (Brown Judaic Studies 2010)

Johnson, David. *Constructive Controversy: Theory, Research, Practice* (Cambridge University Press 2015)

Jones, Van. *Beyond the Messy Truth* (Ballantine 2017)

Kahneman, Daniel. *Thinking, Fast and Slow* (Farar, Straus and Giroux 2011)

Kaminsky, Howard. *Fundamentals of Jewish Conflict Resolution* (Academic Studies Press 2017)

Kendler, Maureen. *All Spoons and No Elbows* (Maureen Kendler Educational Trust 2018)

Klein, Gary. *Sources of Power: How People Make Decisions* (MIT Press 2017)

Kurshan, Ilana. *If All the Seas Were Ink* (St Martin's Press 2017)

Lax, David and Sebenius, James. *3-D Negotiation* (Harvard Business Review Press 2006)

Leslie, Ian. *Conflicted: Why Arguments Are Tearing Us Apart and How They Can Bring Us Together* (Faber 2021)

Lukianoff, Greg and Haidt, Jonathan. *The Coddling of the American Mind* (Penguin 2019)

Maccoby, Hyam. *The Day God Laughed* (St Martin's Press 1978)

McRaney, David. *How Minds Change: The Surprising Science of Belief, Opinion and Persuasion* (Oneworld 2023)

Meir, Moshe. *Hatevuna Hamitchadeshet, Renewed Understanding: the Philosophy of the Study Hall* (Hebrew)

Navarra, Albert. *The Joy of Argument: 91 Ways to Get More of What You Want and Less of What You Don't* (Boyle & Dalton 2015)

Nordell, Jessica. *The End of Bias: A Beginning* (Metropolitan 2022)

O'Brien, James. *How Not to Be Wrong: The Art of Changing Your Mind* (WH Allen 2021)

Oz, Amos and Oz-Salzberger, Fania. *Jews and Words* (Yale University Press 2014)

Patterson, Kerry, Grenny, Joseph, McMillan, Ron and Switzler, Al. *Crucial Conversations: Tools for Talking When the Stakes Are High* (McGraw Hill 2021)

Putnam, Robert. *Bowling Alone: The Collapse and Revival of American Community* (Simon & Schuster, 2000)

Raiffa, Howard. *The Art and Science of Negotiation* (Belknap Press 1985)

Ripley, Amanda. *High Conflict: Why We Get Trapped and How We Get Out* (Simon & Schuster 2022)

Rosen, Jonathan. *The Talmud and the Internet: A Journey Between Worlds* (Farrar, Straus and Giroux 2000)

Rotenberg, Michael. *Sofa lehitkayem, Co-Existence in Controversy* (Hebrew)

Roth, Daniel. *Third-Party Peacemakers in Judaism: Text, Theory, and Practice* (Oxford University Press 2021)

Sacks, Jonathan. *The Dignity of Difference: How to Avoid the Clash of Civilizations* (Continuum 2002)

Sacks, Jonathan. *The Home We Build Together* (Bloomsbury 2009)

Sacks, Jonathan. *Morality: Restoring the Common Good in Divided Times* (Basic Books 2020)

Saiman, Chaim. *Halakhah: The Rabbinic Idea of Law*(Princeton University Press 2018)

Scott, Susan. *Fierce Conversations: Achieving Success at Work and in Life One Conversation at a Time* (New American Library 2002)

Seo, Bo. *Good Arguments: How Debate Teaches Us to Listen and Be Heard* (Penguin 2022)

Sharot, Tali. *The Influential Mind: What the Brain Reveals about our Power to Change Others* (Picador 2018)

Shenk, Joshua. *Powers of Two: Finding the Essence of Innovation in Creative Pairs* (Houghton Mifflin Harcourt 2014)

Stone, Douglas, Patton, Bruce and Heen, Sheila. *Difficult Conversations: How to Discuss What Matters Most* (Portfolio/Penguin 1999)

Storr, Will. *The Science of Storytelling: Why Stories Make Us Human and How to Tell Them Better* (Harry N. Abrams 2020)

Sunstein, Cass. *Why Societies Need Dissent* (Harvard University Press 2005)

Sunstein, Cass. *Going to Extremes: How Like Minds Unite and Divide* (Oxford University Press 2009)

Telushkin, Joseph. *Jewish Humor: What the Best Jewish Jokes Say About the Jews* (William Morrow 1998)

Telushkin, Joseph. *Hillel: If Not Now, When?* (Schocken 2010)

Telushkin, Joseph. *Words That Hurt, Words That Heal* (William Morrow 2019)

Ury, William. *Getting Past No: Negotiating in Difficult Situations* (Bantam 1993)

Wolpe, David J. *In Speech and in Silence: The Jewish Quest for God* (Henry Holt 1992)

Yankelovitch, Daniel. *The Magic of Dialogue: Transforming Conflict into Cooperation* (Touchstone 2001)

Index